GETTING AND SPENDING:
The Consumer's Dilemma

This is a volume in the Arno Press collection

GETTING AND SPENDING:
The Consumer's Dilemma

Advisory Editor
Leon Stein

See last pages of this volume
for a complete list of titles

The Responsibilities of American Advertising

PRIVATE CONTROL AND

PUBLIC INFLUENCE, 1920–1940

OTIS PEASE

ARNO PRESS

A New York Times Company

1976

Editorial Supervision: EVE NELSON

———◆———

Reprint Edition 1976 by Arno Press Inc.

Copyright © 1958 by Yale University Press, Inc.
Reprinted by permission of Yale University Press

Reprinted from a copy in the Princeton
   University Library

GETTING AND SPENDING: The Consumer's Dilemma
ISBN for complete set: 0-405-08005-0
See last pages of this volume for titles.

———◆———

Library of Congress Cataloging in Publication Data

Pease, Otis A
   The responsibilities of American advertising.

   (Getting and spending)
   Reprint of the ed. published by Yale University Press,
New Haven, as no. 2 of Yale publications in American
studies.
   Bibliography: p.
   1. Advertising--United States--History. I. Title.
II. Series. III. Series: Yale publications in
American studies ; 2.
[HF5813.U6P4 1976]   659.1'0973   75-39266
ISBN 0-405-08039-5

YALE PUBLICATIONS IN AMERICAN STUDIES, 2

David Horne, Editor

Published under the direction of the American Studies Program
and with assistance from the William Robertson Coe Fund

The Responsibilities of

OTIS PEASE

American Advertising

PRIVATE CONTROL AND

PUBLIC INFLUENCE, 1920–1940

New Haven: Yale University Press, 1958

TO MARY

I OBSERVED that the vitals of the village were the grocery, the bar-room, the post-office, and the bank; and, as a necessary part of the machinery, they kept a bell, a big gun, and a fire-engine, at convenient places; and the houses were so arranged as to make the most of mankind, in lanes and fronting one another, so that every traveller had to run the gauntlet, and every man, woman, and child might get a lick at him. Of course, those who were stationed nearest to the head of the line, where they could most see and be seen, and have the first blow at him, paid the highest prices for their places; and the few straggling inhabitants in the outskirts, where long gaps in the line began to occur, and the traveller could get over walls or turn aside into cow-paths, and so escape, paid a very slight ground or window tax. Signs were hung out on all sides to allure him; some to catch him by the appetite, as the tavern and victualling cellar; some by the fancy, as the dry goods store and the jeweller's; and others by the hair or the feet or the skirts, as the barber, the shoe-maker, or the tailor. Besides, there was a still more terrible standing invitation to call at every one of these houses, and company expected about these times. For the most part I escaped wonderfully from these dangers, either by proceeding at once boldly and without deliberation to the goal, as is recommended to those who run the gauntlet, or by keeping my thoughts on high things, like Orpheus, who, "loudly singing the praises of the gods to his lyre, drowned the voices of the Sirens, and kept out of danger." Sometimes I bolted suddenly, and nobody could tell my whereabouts, for I did not stand much about gracefulness, and never hesitated at a gap in a fence. I was even accustomed to make an irruption into some houses, where I was well entertained, and after learning the kernels and the very last sieveful of news,—what had subsided, the prospects of war and peace, and whether the world was likely to hold together much longer,—I was let out through the rear avenues, and so escaped to the woods again.

HENRY DAVID THOREAU, *Walden*

Preface

MODERN ADVERTISING in America is at least forty years old. Thoughtful citizens who have strained their eyes at the current growth of television and who have pondered with disquiet the evidence of massive hidden persuaders in their culture find it difficult to remind themselves that most of the advertising they now see was foreshadowed and substantially conceived in previous decades, now increasingly remote and more readily accessible to historians than to present memories. It is not easy, for example, to recognize that there is less new than old in today's four-color magazine, less new than we suspect even in last evening's electronic commercial. We note with concern, if we are sensitive to the forces that govern us, that political campaigns in the late 1950's are managed to an obviously unprecedented degree by advertising experts. Our concern, I suspect, is entirely legitimate. The fact itself should remind us, nevertheless, that, ironically, an old debt is being merely repaid, for historically the techniques of advertising and politics have never been completely independent of each other, and politics in all likelihood came first.

If the past on which the power of present advertising depends seems obscure and irrelevant to us, we may blame in part our cultural and institutional historians. As long ago as 1940 the advertising industry had become a social institution of immense power in American life; yet no careful study has even yet been made of the attitudes of this industry toward the public, its concepts of responsibility, or the intellectual assumptions which have underlain its operations. Writings by advertising men for the benefit, comfort, and instruction of other advertising men of course have been numerous. Equally plentiful have been writings of both publicists and polemicists in praise or dispraise of this or that feature of the advertising business. Few of these endeavors have been especially judicious or impartial, though their value to the historian of recent culture is often as real as it is unsuspected and unintentional. Indeed, for the history of American advertising, only two studies are competent and objective enough to warrant serious attention. One is Neil F. Borden's monumental project, *The Economic Effects of Advertising* (1942), which, despite the fact that in a few respects it stands as an *apologia* for the advertising industry, should preclude for many years the need for a new interpretation of that subject. The other is Ralph Hower's *History of an Advertising Agency* (1949), a carefully documented and sympathetic account of the origins, growth, and operations of a single large agency, N. W. Ayer and Son.

These are essentially economic studies; although the advertising industry was called into being by predominantly economic forces and has remained a responsive instrument of business enterprise, its extraordinary relationship to American society during the past several decades ought to invite more than an economic analysis. It is just as important, in fact, that historians of 20th-century America recognize advertising as a major social force and that they scrutinize and assess the growth of its influence with the same care they give to that of the school or the church or to the major intellectual currents of our recent past. Yet no single first-hand study of the American advertising industry in all its historical and institutional aspects has ever been written, and none seems imminent. Advertising in America has been a sprawling and diffuse enterprise, and the materials which bear on its study as a whole are for the most part too unorganized and unworked at the present time to permit any single individual to encompass and digest them. Few of the preliminary investigations on which the interpretive historian will necessarily depend have yet been made. As a consequence, he must for the moment content himself with making forays of more modest size, where the capacity for insight may be permitted to compensate for restricted dimensions.

I have therefore made no effort here to write the whole history of American advertising between 1920 and 1940. Rather this book analyzes the extent to which concepts of public responsibility existed in the national advertising industry during a critical period of its recent history, and interprets the attitudes of important segments of the industry toward the consumer and toward the general problems which arose from the relationship between advertiser and consumer in a democratic, economically abundant society. I shall attempt to describe the important challenge which the consumer offered to the concepts and practices of national advertising and, finally, to examine the ways in which this challenge was resisted and overcome, leaving the national advertising industry by 1940 in a more impregnable position than ever before in its history.

To cover the subject with adequacy and yet to avoid a project of unmanageable size, I have imposed two limitations on its scope —limitations which, however, I believe do not impair its significance.

1. This study is limited to the national advertising industry; it is only indirectly concerned with local or retail advertising. National advertisers and the large national agencies (together with the principal trade journals of advertising) comprise the national advertising industry, that segment of the industry most influential in molding the techniques, the policies, and the operating concepts of American advertising. As a consequence, however, much of the data used herein, and many of the conclusions drawn from them, pertain equally well to local and retail advertising.

2. The relations between advertisers and the mass media and between the media and the public which are pertinent to this study have been confined to the two chief forms of printed media, the newspaper and the magazine. It would have been equally

pertinent to have studied the growth of advertising on radio and television, but to do so might well have entailed a book double the length of this one. Fortunately, the data and conclusions of the present study to a considerable extent are also relevant to national advertising on the radio during the same span of years.

This study has evolved from a doctoral dissertation presented in 1954 in a rather different form at Yale University and awarded the John Addison Porter prize for that year. As every historian must, I willingly recognize that although scholarly writing is a peculiarly personal enterprise, few enterprises in modern life also depend more deeply and cogently on a community of scholarship and thought. I can testify with gratitude to the efficiency and cooperation of the Yale Library, the New York Public Library, the Stanford University Library, the Libraries of the Universities of Texas, Washington, and California (Berkeley), the editorial office of *Printers' Ink,* and the office of the Psychological Corporation in New York. Acknowledgments and thanks are due the publishers of *Printers' Ink, Advertising Agency Magazine,* and the *Saturday Evening Post,* for permission to reprint material from their periodicals. I am also grateful for the financial assistance offered me by the Texas Research Institute and the Institute of American History at Stanford University.

Particularly pleasant is the task of acknowledging the incalculable help of individual persons. For assistance in making available countless pieces of information and in clarifying my ideas, I wish to thank George F. Thomson and René Clarke of the Calkins and Holden advertising firm, Kenneth B. Willson of the National Better Business Bureau, Richard L. Scheidker of the American Association of Advertising Agencies, F. J. Schlink of Consumers' Research, Jerry Voorhis of the Cooperative League, and my father, Frederic A. Pease.

For their essential criticism and willing advice on form and substance at various stages of composition, I am especially grateful to Ralph H. Gabriel, Leonard W. Doob, Richard Ruggles, Waldo H. Heinrichs, Jr., Gilbert Pierce Haight, Frank Holzman, and Harry Woolf, as well as to Barnes F. Lathrop, David D. Van Tassel, Charles H. Taylor, Jr., and Richard O. Goodwillie, for more intangible assistance. To my wife Mary I gladly offer an acknowledgment for the sort of help (editorial, clerical, and familial) that writers with patient and understanding wives should unfailingly appreciate.

Above all else, I am permanently indebted to the continuous inspiration and indispensable guidance of David M. Potter. From its inception this study owes more to his careful and rigorous scrutiny and his persistent intellectual probing than I can adequately express.

It need scarcely be pointed out that however much the merits of this book reflect the help of others, responsibility for the views which it expresses rests solely with myself.

O. P.

Stanford, California
February 1958

Contents

Illustrations

Figure 3 has been reproduced by courtesy of Sunkist Growers, Inc.; 4 by courtesy of Studebaker-Packard Corp.; 5 by courtesy of N. W. Ayer and Son. All figures by courtesy of the Curtis Publishing Co.

1

The Growth of National Advertising

It has been the modern task of advertising to persuade the individual citizen to conceive of himself primarily as a consumer of goods. In an economy which requires for its continued health a continuous increase in mass consumption the advertising industry has virtually been accorded the major responsibility for stimulating and directing that consumption. During the course of its operations, and more for historic than logical reasons, advertising has come to play a central role in developing the principal techniques of modern mass propaganda, and its power has continuously reflected the thoroughness with which it has transformed and underwritten radio and television broadcasting and the nation's press. The control of mass media, and the ability to make efficient use of the techniques of propaganda on a large scale, have always been matters of critical importance to the character and

1

nature of society. The history of how American advertising has defined its own role is a story, then, of a private industry engaged in the business of public influence.

Therein lies a modern variation of an old and common dilemma. Despite its public character, the advertising industry is a commercial enterprise, responsible primarily to those who patronize it. Save for the minimum legal requirements and self-engendered "rules of fair trade" imposed on all industries doing business with the public or with commercial enterprises, the industry has successfully refused to permit restrictions on its behavior. This refusal has stemmed from the operating concepts which advertising men have evolved for their trade, its function, its social value, and its responsibility toward the public. These concepts first became articulate in the period between the two world wars. In that period advertising in the United States developed most of its present influence and simultaneously faced and resisted successfully an explicit challenge which a group of opponents and skeptics offered to its power. Partially in answer to this challenge, the national advertising industry formulated concepts of its own responsibility, attempted to utilize those concepts as arguments against further public regulation of advertising, and at the same time strengthened its own position against further challenge by constantly improving the effectiveness of advertising itself.

This study, then, properly concerns itself with the period which begins with the close of the first World War and ends at the eve of the second. To define more sharply what took place during those years, however, I will first review the significant way in which national advertising had come into existence and was to grow in the generation preceding the 1920's.[1]

1. The material which follows in this chapter, where not otherwise noted, is drawn from several general studies in the field of advertising: Neil H. Borden, *The Economic Effects of Advertising*, Chicago, Richard O. Irwin, Inc., 1942; Ralph M. Hower, *The History of an Advertising Agency: N. W. Ayer and Son at Work, 1869–1949*, Cambridge, Mass., Harvard University Press, 1949; Edward Jackson Baur, "Voluntary Control in the Advertising Industry," dissertation, Chicago, 1942; Frank Presbrey, *History and Development of Advertising*, New York, Doubleday, Doran, Inc., 1929; *Printers' Ink: Fifty Years, 1888–1938*, New York, Printers' Ink Publishing Co., 1938; George B. Hotchkiss, *Milestones of Marketing*, New York, Macmillan, 1938; Alfred McLung Lee, *The Daily Newspaper in America: the Evolution of a Social Instrument*, New York, Macmillan, 1937.

Modern advertising is primarily a marketing technique for business enterprise. It has flourished chiefly in countries and in periods in which private industrial capitalism has been able to provide a significant quantity of surplus wealth and to support a considerable degree of leisure and a high standard of consumption for large numbers of people. Advertising in some form has operated in societies whose markets have been state-controlled, and to a small degree it once flourished in pre-industrial America and in 18th-century England, but in neither form did it particularly resemble the advertising which has developed during the past generation in the English-speaking nations and particularly in the United States.

The unique importance and complexity of American advertising plainly stem from a large number of factors which, though not individually restricted to the United States, have been combined possibly more favorably in the United States than elsewhere. The industrialization which accompanied and followed the Civil War required manufacturers to seek ever larger markets in which to dispose of their expanding production, and nationwide advertising proved to be an unusually efficient technique in gaining such markets. The successful absorption of throngs of immigrant peoples swelled the demand for goods, while advertising soon became cheaper than other means of selling in an economy where labor costs remained high and distances great. Simultaneously mass media also expanded on a scale made possible by the cheapness of newsprint, by new techniques in periodical publishing, by a mobile population, and by the generally powerful political influence of publishers, who were able to obtain legislation favorable to a wide circulation of periodicals at low cost to themselves.

It was in such a climate that American advertising became an industry, but of critical importance to its growth was the change of character which took place when one segment of the industry, "national" advertising, grew to a position of dominance and influence which no other segment of the industry could match.

Because of the size of operations needed to sell in a nationwide market, national advertising has acquired qualities and attributes which distinguish it from advertising in general. Yet curiously it has always eluded precise definition. By general consensus anyone

who advertises a product or service in media of general circulation
or attempts to convey a commercial message to substantially large
segments of the nation is a national advertiser. To buy space in the
Saturday Evening Post or time over a nationwide radio network,
or to send a form letter to three million prospects scattered through
forty states would automatically impart to a firm the unofficial
status of a national advertiser, though a single unrepeated effort
of this kind would hardly entitle it to membership in the Association of National Advertisers. In like fashion General Motors
could be regarded as a national advertiser solely on the strength
of its nationwide newspaper advertising for Chevrolet, though
these advertisements may be placed locally by its dealers and may
vary in content from one state or region to another or even from
one newspaper to another. When one takes into account the
nebulous and shifting boundaries which separate national from
local or retail advertising, one is not surprised to find that, although the volume of national advertising placed in periodical
media has been reliably calculated for the period since 1915, at
present no statistics on national advertising as a separate entity
exist for the years prior to 1935. In that year the proportion of
national to total advertising was almost precisely one half; since
1940 it has climbed to about three-fifths.[2]

Ninety years ago, national advertising could scarcely be said
to have existed. Until the end of the Civil War effective buying
and selling in the United States was restricted to local areas. The
country store and the wholesaler dominated the market, for
they enjoyed a monopoly position based on location which dis-

2. For comment on the problem of defining "national advertising," see *Printers'
Ink (P.I.)* (Dec. 23, 1926), p. 57; (Oct. 29, 1948), pp. 57 ff. For estimates of
national advertising since 1935 see *Printers' Ink Guide to Marketing for 1957*,
Sec. 2 of the Aug. 24, 1956, issue of *P.I.* National advertising alone between 1920
and 1940 supplied, on a rough average, about 20 per cent of the total revenue
of the nation's newspapers and nearly 40 per cent of the total revenue of the
nation's magazines. Local advertising supplied an additional 45 per cent and 10
per cent respectively. See Borden, pp. 55, 68–71.

Today national advertising receives formal recognition to the extent that it is
charged special space rates, is placed through officially recognized agencies, and
provides an exclusive basis for membership in one of the most powerful trade associations in marketing, the Association of National Advertisers (ANA).

appeared only with the rapid extension of railroads. Some stores in small communities succumbed to the specialized market centers to be found in a few growing cities, but many others, especially the strongly entrenched wholesale houses, survived to become department stores (such as A. T. Stewart, Marshall Field's, and Wanamaker's) which bought directly from the manufacturer and sold his goods anonymously under a private or wholesale brand name at "bargain" prices. Indeed the more powerful merchants attempted to control the disposal of a manufacturer's entire output and frequently forced him to give ground in matters of price and design. Few manufacturers were in a position to resist. They sold almost nothing directly to the consumer and were little known to him; nor did they exercise much control over the retailer, who bought his wares from jobbers or independent wholesalers. Advertising, except for patent medicines, remained largely in the retailer's hands. Until close to the end of the century, in fact, the most spectacular and effective advertising copy was generally sponsored by large retail stores and mail order firms whose writers, such as John Powers of Wanamaker's, were often the most gifted innovators in the field.

The rapid growth, in numbers and size, of manufacturing enterprises during and after the Civil War gradually changed the conditions which retailers found so favorable. Innovations in the management of business firms, the proliferating spread of railroads, and the success of more efficient techniques of production afforded manufacturers for the first time the opportunity and the incentive to control the ultimate sale of their products. Anxious to use whatever weapons would help them, they proved warmly receptive to the agents and missionaries of advertising.

It is now generally agreed that those most responsible for encouraging manufacturers to use advertising were the agents of commercial publishing houses who sold space either as direct representatives of newspapers or magazines or as independent space jobbers whom the publishers paid on commission. Publishers welcomed the stability which the advertising revenue from dependable businesses could provide, and their enthusiastic representatives sought to persuade sales managers that advertising could create and increase a direct demand for a product by acting as "an irresistible force of suction that would draw goods through dealer and wholesaler." [3] Such advertising attempted to establish, if not "brand loyalty," at least a widespread recognition of the manufacturer's slogan or trade mark ("Uneeda Biscuit." "Children Cry for Castoria.") Publishers were quick to insist that this could be done most efficiently by national advertising in newspapers and magazines. Consumers would be encouraged to ask for particular brands, and retailers would consequently be forced to stock them. To provide the manufacturer with his nationwide "audience," publishers began to revamp their newspapers and magazines to attract wider readership and to offer better facilities for printing advertisements. Typical of such publishers were Cyrus Curtis and Edward Bok of the *Ladies' Home Journal,* who proselytized manufacturers and publishers alike to help establish the magazine as a powerful advertising medium. Partially in consequence of publishers' efforts, partially as a result of the growing influence of independent advertising agencies (the J. Walter Thompson agency, for example), magazine advertising nearly tripled its volume in the 1880's, and its revenues soon surpassed those derived from the sale of billboard space, which had previously dominated advertising media. [4]

Advertising agencies soon became persistent missionaries for the use of national advertising. In addition to the J. Walter Thompson company, the firms of Calkins and Holden and N. W. Ayer and Son tried to persuade large manufacturers to utilize national advertising. [5] As early as 1890, the Ayer agency had gradually ceased to do business with retailers and henceforth, as one of its members declared, was to write advertising for "manufacturers who sold through dealers and retailers but preferred to get control over their ultimate market." [6] The true object of news-

3. Hotchkiss, *Milestones of Marketing,* p. 53.

4. Presbrey, *History and Development of Advertising,* pp. 339–41. Presbrey ascribes the decline in popularity of billboards to the growing rate of literacy.

5. Earnest Elmo Calkins, *"And Hearing Not—": Annals of an Adman* (New York, Scribner's, 1946), pp. 210–12.

6. Hower, *History of an Advertising Agency,* p. 207.

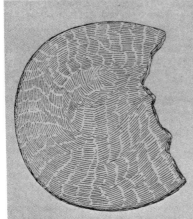

There is a peculiarity about **Uneeda Jinjer Wayfer**. The more you eat the more you want, but you can eat to your satisfaction without eating too many. It's the delicacy of a **Uneeda Jinjer Wayfer** that makes it appetizing; it's the goodness of a **Uneeda Jinjer Wayfer** that makes it wholesome. Every

Uneeda Jinjer Wayfer

The first bite you take is a revelation.

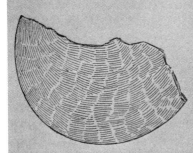

The last bite you take gives you an appetite for more.

is just right. It contains a touch of ginger to make it delicious; it contains the best of everything to make it good. It reminds you of the old-fashioned Ginger Snap—it's so different. Have them on the table; give them to the children; never let your supply run short. Sold everywhere in air-tight, moisture-proof boxes, just like the famous **Uneeda Biscuit.** Made only by

NATIONAL BISCUIT COMPANY

Proprietors of the registered trade-mark, "**Uneeda**"

1. A typical example of national advertising in the 1890's, embodying the technique of simple announcement.

2. Testimonials exploiting public interest in notable personalities were common in late 19th-century advertising for patent medicines and soap.

3. By 1916 a few leading national advertisers, while not abandoning the "announcement" theory of copy, were displaying some imagination in their techniques.

paper advertising, wrote the Ayer firm to a customer in 1903, "should be to convince the consumer of the value of your product. That done, some dealer will have to keep it . . ." [7] And in 1905, H. N. McKinney, an Ayer vice-president, declared in a report to his staff: "The most dissatisfied man today is the manufacturer. He does not sell his goods or make a reputation for himself, but he makes it for the jobber. The manufacturers are waking up to that fact; and our great business is to show the manufacturer that he ought to own his own trade by making the demand direct from the consumer." [8]

National advertising, then, was "sold" to the manufacturer as a competitive tool which was supposed to assure him a measure of control over his prices, his merchandising policies, and his margin of profit. It is true that a few mail order houses and large retail stores found a degree of national advertising profitable, but by the end of the 19th century the task of advertising to large numbers of ultimate consumers involved techniques and aims which set it apart from the still larger quantity of local and retail advertising. Presbrey's study sets 1890 as the date when the dominance of brand names, won by national advertising, had begun to establish for a score of manufacturers a large degree of independence from the wholesaler and retailer.[9] By this time manufacturers of Sapolio, Ivory and Pears soap, and Royal Baking Powder, the first four consistent national advertisers, characteristically sought nationwide prominence for a single brand, while others who made packaged food, soaps, typewriters, bicycles, pianos, tobacco products, and certain items of clothing soon followed them. The continuing movement of population into urban industrial centers gave specialized manufacturers, regardless of their location, an increasingly wider market and an opportunity to compete favorably with rival manufacturers in their own localities. George B. Hotchkiss has suggested that by 1914, "the whole conception of the domestic market had changed. It was no longer a definite place, but people. The manufacturer was able

7. Quoted in Hower, p. 361.
8. Quoted in Hower, p. 260.
9. Presbrey, pp. 338–9.

to consider as his market all potential customers, wherever located, since he had a means of reaching them with his products, and with information about his products." [10]

By the end of the first World War the advertising industry was in the process of becoming a reasonably stable economic service. It already embodied a complex of private associations replete with rituals and other devices for their preservation and enhancement. Economically, advertising men, as did all businessmen, measured success by the profit derived from the sale of their services. Socially, the industry sought fervently to acquire prestige and respect among businessmen and the public, and these characteristics were apt to hinge on the reputation of national advertising as a successful and "ethical" business technique. Soon a variety of organizations representing national manufacturers, publishers, and agents, as distinct from retailers and other local advertisers, emerged to dominate the industry. Salesmen from national firms were constantly "educating" local dealers to sell more efficiently, to stock national brands and to "tie into" national campaigns. This process of education continued for the next twenty years to absorb a large part of the marketing efforts of national firms.

As the techniques of advertising and mass selling spread from the large commercial centers to smaller communities, local advertising men formed clubs for mutual social and economic benefit and generally affiliated their clubs with national organizations. Catering to a broad membership practically indistinguishable in form or purpose from local Chambers of Commerce, they were eventually to discover that national advertisers sought benefits unrelated to and even incompatible with the goals of local members. The Associated Advertising Clubs of the World (AACW), for example, was formed in 1914 from a loose federation of local clubs but was financed largely by national advertisers for the purposes of establishing rules of "fair trade" on a national scale and of promoting the spread of national brands. But the majority of its members remained local clubmen who sought from their associations a means of conviviality, social prestige, and fulfillment for their own local aims. They were unwilling to pay heavy

10. Hotchkiss, p. 220.

dues to a national organization which catered to other interests. A split occurred, and by 1920 national advertisers had erected a collection of trade associations distinct from the AACW. One of the most important was the American Association of Advertising Agencies (AAAA), founded in 1917, which catered to the interests of the "elite" agencies most closely connected with national advertising and which frequently opposed the methods of small local agencies. Equally important was the Association of National Advertisers (ANA), which broke away from the AACW in 1915 and became the official spokesman for exclusively national advertising interests, at times arrayed not only against retailers, distributors, and uncooperative small manufacturers but also against publishers and agencies. Together with such institutions as the American Newspaper Publishers' Association (ANPA), and the Advertising Federation of America (AFA), which superseded the AACW in 1929, they compiled research data, standardized contracts and practices in rate-setting, and served the nationwide interests of their members.

Despite the sanguine promises of enthusiastic agents and publishers, not every manufacturer was in a position to benefit from national advertising or to create brand loyalty for his product. It has been observed that producers of oranges have profited from national advertising, but producers of walnuts have not, and that sales of sugar, salt, lettuce, sheeting, and many items of clothing have depended very little on national advertising. Products with significant hidden qualities, not immediately or objectively available for consumer inspection, were more readily advertised on a larger scale than others. Many products easily associated emotionally with health, personal success, attractiveness, or security, for example, proved decidedly responsive to consumer advertising. A more important criterion was whether a firm's operations could provide substantial sums for advertising, a possibility, Borden suggests, which was apt to depend on the number of units marketable in a given time, the margin of revenue per unit, the degree of competitiveness in the industry, and the relative advantages of advertising a product over other means of selling it.[11] Even when national advertising proved economically

11. Borden, *Economic Effects of Advertising*, pp. 844-7.

feasible, most manufacturers soon discovered that they could gain from it no more than partial control over their distributors. In industries where a few firms supplied most of the demand—such as automobiles, refrigerators, cigarettes, canned soups, soap, dentrifices—manufacturers were able to dominate the selling process. In other industries, however, (canned foods, for example,) distributors competed successfully with manufacturers, and did so less by advertising than by direct selling. And it was everywhere axiomatic that the failure of a national advertiser to secure the extensive cooperation of his retailers meant failure to sell the product. The convenient assertion of early publishers and their agents that the sheer force of advertising copy would sell a product in the face of a dealer's antagonism was quickly disproved by experience, though as recently as 1942 an expert on marketing felt it necessary to warn that "for only a relatively few products is the pull of advertising upon consumers strong enough to force retailers to handle them." [12]

By 1920, nevertheless, national advertising associations had built a durable foundation for the spectacular triumphs of advertising as a whole. They had managed to stabilize the function of space-buying, to enforce the observance of a "fair price" for agency services, and to demonstrate periodic concern over the effectiveness and utility of advertising techniques. Somewhat earlier, psychologists had "discovered" advertising, as had the planners of university curricula. In the more active centers of agency enterprise, principally New York, Philadelphia, Chicago, and Detroit, enthusiastic trade journals had begun to formalize and publicize the expanding body of rules and practices which they often described with an excess of assurance as the "science" of advertising.

The national associations did more. They helped increasingly to formulate and sustain the mythology, rituals, and rationale of advertising and of the economic structure which it served. They gave status to individual clubs, provided the solidarity of convivial entertainment, afforded opportunities to establish a jargon which would at once unite and bestow distinction on members of a

12. Ibid., p. 108. Since 1900 Starch, Copeland, Hotchkiss, and others in books and trade journals have expressed the same opinion.

nationwide occupation, and sponsored enormous conventions at which notable public figures, from England as well as America, were moved to remind their audiences of the universality, humanitarianism, virtue, honesty, and indispensability of advertising. At these gatherings one could engage variously in business, recreation, and worship, for the agenda as likely as not called for banquets, communal breakfasts, lay preaching in churches, dramatic skits, singing, oratory, parades, dances, and, not least, travel to and hospitality shared in remote cities and even foreign (usually English-speaking) lands. The enormous efforts and costs which the participants cheerfully assumed attests to the extraordinary importance for them of the quasireligious "booster" spirit which all this activity provided.[13]

The prophets of advertising had reason to glow. Like the most ardent boosters of local civic expansion (indeed, they were often the same people), they put their faith in upward-soaring statistics, and their faith was spectacularly rewarded. In the postwar years of the early 1920's, expenditures for advertising in America shattered every previous record. During the war many businesses had curtailed their "product advertising," but in order not to lose their public they increased their expenditures for good-will and other institutional advertisements. With the rapid revival of business activity in 1919, most firms resumed their former advertising appropriations, and some were induced by a wave of labor unrest to continue their good-will advertising as well. Other businessmen began to advertise extensively for the first time: prominent among them were bankers, who were impressed by the success which had accompanied wartime efforts to advertise Liberty Bonds, and producers of women's goods, who were discovering an expanded market for cheap dresses, cosmetics, canned food, and household appliances in a society where women remained less frequently at home, entered more jobs, and earned and spent more money. In these years, moreover, most businesses found that to advertise cost them little, for the wartime excess profits tax, passed in 1917, encouraged corporations to increase their

13. Baur, "Voluntary Control in the Advertising Industry," p. 186. A large amount of published material on advertising conventions and social activities exists in the trade journals and in separate publications.

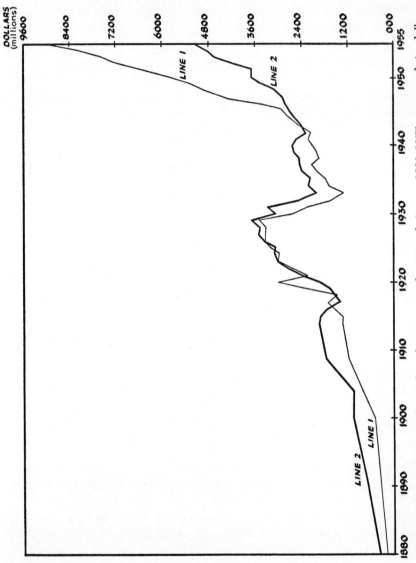

Fig. 1. Total yearly expenditure for advertising in the United States, 1880–1955: expressed in dollars (line 1); expressed in dollars weighted to reflect constant purchasing power for base year 1926 (line 2). Sources: see n. 14.

"legitimate" expenses, of which advertising was one. It is certain that many firms found it more difficult to reduce their advertising expenditures than to continue them; in any event the excess profits tax was repealed in 1922 with no noticeably adverse effects on the volume of American advertising.

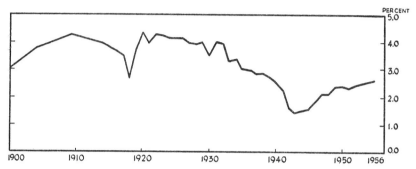

Fig. 2. Total yearly expenditure for advertising in the United States as a percentage of national income, 1900–55. Sources: see n. 14.

At almost precisely this moment, another factor had begun to affect the nation's investment in advertising. Until the 1920's the market for consumers' goods in America proved generally to be a "seller's" market, in which producers found it relatively easy to persuade buyers to enter the market at a given price. The steady expansion of advertising in this market can be attributed mainly to the increase in the volume of business as a whole. The period between the two world wars, however, encompassed two sharp business recessions and a major depression, and in this period, particularly between 1922 and 1939, the market was commonly considered a strong "buyer's" market. In such a market, where producers found it more difficult to persuade buyers to enter the market at a given price, the advertising industry was called on to expand, to adopt more efficient techniques, and to promote its services more aggressively. A general decline in profits, further-more, led businessmen to consider advertising as an increasingly attractive substitute for other forms of market competition (price-cutting, for example) which for some time had been circum-scribed informally by collective, private action and fair trade agreements. By 1940, then, the advertising industry had survived

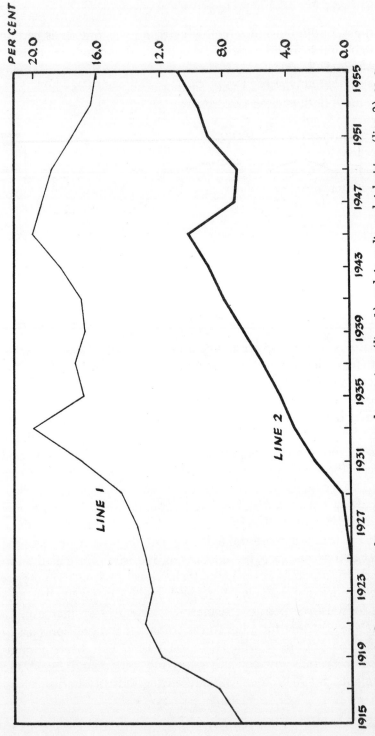

Fig. 3. National advertising expenditure in newspapers and magazines (line 1) and in radio and television (line 2) as a percentage of total advertising. Source: *Printers' Ink Guide to Marketing for 1957.*

a temporary slump, had consolidated its earlier rapid gains, and was about to set off on a course of renewed expansion unmatched in its history. If one discounts the momentary circumstance of war and the universally dispiriting depression, the volume of wealth spent on advertising in the United States, even when measured in dollars of constant purchasing power, has demonstrated in its growth since 1918 an awesome persistence, while throughout two generations the American advertising industry has continued to absorb, except for years of war, over 2 per cent of the nation's total income each year.[14]

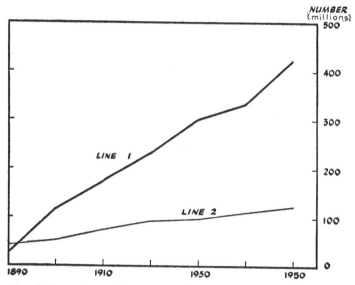

Fig. 4. Comparison of literate population with printed media circulation in the United States: total circulation of newspapers and magazines (line 1); literates ten years or older (line 2). Source: *P.I.* (October 19, 1948), pp. 100 ff.

14. On the question of the excess profits tax, see Carl F. Taeusch, *Policy and Ethics in Business* (New York, McGraw-Hill, 1931), p. 460. For yearly advertising volume, see *Printers' Ink Guide to Marketing for 1957.* In translating the dollar volume into dollars which would represent constant purchasing power, I made use of the Wholesale Price Index for All Commodities, United States Bureau of the Census, *Statistical Abstract of the United States,* (1928), p. 320, and (1955), pp. 311–13. The figures for national income were obtained from the following sources: for 1900–29 the estimates of the Bureau of Economic Research, as reported in *P.I.* (Oct. 29, 1948), pp. 100 ff.; 1929–48, from the *Statistical Abstract* (1949), p. 281; 1949–55, from the *Abstract* (1955), p. 287.

Growth and power were not easily won and did not go un-challenged. Within this period the advertising industry was forced to strive endlessly to gain the patronage and respect of other business firms and the trust of the public which it was expected to influence. Well before the first World War it had faced a skepti-cal public. Nationwide indignation over irresponsible business practices had led to the adoption of the Pure Food and Drug Act of 1906, and soon spilled over to touch nearly every phase of the relations of business to the people. In such an era the conspicuous examples of misrepresentation and falsity in advertising could scarcely have gone ignored. While the largest and most con-spicuous advertisers in 1910 were less prone to outright dishonesty and deception than they had been a generation previous, many more firms were advertising, and it was doubtful whether the average behavior of the industry had improved. The muckraking efforts of a few notable publishers temporarily eliminated the worst examples of fraud from a few magazines and newspapers, but they could not be said to have established any significant con-fidence in advertising except, perhaps, that which appeared in their own publications. Inspired equally by individual revulsion at the existence of muck and by the discovery that a temporary increase in circulation more than made up for the loss of a few indignant advertisers, publishers who sponsored muckraking de-pended on the sensationalism of exposure to sustain public in-terest. Nevertheless, skepticism of advertising and demands for its reform never wholly died away, and by the middle of the 1920's the need for more drastic selling tactics led to new methods of appeal in advertising, some of which produced tension and even hostility within the advertising industry and between the industry and portions of its public.

Until at least the 1930's, however, national advertising men were less concerned over their public popularity than over their standing with business clients. Many agencies and all of the trade journals of the industry persistently attempted to convince indi-vidual firms and even entire industries of the economic advantages of advertising. Their commonest argument was that national ad-vertising was the most efficient device for obtaining a mass market and a mass market would save a manufacturer more than it cost him to advertise for it; that, in short, it almost invariably paid to advertise.[15] Year by year this contention gained validity as advertising became a noticeably better buy. The first World War, meanwhile, afforded opportunities for advertising men to serve their country while remaining in business, and the success of their war work doubtless contributed to their enhanced prestige. George Creel, chairman of the Committee on Public Information, which had utilized the advertising talents of the nation on behalf of Liberty Bonds and morale posters, once declared that up until 1917 most advertising men were regarded as in a class with sideshow barkers and check-suited salesmen, socially rejected, morally suspect; the trade was hardly worthy of recognition by a government agency, to say nothing of a respectable business firm; but during the war advertising men were able to convince Creel that they could effectively serve the national interest by building public support for the war policies of the government.[16]

Advertising men took pride in the success with which they had helped to persuade a nation at war to invest in Liberty Bonds, to forego sugar and meat, to drive its women into munitions plants, and to think of the unpleasant work of trench warfare as a crusade to kill Huns.[17] With the return of peace they were reluctant to surrender their newly won prestige, and henceforth, in the fervent promotion of their craft, they stressed that advertising had proved that it could instill ideas and that ideas could sell products. George French, editor of the trade journal *Advertising and Selling*, encouraged his readers and their clients alike to consider advertising an immensely powerful weapon for the education of consumers. "As a motive power in social, economic, religious and commercial life," French wrote in 1920, "advertising is more effective than any other in disseminating the truth."[18]

15. These general sentiments may be found in countless places in any of the trade journals of advertising in the 1920's and 1930's. The AAAA occasionally sponsored advertisements which conveyed similar arguments. *Advertising Yearbook for 1922* (New York, Doubleday, 1922), p. 208. *Advertising and Selling* (A.S.) (May 1938), p. 36.

16. George Creel, *How We Advertised America* (New York, Harper, 1920), pp. 156–65.

17. *P.I.* (May 9, 1918), p. 25; (Jan. 2, 1919), p. 61.

18. *A.S.,* (June 12, 1920), p. 3.

Others reminded businessmen that advertising could stimulate a demand for new and unfamiliar products by helping to discredit social taboos and puncture inconvenient consumer prejudices. Manufacturers of chewing gum, for example, could expect advertising to counteract the stigma of vulgarity and childishness which school teachers generally placed on it. Still others asserted that advertising men were capable of merchandising on a national scale not only medicine and pianos but "ideas" such as hygiene, Santa Claus, patriotism, and a distrust of subversives.[19]

Although hygiene and Santa Claus could be turned to commercial advantage, if carefully handled, the promotion of patriotism was apt to strike the average manufacturer and his sales manager as scarcely worth their attention. It was hard enough to credit the rasher claims which a few advertising enthusiasts were asserting on behalf of their collective talents, and some businessmen were not entirely convinced that appropriations even for product advertising deserved a place in their budgets, much less the advertising of "ideas." Hardboiled salesmen tended to scorn copy-writing as a frivolous waste of time and money, while business executives, raised in an era when greater productivity seemed to be the only business goal morally worth striving for, often distrusted the apostles of this new creed, which seemed to be based on the theory that consumption could be stimulated by verbal and pictorial sleights-of-hand.

Despite the fact, then, that the advertising industry had become by 1920 a powerful, permanent force in business and social life, its practitioners had still to solve what they were apt to consider their most bothersome problem, the problem of winning a secure position for advertising in the face of consumer and even occasional business skepticism. Those who were convinced that advertising was wasteful or that it needed control in the public interest could scarcely be won over with a few speeches at festive conventions or with limited gestures of self-control. In the period between the two wars advertising men encountered consumer resistance to their purposes. They responded to this resistance by developing techniques which would allay it without

19. *P.I.* (Jan. 2, 1919), p. 61; (Mar. 14, 1918), p. 17; (July 8, 1920), p. 17. *A.S.* (Mar. 12, 1921), p. 5. *P.I.* (Feb. 10, 1921), p. 57.

surrendering to it. They solved their problems, as shall be seen, in a way that left them confident that the future would bring newer and expanded opportunities for the unchallenged exercise of their power.

2

National Advertising and the Good Life

THE YEARS which followed the first World War were years of confidence for the American advertising man. Not only did the volume and profits of his business expand; so, more significantly, did his aims and techniques. He had come to think of himself as an instiller of "ideas," and it was clear to him in consequence that his role could be compared favorably with those of educators, editors, and all others who powerfully affected social thought. He could not help feeling, in fact, that the comparison flattered him, for he was convinced that among those whose duty was to instruct and persuade he alone was in a position to assist at the birth of a free and abundant business economy on which all that was good in life so plainly depended. For the most part he became proud of what he now chose to call his profession, and it would not be an exaggeration to say that throughout most of the generation between the two world wars he tended to look upon himself as an economic reformer, a pioneer for a new social order. This attitude was to prove immensely significant, not necessarily because it was correct but because it created distressing contradictions and dilemmas concerning the image he held of his responsibility to society.

The advertising man sought to realize his social role through the attainment of at least three goals which he had only just begun to consider desirable and within his reach but which in time were to influence the entire business of advertising. One was the belief that in an economy increasingly dependent for its stability on mass consumption, advertising could become a powerful stimulant to consumption and an essential creator of new wants. Another was the growing conviction that advertising could win public good will for individual businesses and for business enterprise in general. A third was the confidence that advertising could be liberated from the confines of simple announcement and henceforth would be in a position to adopt complex and sophisticated principles of persuasion. These goals sprang from a mixture of faith and fact, a growing awareness both of what advertising ought to be capable of doing and of what in fact it was beginning to accomplish with ever-increasing skill. Though the practice of new techniques was slow to catch up with principle, the advertising man was now to make of his pages in the mass media an influential show window in which he began to display before a susceptible public what he hoped were the persuasively alluring models of the Good Life. An examination of these goals is essential if one is to understand the subsequent relations of the advertising man to his public.

Like clergymen and teachers, advertising men appeared to derive an important sense of satisfaction from their belief that while serving their profession they were also inspiring citizens to live a more abundant life, but crucial to this belief was the conviction that a more abundant life meant a life of ever-increasing material wants, the sort of life which advertising was particularly well designed to encourage. The social mission of advertising thus depended by necessity on a doctrine of material progress. Progress allegedly resulted from a state of discontent with things as they were, and advertising bred healthy discontent. "Advertising is the art of creating a new want," one advertiser expressed it typically. Most products advertised in modern nations were not necessities of life but were "wanted" as a result of culturally-imposed values, and advertising helped mold those values. For what purpose? "By making the luxuries of today the necessities of tomorrow," advertising creates prosperity, alters social beliefs, and advances civilization.[1] And what task could prove more urgent or more timely? Of all of the economic problems which the American nation faced in the period between the two wars, possibly the most crucial was the problem of underconsumption.

Scarcely had a buyer's market developed in the early 1920's when advertising men began to assert their competence and their responsibility to promote consumption as an economic and social need. In time of depression they were to claim for themselves the power, and by inference the responsibility, to rescue the entire economy by stirring up among flagging consumers a will to consume. Similarly in a period of overproduction and apparent prosperity they were to insist that advertising was in large part responsible for the existence of leisure and wealth. To meet this responsibility, they developed at least two important operating theories for the planning of advertisements: the encouragement of a dread of obsolescence, and the stimulation of primary demand through cooperative advertising. In either case they considered that advertisements should create in their middle-class readers a frame of mind that constantly sought new acquisitions. Worried over public indifference to obsolescence, a number of watch and silver manufacturers in 1928 revealed a deep concern over the problem of underconsumption. Too many families, they observed, had been clinging to ancestral heirlooms "woefully outmoded." "We were losing an important volume of trade, year after year, due to this misapplied sentiment." It was their view that any article "which refuses to wear out is a tragedy of business." Consequently, silver and watch manufacturers alike sought relief in advertising: "ridicule of the past from which the silver was handed down proved to be the best plan." It made the owners of old

1. Truman DeWeese, Director of Publicity, Shredded Wheat Co., A.S. (June 11, 1921), p. 7.

articles "self-conscious" and aimed at "shaming them into a more liberal viewpoint." [2] Advertising, urged an executive of the General Motors Corporation at a sales convention in 1929, must make people "healthily dissatisfied with what they now have in favor of something better. The old factors of wear and tear can no longer be depended upon to create a demand. They are too slow." [3] On this critical issue Earnest Elmo Calkins, one of the most distinguished and respected advertising agents, reflected the convictions of most advertising men when he wrote in 1930 that in a period of slump consumption was the most important goal of the economic system. Advertising men must strive to become engineers of consumption. "Consumption engineering must see to it that we use *up* the kind of goods we now merely use." If the public could be more easily persuaded of obsolescence, last year's cars could be made to go the way of a used tube of toothpaste. "Consumption engineering," warned Calkins, "does not end until we can consume all we can make." [4]

The increasing enjoyment of material goods, in other words, was regarded by a happy coincidence as desirable not merely for its own sake but because it assured increasing consumption and hence production. The rate of production, whatever it might be, was sanctified as a sort of absolute, an end in itself, and consumption was required largely as a means of disposing of the product at a profit, thus enabling the productive function to continue. Advertising, wrote an editor of *Printers' Ink* in 1926, enabled manufacturers to "set up before the masses of wage-earners . . . certain definite, tangible goals of desire. . . . Whatever adds to a man's desire to own more wealth adds to the wealth of the nation." [5] Such a fortunate instrument of civilization seemed almost as morally blessed as the self-regulating mechanisms exalted in 18th-century political theory, in which the State and the Order of Nature perpetually reinforced each other for the benefit of God's principal creation, Man. Indeed a theory of free capitalistic

2. *P.I.* (May 10, 1928), p. 77. This theme was seldom made very explicit in their advertising.
3. *P.I.* (Oct. 10, 1929), p. 25.
4. *P.I.* (May 22, 1930), p. 49.
5. *P.I.* (Aug. 12, 1926), editorial.

enterprise, which most businessmen explicitly assumed when they sought to justify advertising, premised a self-correcting conflict of diverse, even hostile, interests, wherein every individual, employing whatever market tools assured him a maximum profit, automatically furthered the ultimate best interests of every other individual. The literature of advertising abounds with slight variations of this theory.

In the years before the Depression several major industries were regularly producing more than the public could be persuaded to consume. Frequently unwilling to abide the consequences of a reduction in price or in output, yet anxious to bolster their markets, many of them sponsored cooperative campaigns of advertising which attempted to stimulate a greater "primary" demand, that is to say a demand for an entire industry or class of product. Advertising of this sort was apt to originate with trade associations, which had spent only $40,000 for promotional campaigns in 1919 but over $6,000,000 for them in 1929.[6] Cooperative advertising offered copy writers an almost unprecedented opportunity to try to increase or change general habits of consumption. Those who were asserting enthusiastically that advertising could "educate" consumers were now permitted, for example, to promote not only Lux soap at the expense of Ivory but a greater use of soap in general by a larger number of people. Prominent among such industries were soap, fruit, lettuce, lumber, and cotton textiles.

An example or two will suggest the character of these efforts to bolster consumption. The Association of American Soap and Glycerine Producers, established in 1927, represented 80 per cent of the soap industry. Its purpose, according to its manager, was to increase the market for soap, and it expected to achieve this purpose in a number of ways: by advertising to the American lower classes the high standards of cleanliness expected of citizens of the cleanest country in the world; by "cooperating" with schools, boards of health, and medical men in promoting more certain habits of soap consumption, not only in family life but through cleaner buildings, window-washing, and the like; and especially

6. Philip P. Gott, "Trade Promotion by Trade Associations," *Public Opinion Quarterly* (Jan. 1937), p. 126.

by "cooperating with other business people who are going our way," which was to say plumbers and manufacturers of hot water appliances, towels, and bathroom equipment. The Association itself sponsored both general and local advertising geared not only to the less unwashed but to the already washed: there could not be too much consumption of soap in any American home.[7]

If soap producers felt insufficiently patronized, however, large food industries, faced with a decline in the quantity of food per capita consumed in the United States, regarded their plight as far more desperate. The advent of the depression encouraged some growers to hope that with skillful and continuous effort they could recapture a good part of the consumer's family budget, recently lost to automobiles, home appliances, and radios; for, they pointed out, even in a depression people have to eat.[8] To encourage a greater consumption of food, advertising men recommended cooperative campaigns for each major crop. Stated Don Francisco of the Lord and Thomas agency to a gathering of fruit growers: if the advertising for Sunkist oranges has deprived apple growers of their market, let apple growers advertise. When they have regained an apple market, let Northwest apples compete with Northeast apples. Some products might require new appeals: consider how the lemon growers proposed that lemon juice be tried as a face and scalp wash. The added consumption of a little more daily fruit for each family in the United States would not cost anybody much of anything, yet the market would be made safe for all fruit growers.[9]

Thus would advertising lead to more advertising. In a book published in 1928 and entitled *America's Prosperity*, Paul Mazur, an economist, stated the concept still more clearly. The commonplace battles between manufacturer and retailer, Mazur asserted, were no longer important compared with the real battle to break down all consumer resistance to nationally advertised products wherever sold. Whole industries would battle for an increased share of the consumer's dollar. Gigantic cooperative campaigns

7. *P.I.* (Sept. 6, 1928), p. 53.
8. *P.I.* (Oct. 30, 1930), p. 110.
9. *P.I.* (Sept. 6, 1928), p. 64. For an instance of cooperative lumber advertising, see *P.I.* (Nov. 3, 1927), p. 153. For lettuce growers, *P.I.* (Jan. 8, 1931), p. 80.

should utilize every known advertising skill to assault the public, each sponsored by an entire industry. Nobody could lose, for as the products were not directly competitive with each other, the advertisements for them would no longer work at cross purposes; automobiles would vie with radios, cigarettes with candy, but the public, induced to want both products, would find the means to buy both. The problem of overproduction would vanish, and America's prosperity would increase indefinitely.[10]

Any group which attempted with such confidence to prescribe a remedy for underconsumption almost necessarily had to express opinions on the question of the distribution of income. With regularity and conviction advertising men spoke out on behalf of high-wage policies and effective bargaining power for wage earners. "If we encourage Gusseppi [sic], the track laborer, to wear silken pajamas," cautioned a *Printers' Ink* editorial in 1919, "we must not complain when he strikes for more pay." [11] Many advertising men, of course, preferred to regard the problem in much the same way as did the average businessman: the disparity between wants and wages was self-correcting, for workers, induced to want more, would be led to work harder and longer to earn more. But frequently men engaged in the production of advertisements found themselves aligned with spokesmen for labor and for a more progressive economic philosophy, which held that a stimulus to consume, however effective, was insufficient in an economy where a large proportion of income had been funneled into savings, speculation, or an expansion of production.[12]

A crisis as severe as the Depression of 1929–33 is apt to uncover and sharpen any inconsistencies in the underlying assumptions on which a social group may conduct their operations but which are normally obscured from outside view. The Depression brought into open view a significant cleavage of opinion between advertising men and their fellow businessmen over its remedies and the economic lessons it held for the future. During the first shock of the crash few businessmen would admit that re-

10. Mazur's book was enthusiastically reviewed in *P.I.* (Mar. 22, 1928), p. 119.
11. *P.I.* (Oct. 23, 1919), p. 156.
12. For example, *P.I.* (Aug. 9, 1928), p. 41. Numerous comments of a similar nature can be found in published advertising records in the mid-1920's.

covery would require anything more than a psychological adjustment on the part of millions of consumers. Fear of buying had brought panic, and panic had induced fear. Advertising faced a crucial test of its power and responsibility. Was it not in a position to break this vicious spiral? Businessmen should persuade the consumer to hold fast to his duty to consume. Such a "psychological" view assumed a fundamental soundness in the economy and in the existing distribution of income, an assumption to which both the Federal Administration and business associations publicly subscribed. If mere fear had dammed up purchasing power, advertising had but to pry open the gates, and the flood of prosperity would return.[13] Trade associations bought space to plead for a national buying spree: money must be spent; hoarding was unpatriotic. "Buy something from somebody: we all prosper together," pleaded a utilities association in large newspaper copy in 1932.[14] "We'll go to the movies—that's one way to spend," ran one advertisement which the Hearst Press sponsored in the same year. Emergency committees to discourage the layoff of workers and to promote national confidence in recovery obtained the voluntary services of prominent advertising men, many of whom had been called to write messages of public import in 1918.[15]

But as the Depression, impervious to doses of mass persuasion, continued to spread and fester, many advertising men offered a different diagnosis and prescription. They asserted that prosperity had collapsed not from a general "failure" in consumer demand but from an inadequate distribution of wealth, short-sighted banking policies, and mistakes of national leadership.[16] In their view advertising had been all too effective: installment buying and the feverish activity of prosperity itself attested to a selling job well done. But selling was not enough. Writing from Washington in the spring of 1933, Roy Dickinson, an editor of *Printers' Ink,*

13. *P.I.* (Feb. 6, 1930), p. 163; (Aug. 18, 1932), p. 82.
14. *P.I.* (Aug. 18, 1932), p. 82.
15. *P.I.* (Dec. 11, 1930), p. 42; (Feb. 11, 1932), p. 41. See also (Oct. 15, 1931), p. 33, and (Oct. 12, 1933), p. 3, for information on federal sponsorship of advertising to solve problems of depression.
16. For example, *P.I.* (Jan. 7, 1932), p. 3. See also the comments of two businessmen in 1931, as quoted by Stuart Chase, *The Economy of Abundance* (New York, Macmillan, 1934), p. 278.

forecast a new spirit and a new power in American advertising. Henceforth the advertising agent should broaden his operations. He should be allowed to take a hand in planning production in order to obtain a maximum response from consumers. He must become an expert in marketing, a producer of consumers. Thus the advertising man would act as an agent for reform in the American economy.[17] Like the newly-formed NRA, declared Dickinson in the early weeks of the New Deal, "the fundamental purpose of advertising is to offer a better, fuller life for the masses." It must attack the "tradition of thrift" entrenched in a society where people have been taught to save rather than buy. "Orthodox and conservative policies were tried by the bankers and the old leaders and they failed." [18] In these remarks, Dickinson articulated a view which many of his readers shared. Through his advertising the modern businessman must and would attempt to strengthen public faith in a new social order in which the driving force for greater production was to be a nationwide desire to consume more goods. A new era was now at hand. Before the 1920's advertising men had not explicitly conceived of their role as one that offered promises of lessening or eliminating underconsumption, and the fact that they were now doing so and would continue to do so indicates a distinct advance in the potential influence of national advertising in American society.

National advertising, meanwhile, had been allotted still another role, that of providing general publicity and propaganda on behalf of its clients. Commonly called institutional, or public relations, advertising, it had been considered practicable and useful only with the advent of a wartime economy, when many firms, unable to supply civilians with goods, preferred to advertise their names rather than their non-existent products.[19] In periods of normal economic activity businessmen usually made no secret of their contempt for the "glittering generalities" of institutional advertising. In order to sell, an advertisement was supposed to focus

17. *P.I.* (Apr. 20, 1933), p. 3. See also, E. E. Calkins, *P.I.* (May 22, 1930), p. 49.

18. *P.I.* (July 6, 1933), p. 3.

19. *P.I.* (Jan. 3, 1918), p. 95; (Nov. 7, 1918), p. 44; (July 10, 1919), p. 93.

on the thing sold; one which did not sell could not pay its own way.[20] Because the effectiveness of institutional advertising was even more difficult to measure than the effectiveness of other kinds, it was considered a likely refuge for incompetent agents and poseurs. But despite this undercurrent of suspicion, institutional advertising grew markedly in the 1920's and soon established itself as an important adjunct of commercial advertising in general. One well-known agent, Theodore F. MacManus, who was responsible for the advertising of the Cadillac automobile, invoked in these years a vision of the potentiality and scope of institutional advertising which seemed almost intoxicating:

> Think of the same mental flash repeating itself over and over again—on farms, in county seats, small towns, small cities, big cities, metropolitan centers; in homes, stores, railroad trains, boats, clubs, crowded streets, quiet country lanes. Think of an invisible cloud of friendly, favorable impressions rising up from that mass—a warm breath of good will— coming, going—all over the nation. Think of its speaking the needed word: silently, insidiously, unconsciously, influencing the buying effort.[21]

Institutional advertising flourished, it seems to me, not because its critics were wrong but because it was able to advance far beyond the original techniques and uses to which its critics principally objected. In prewar America institutional advertising had become overlaid with accepted conventions; typically it consisted of a large lithograph of the company plant, idealized, surrounded with portrait ovals from which were apt to glare the engraved likenesses of the founder, his first treasurer, and the present manager. Younger businessmen, disdainful of such uninspired practices and remembering successful instances of "personality" publicity in war, virtually succeeded in raising what had been an unsophisticated use of the pathetic fallacy into a sort of advertising first principle.[22] In 1925 the Association of Advertising Clubs

20. A.S. (Dec. 11, 1920), p. 12. Sentiments of this nature were frequently expressed in the 1920's.

21. *P.I.* (Feb. 10, 1927), p. 85.

22. See, for example, *P.I.* (June 12, 1919), p. 37; (Jan. 1, 1920), p. 61; (Jan. 8, 1920), p. 29.

of the World (AACW) published a book by Amos Stote, an authority on public relations, in which he stated that the principal concept of advertising to emerge since the World War was the humanization of business. It was no longer enough to glorify the firm; one must emphasize the loyalty, friendliness, and respect between consumer, manager, and worker that prevails between members of families. Customers did not necessarily offer a seller their loyalty simply because they had patronized him; they were often "as fickle as their average intelligence is small." Stote viewed the task of modern advertising as that of substituting for a purely market relationship of buyer and seller a broader social relationship. He urged that even as businessmen sell products they should also sell the totality of a corporate enterprise, its impact on American life, its role in the social structure.[23] The consumer, Stote had declared in an earlier article, "must be made to feel that big business is his big brother." [24]

Rather than sell an inanimate object or a service, then, a firm should attempt to sell a "personal" relationship instead; many who did so were primarily interested in winning the sympathy of their employees and the public for their labor policies. Advertisements for the Cleveland Hydraulic Pressed Steel Company, according to a statement of the management, were written to establish the impression that the company was a person—complete with soul and conscience—talking man-to-man with the other persons who happened to work for him: here at Hydraulic we are all equal, all "fellows," fighting a common enemy, dehumanization.[25] The Billings-Spencer Company, manufacturer of machine tools, promoted a similar image of its labor relations. The company was a human being, for which all of its workmen had an "affection" born of their "love of steel"; they worked not only for wages, "the lesser reward," but for satisfactions of craftsmanship and out of an affectionate appreciation for their employer.[26] Meat packers, following the publicity given their operations at the beginning of the century, were occasionally vociferous

23. Amos Stote, *Why We Live*, New York, Doubleday, Page, 1925.
24. *P.I.* (Apr. 24, 1924), p. 10.
25. *P.I.* (July 31, 1919), p. 3.
26. *P.I.* (June 26, 1919), p. 33.

in support of "educational" advertising. A large corporation, stated an executive of the Swift Packing Company in 1920, must possess "character," not based simply upon meritorious services or products but upon the total image which the public has of the corporation. Swift advertised in order to present the public with the facts of business life and with the principles on which any business must be conducted under a profit system.[27] "Our advertising," wrote Mr. A. H. Smith, president of the New York Central Railroad in 1920, "is, so to speak, an accounting of our stewardship. We feel that it is due the public and due us." [28]

Public relations advertising soon became the particular hallmark of utilities, insurance companies, and a few large trade associations. Many businesses of this sort felt themselves victimized by local public regulatory bodies seeking to force them to lower their rates, offer additional services, or even to pass out of existence. Local governments often regarded large national industries as likely sources of tax revenue, and a crusading political orator could easily pin blame on a large utility for local ills and troubles. Utilities were consequently eager to make use of whatever policies of publicity would best serve them. The Great Northern Railroad in 1924, for example, advertised extensively in local papers that served the communities through which it ran; its message stressed not travel but the economic advantages which the railroad brought to the region, the "human interest" stories of personnel and operations, and the reasons why a large corporation could make more profit at less cost to the customer than a small one.[29] A group of manufacturing firms in Wisconsin ran an "educational" series in their local papers to forestall "unfair" regulatory action by the state legislature and to urge a lower tax rate on corporations.[30] The National Lumber Manufacturers' Association advertised nationally from 1922 to 1929 in order to promote not only the sale of lumber but a favorable public image of the lumberman as a public-spirited conservator of the nation's forests, a man

27. *A.S.* (Sept. 4, 1920), p. 12.
28. *A.S.* (July 3, 1920), p. 9.
29. *P.I.* (Oct. 2, 1924), p. 3.
30. *P.I.* (Dec. 4, 1924), p. 10. The "unfair" action which the Legislature was contemplating was the enactment of an eight-hour day and an employee insurance requirement.

on whom regulations of local and state governments fell as an unfair burden.[31]

Until the 1930's, national advertising was rarely used to win favorable attitudes toward business in general or to promulgate a point of view toward political or economic questions of national interest. But as the Depression deepened, voices could be heard expressing cautious hope that the national advertising industry might help to refurbish the social reputation of American business and to create public allegiance to the structure of values on which both business and advertising were thought to depend. In the same year in which the Supreme Court ruled the NRA unconstitutional, a number of prominent corporations, including General Motors and U. S. Steel, were sponsoring advertisements on behalf of all American business. General Motors' advertising declared that whoever serves Progress serves America, that Business benefits the consumer while Government taxes him, and they warned that the American way of life was in danger from ambitious schemers.[32] Foremost among those who encouraged this use of paid advertisements was Bruce Barton, a leading advertising executive who argued, typically, that no industry had any right to be "misunderstood" by the public, for "by its unpopularity it poisons the pond in which we all must fish." In December 1935 Barton told businessmen that if they wished to save themselves, they had better use advertising to win the next election. The story of what business means to America, he warned, "should be told just as continuously as the people are told that

31. *P.I.* (Jan. 3, 1924), p. 93; (July 12, 1928), p. 53. A Congressional investigation of conservation practices no doubt contributed to the lumbermen's eagerness to employ national advertising, as was also the case with public utilities. To advertise one's virtues in the local papers frequently served the dual purpose of creating a favorable public image of one's company and rendering the paper itself—often the only organ of local opinion—significantly grateful for essential revenues. In a report published in the *New Republic* (Jan. 20, 1926) many country weeklies, squeezed by rising costs of publishing and increased competition from large city dailies, were cited as having been forced to compete for lucrative "foreign" (i.e. national) advertising by offering editorial support to the advertiser himself. This foreign advertising was placed chiefly by electric utilities, manufacturing companies, and railroads. It was designed not to sell goods but primarily to develop good will toward its sponsors and toward the general economic system.

32. S. H. Walker and Paul Sklar, *Business Finds Its Voice: Management's Efforts to Sell the Business Idea to the Public*, New York, Harper, 1938.

Ivory Soap floats or that children cry for Castoria." [33] Throughout the ensuing eleven months other advertising men echoed Barton's plea, but the one-sided presidential victory in November 1936 apparently led many businessmen to doubt whether ideas of such a general nature could sway the public, and corporations reverted once more to institutional advertising.[34]

By 1940 enough firms had regularly engaged in public relations advertising to create virtually a new occupation: whereas advertising men in the 1920's had tended to sneer at the lowly "press agent," by now they were enthusiastic about his more respectable offspring, the "public relations expert." In 1949, Ralph Hower reported in his history of the N. W. Ayer advertising agency: "The clear and inescapable authority with which an advertiser could inform the public *on a wide range of subjects* . . . led Ayer to [declare], 'Advertising is a specialized technique for mass communication.'" [35] The agent, according to Hower, anticipated becoming a business advisor in the broadest sense of the word, an advisor for all of a firm's policies of "communication." Plainly, whatever views on a "wide range of subjects" a firm chose to "communicate" would henceforth be promulgated by every available technique of advertising that had been proven effective in influencing the public to purchase consumer commodities. Equally plain was the fact that although the services of advertising agencies were available to anyone who had the required amount of money to spend, some institutions had more money to spend than others, and consequently those views held by institutions not wealthy enough to afford the cost of "communicating" them by the well-developed techniques of advertising could scarcely compete with the views held by institutions which could afford it.

In the first quarter of the 20th century the techniques and the tone of American advertising underwent profound and significant change. The average national advertisement written in 1910 characteristically limited itself to a simple illustrated description

33. *P.I.* (Dec. 12, 1935), p. 17.
34. *P.I.* (Apr. 30, 1936), p. 7; (Oct. 15, 1936), p. 49; (Aug. 18, 1938), p. 6.
35. Hower, pp. 183–4. Italics mine.

of a product. The description was not necessarily truthful: it may have distorted or even misrepresented the facts, but more often than not it overflowed with specific claims for the product and what the product could do. Lemons (pictured) may be used in three ways (described). Pear's soap was the best soap for cleansing the skin (illustrated with a woman's face). As a rule the copy attempted to argue or discuss its claims; examples of fantasy and the use of arresting human action irrelevant to the product were rare. Such advertising seldom attempted to sell an attitude or a way of life. But by the 1920's the world of the American advertisement had become distinctly more complex. Passing gradually from simple methods of announcement to complex methods of emotional and nonrational appeal, national advertising attempted to traffic in beliefs concerning the Good Life.

Some manufacturers found that merely a statement of quality and an illustration of the product were insufficient to sell it, that to sell a product, one must sell more than the product: one must sell its use and service, indeed an entire pattern of consumption. An advertisement must be capable, for example, of persuading a reader to buy not just an orange but health and refreshment, not a furnace but heat and comfort. So advertising began to evoke from the product a cloud of subjective values, and this change in emphasis led to an important change in appeal and tone. For as soon as copy writers released themselves from the confinement of factual description, they increasingly substituted for it a world of fantasy and verbal euphemism bordering on the irrational.[36] A description, for example, of a Simmons bed, its length, width, mattress, cost, and model specifications riveted no one's attention and merely pointed up the possibility that other makes of bed might be cheaper and just as serviceable. But to advertise quiet "noiseless" sleep [37] was eventually to allow one's artist, photogra-

36. A.S. (Jan. 25, 1919), p. 13. Investigation of national advertisements selected from four evenly spaced years (1895, 1906, 1917, 1928) led me to these conclusions, and comments by other observers would seem to confirm them. See A.S. (July 17, 1920), pp. 10–12; P.I. (Aug. 12, 1920), p. 73; Hower, p. 264; Daniel Starch, *Principles of Advertising*, New York, H. W. Shaw, 1923; Joseph H. Appel, *Growing Up with Advertising* (New York Business Bourse, 1940), pp. 93–101.

37. P.I. (Apr. 21, 1921), p. 41.

pher, and copy writer a field day in self-expression, and to cele-
brate rest with an illustrated poem, or to suggest that one's bed
should confer prestige, security, and heightened sexual facility as
well as sleep, would presumably assure Simmons a wider readership, a unique set of virtues, and a means of discouraging a factual
comparison of products. "I want advertising copy to arouse me,"
pleaded the associate editor of *Advertising and Selling* in 1919,
heralding what he hoped was a new era in salesmanship, ". . . to
create in me a desire to possess the thing that's advertised, even
though I don't need it." [38]

By 1930 advertising men had begun to explore a range of
techniques scarcely touched before the first World War. Arresting
layouts and a striking use of photography augmented their
sophisticated creation of "human interest." These developments
were particularly noticeable in advertisements for cigarettes, tires,
dental products, and cosmetics, which, though they accounted
for only one-fourth of all paid space, attained after 1920 a unique
prominence through an original and imaginative use of headlines, newspaper layouts, publicity stunts, and testimonials, and
through an ability to attract and disarm readers by offerings of
entertainment and human anecdote. Yet it would be misleading
to suggest that emotional copy universally replaced rational ex-
position and factual argument. The attention which some industries incurred by their spectacular advertising tended to conceal
the fact that as of 1929 the many advertisements in the general
and women's magazines were written for producers of canned
food, clothing, home appliances, and furniture, whose advertising techniques on the whole remained conventional and conservative. [39]

The advertising of the automobile industry exerted perhaps

---

38. *A.S.* (Jan. 25, 1919), p. 13.

39. A survey conducted by *Tide* (Sept. 1929), p. 3, of the *Ladies' Home Journal*
for September 1929, revealed that of 100 full-page advertisements, 14 exploited
testimonials, 26 employed other sensational or "human interest" devices, 4 were
public relations or institutional advertisements, and the remaining 56 consisted of
"rational" argumentative copy, advice, or recipes, or the product pictured by
itself. Independent investigation of the same magazine issue indicated to this
writer that, given an extremely broad conception of rationality, the findings of
Tide were generally valid.

the strongest pull toward intangible, subjective copy. Next to
soap products, automobiles have accounted for more national
advertising than any other industry in the country, and the copy
practices of their agents have helped to influence the style of
national advertising in general. Prewar advertising for automobiles had often featured technical and expository argument and
was written for men. But by the late 1920's few automobile advertisements mentioned motors, parts, or performance in any but
the most evasive terms; their copy and illustrations were increasingly directed at middle-class women, and ownership of an automobile was first being made to seem not only a key to goals desirable for their own sake but a social necessity and a moral duty.
A command to "try our new Chevrolet" was merely an invitation
to consume and had characterized most advertising throughout
time. But gradually in its place came the more elaborate proposition which tended to assert, implicitly if not directly, that he who
gave up his cheap Chevrolet for an expensive Cadillac would not
only drive faster but live better, earn more, climb more easily
into a bigger home and job, and be asked with his wife to join
the country club.[40] One of the earliest successful campaigns to
"institutionalize" an automobile, in fact, was managed by Theodore MacManus for Cadillac. He constructed successfully what
was in effect a subjective and unprovable prestige value that led
virtually a whole society to think of the Cadillac as "the best,"
the "number one" among American cars, an attitude shared
equally by those who could afford to buy one and those who could
not.[41]

By 1930 the automobile in American advertising had evolved
into a great symbol of aspiration, pictured in a setting as ritualistic
as the iconography of a cathedral window, and its functions in
some ways were similar. Copy writers almost invariably surrounded their products with wealth, glamour, and country estates,
filled them with leisure-class residents of Newport or the Main
Line, handsome, windblown couples driving to a lawn party, or
rosy children warm and safe in the back seat. Such advertisements

40. For examples of this sort, see *Saturday Evening Post* (Jan. 24, 1925), p.
45; (Jan. 7, 1928), p. 77.
41. *P.I.* (Oct. 4, 1923), p. 33.

ONLY
PACKARD
CAN BUILD A
PACKARD

A MAN IS KNOWN BY THE CAR HE KEEPS

In the old days men were rated by the homes in which they lived

and few but their friends saw them.

Today, men are rated by the cars they drive

and everybody sees them—

for the car is mobile and the home is not.

To own a Packard is an evidence of discriminating taste.

Woman, with her observing eye, has known this for twenty-five years.

And woman, proverbial for her greater thrift, will insist upon the family motor car being a Packard once she learns that the Packard Six costs less to own, operate and maintain than the ordinary car the family has been buying every year or two.

Packard Six and Packard Eight both furnished in ten body types, open and enclosed. Packard's extremely liberal monthly payment plan makes possible the immediate enjoyment of a Packard, purchasing out of income instead of capital.

A S K   T H E   M A N   W H O   O W N S   O N E

4. While most automobile advertisements in 1925 remained factual and "rational" in technique, a few were already cultivating an appeal to intangible values.

tried to assure their readers of the permanence and desirability of a way of life whose very core was the ownership and consumption of an automobile; they were making it possible for a nation of car owners to believe, and not without reason, that they owned more than a car; with a car came membership in a special brotherhood which possessed a dream world of its own; and they were helping to reinforce public faith in the automobile as a social institution. Automobile advertising, summarized John B. Hardee, one of its practitioners in 1929, has established the fact that "no matter what you pay for your motor car, it will give you prestige and social recognition." [42]

More explicitly educational were the advertisements published in these years by the Metropolitan Life Insurance Company, and it is perhaps significant that they won constant acclaim from advertising men for their ideal of "public service." A few of them received an award for disclosing "the highest type of idealism in business," and another received a Harvard Advertising Award for literary merit.[43] In substance Metropolitan advertisements were editorials which offered middle-class readers popular advice, publicity on personal health and hygiene, the care of one's family, discoveries in the treatment of disease and illness, advances in public health, and patterns of personal and social behavior. They stressed that communities gain when individuals cooperate to make homes safe and healthy; they encouraged the support of welfare agencies, waste disposal, traffic safety, the welcoming and care of immigrants, programs of immunization, and fresh air camps for city children. To American families their advice, endlessly repeated, was unambiguous: invest money regularly, save for the future, buy insurance to guarantee a regular income for your wife and children, see your doctor frequently, eat wisely,

42. *P.I.* (Dec. 12, 1929), p. 197.

43. See *An Adventure in Advertising,* a pamphlet published in 1925 by the Metropolitan Life Insurance Company, in which 32 of their advertisements, circulated in national magazines, were reproduced. See also *P.I.* (Oct. 24, 1929), p. 3; (Aug. 20, 1931), p. 44; (Aug. 16, 1934), p. 97. The Harvard Advertising Awards were begun in 1924 by E. W. Bok, who sponsored them with funds given to the Harvard Business School for establishing a yearly contest to determine the best advertisement, or series of them, according to criteria of service to advertising, effectiveness of composition, etc.

vote, clean your teeth, control your weight, repair your home, learn to enjoy leisure, drink milk, support the Child Labor Amendment, be a better employer and a kinder neighbor. This advertising often implicitly underscored a number of general social themes: the modern American family is surrounded with a protective wall of institutional services consisting of nurses, doctors, chemists, and insurance companies, who wage a heroic battle against invading hosts of germs and an unfriendly Nature; social progress is inevitable if every man joins to eradicate squalor and poverty; through work, thrift, and hygiene an era of social prosperity will arrive.

Advertisements for Metropolitan Life were unique in their imaginative display of a social conscience. Impeccably discreet, their messages served the public by serving their sponsor. Advertisers were understandably envious of such a corporation; here for once it was possible to find in virtue an economic necessity. Metropolitan advertisements were truly a special case. Nevertheless, in promulgating a doctrine of faith in progress they had much in common with the important and far more conspicuous segment of American advertising which was first beginning to present a world of middle-class dreams. In this world one could now find a few basic themes embodying a distinctive set of social values scarcely visible in advertising ten years before.

Two of the most common themes in American advertising in the 1920's may be expressed roughly as follows: [44]

1. The American family at home. Home is never an apartment but a house, usually owned. It sanctifies leisure and recreation. It is invariably a "white collar" home. No one works or sweats; families only play at home. A housewife plays with her kitchen and her laundry; the husband plays with his boys or his radio.

44. The following analysis is based on a study of the advertising found in three issues of the *Woman's Home Companion:* May 1928, February 1929, September 1929. For each basic theme, recurrent enough to warrant consideration, I devised a system of evaluating its strength and frequency of impact. For advertisements in which the basic theme predominated, I set the following "point" values: double page, 5; single page, 3; half page, 2. Color pages and unusually spectacular effects were allotted 1–3 points extra. For advertisements with more than one theme conspicuously present, I counted the value for each theme. A few themes predominant in women's magazines failed to score heavily in general magazines, and vice versa.

Homes usually have two cars and a dog. Mothers-in-law, uncles, and grandfathers live elsewhere. Single men and women do not exist. A successful man is a husband who is unfailingly cheerful, "sincere," and upwardly mobile. He may often acquire these virtues by correspondence courses and by other expenditures of money, but his failure to possess them would be a sign not of poverty but of defective character. The worries, insecurities, and fears of modern men and women stem from failure to be liked, to adjust to one another, to find adequate sexual satisfactions, but especially from failure to live amid the accoutrements of leisure. These criteria of security are surpassingly important to all families. To possess them is to be free from tension and misery. Harmony and happiness in fact depend on the rate of consumption of gadgets. Friends are always dropping in to view the Frigidaire or dance to the Philco. No more than a good meal and a quiet deodorant are needed to keep the affection of one's husband and children. The preparation and serving of food, to be sure, is a complex function; but the housewife may trust the food industry for advice and guidance. Other large institutions perpetually bolster the family: banks, insurance companies, and utilities stand ready to protect its security and preserve its happiness. Money spent in these institutions is never an expense but an investment.

2. *The importance of romantic love.* The satisfactions of sex and the criteria of romantic love are inextricably intertwined; but whereas romantic love is indispensable to sexual satisfaction, the reverse is not the case: romantic love is desirable in and of itself and is bound up with other ends, such as prestige, social success, power, and wealth. The criteria of romantic love can be acquired cheaply by purchase: youth, smoothness of skin, a prominent bust, a deodorized body, a daily ritual of body care, handsome or alluring clothes, outward manners, and a ready affirmative response to these criteria in the other person. (Some women age so young and fade out—constipated. The wife of the Pretender to the throne of France is irresistible; she possesses the power to love; she commands attention; she uses Ponds. Look like a schoolgirl all your life; use Palmolive for your skin—it is made from natural African beauty oils.) Romantic love is available

only to those who retain the appearance of youth. Men and women over forty are Mothers, Fathers, Grandmothers, Grandfathers, Business Executives, Professional People; they are no longer capable of romantic love or, therefore, of sexual interests. They seek, instead, prestige and social success; they are content merely to conform to their assigned roles as Mother, Father, etc. Romantic love is also a function of wealth and the ability to consume it. Romantic love depends on leisure time, shopping, parties, sports, vacations, cruises, night clubs, and usually on the premise that the pair are not yet married. Real satisfaction is attainable from sex only upon acquiring the criteria of romantic love.

The most striking new element in the social content of national advertising in the 1920's and 1930's was a conspicuous preoccupation with leisure and the enjoyment of consumption. In 1925 a national advertisement for a commercial bank was headed: "May your child's disappointment always be equally trivial." There followed an illustration of a small boy who was crying because a balloon had just escaped from his chubby hand. The text continued:

> His heart is broken . . . But Daddy will soon make good the loss. A new balloon of gorgeous color will quickly turn the clouds into sunshine. That seems to be Daddy's perennial job to keep the clouds away and to make his children's lives one continuous day of sunshine. And, as they grow . . . it requires more expensive and more skillful planning. Instead of a balloon your son wants financial backing . . . your daughter wants vocational education. You want them both to have a trip to Europe, and other advantages which perhaps you never enjoyed.[45]

The overt intention of this advertisement was to encourage investment and savings, but the stimulus which it employed was of a different and far more representative character. Leisure to consume and to enjoy material goods was an effective guarantee of happiness.

The importance of this doctrine, explicit in the advertisements

45. Quoted in *P.I.* (Dec. 10, 1925), p. 49, under the title, "Advertising—Arch Enemy of Poverty and Disease."

themselves, was deliberately stressed by the men who wrote them. Those engaged in 20th-century advertising in the United States looked on themselves, in effect, as crusaders for the liberation of a middle-class people from the tyranny of Puritanism, parsimoniousness, and material asceticism. Has advertising lured Americans into living beyond their means? asked *Printers' Ink* in 1930. Ten years ago, went the answer, this question might have been a real one, but not today. Americans have now been persuaded that it is "wholesome to live and to enjoy abundantly, that happiness in the hand is in itself like money in the bank. . . . To live and to enjoy—that is the basis of modern economics." [46] When defining the subject of advertising for the *Encyclopedia of Social Sciences* in 1933, Everett S. Lyon was to ascribe to the advertiser a central role in a new society:

> This great advertising activity has been largely due to the fact that advertisers have accepted increased productivity and, more important, its corollary, increased consumptivity. . . . In accepting consumptivity they have been alone. The bankers have preached investments; the economist has taught saving; the schools have inculcated thrift. Our tradition is a tradition of careful frugality. . . . Consumer advertising is the first rough effort of a society becoming prosperous to teach itself the use of the relatively great wealth of new resources, new techniques and a reorganized production. . . . Advertising . . . is almost the only force at work against puritanism in consumption.

Advertising men set out deliberately to combat what they considered to be the archaic attitudes of an earlier society, namely, that to crave and enjoy material goods was sinful, that to consume with abandon or on mere whim was a waste and consequently immoral. In the 1920's the business leaders of America were still steeped, it appeared, in the ethic of producers, who considered thrift and frugality to be virtues, who distrusted the attitudes of the spendthrift, and who even scorned preoccupation with leisure, a primary fact of their contemporary society, as morally degenerating and as destructive of the social order. Such men, it has been suggested, measured success by one's pecuniary

46. *P.I.* (Jan. 23, 1930), p. 81.

standing, but only because pecuniary standing measured productive ability and not because it might enhance one's skill in consumption or enthusiasm for it.[47] A society which had so long revered these qualities now, it seemed, had to be taught to approve and engage in uninhibited consumption. Into a world of older values, then—the values of an earlier capitalistic ethic—the advertising man came as a self-consciously rebellious reformer.

Yet in two important ways the advertising industry compromised with the traditional ethic even while attempting to reform it. On the one hand, most advertising men continued to insist that the principal virtue of high consumption was its tendency to stimulate production. Much as the hardness of a pew in church could serve to keep a sinner awake to the sermon, so might the discontent and frustrations induced by modern advertising spur a productive society to a high rate of growth. "An absolute resignation to things as they are is found among the fatalistic inhabitants of India and China," an advertising man wrote in 1930. In happy contrast, he pointed out, "dissatisfied customers" create new markets, and American advertising "helps to keep the masses dissatisfied with their present mode of life." [48] Secondly, most national advertisements continued throughout the 1920's and 1930's to operate on the principle that consumers had to possess direct and conscious reasons, or what would pass for such reasons, to consume anything. It was important, particularly in a period of economic depression, to cast an aura of scientific and logical rationality over a stimulus to buy, whether the stimulus itself was rational or not. It is notable, however, that by 1940 advertising men found it possible and occasionally desirable to reduce or to abandon these partial concessions to an older ethic, and even where these concessions were not abandoned they did not greatly hinder the persistent effort of national advertising to break down the psychological barriers which hindered consumption.[49]

But the ultimate development of social significance in national

47. For a persuasive study of this ethic and the extent to which it pervaded the business world of the 1920's see James W. Prothro, *The Dollar Decade* (Baton Rouge, Lousiana State University Press, 1954), pp. 209–41.

48. *P.I.* (Feb. 6, 1930), p. 163. This general view is rife in all advertising literature in the late 1920's.

49. Further discussion of this trend will be found in Chap. 7, below.

advertising between the two wars was that it had become a form of literary art, or was at least performing some of the functions of literary art.[50] Offering ritualistic symbols to evoke a dream world of desirable consumption, advertising enabled and encouraged the reader to apprehend this world directly from the symbols and to discover in it an object of aspiration. Not only did it teach the public how to consume and how to behave with material goods, it also helped make the *problem* of how to consume of fundamental concern to everyone. In an economy of abundance, American advertising soon became a guide to social competence and social success. Man, said the practitioners of advertising, lives by his desires and his wants. Advertising, like literary or religious art, simultaneously expressed man's desires and exhorted him to fulfill them.

Within a few years advertising men created for themselves a complex role. In their struggle to sell goods and services, they learned to conduct a continuous traffic in ideas; they attempted to reinforce and encourage attitudes helpful to businessmen in an economy threatened with a serious lag in consumption; and they successfully mirrored for a nation of consumers a specialized and popular image of the Good Life. The new role of advertising called for the ceaseless exercise of influence and social power, and as its powers grew there soon developed an internal struggle to harness and safeguard it and to preserve its role as an increasingly secure and profitable auxiliary of business capitalism. At issue in this struggle were not the goals of advertising but the methods for reaching them. Advertising men, as will be made clear, were anxious to forestall the insistent public questions which their methods had begun to raise, and they were to hope that the internal regulation of methods would render the goals immune from any conceivable assault.

50. For two perceptive views of advertising as a form of literary art see Elizabeth Corbett, "The American Legend," *Century Magazine* (Jan. 1929), p. 303; Paul Parker, "The Iconography of Advertising Art," *Harper's* (June 1938), p. 80.

3

The Limits of Internal Regulation

In 1927 a mattress manufacturer was brought into a California court on the charge of having violated a state statute which outlawed fraudulent advertising. The court found not only the manufacturer but his advertising agent guilty of fraud and supported its verdict with an opinion that the agent represented a firm of advertising men who ought always to be considered responsible for upholding a professional standard of ethics.[1] Thus the behavior of an advertising man was condemned, because in addition to being fraudulent it was declared detrimental to the professional interests of advertising. The case may stand as a symbol for the fact that by 1927 the interpretation of what constituted these professional interests or responsibilities had become an over-riding issue for the national advertising industry in the United States.

For many years advertising men had referred to their trade as

1. *P.I.* (Oct. 6, 1927), p. 112.

a "profession." Though some of them deprecated the pretensions of the label, most regarded themselves as responsible in a "professional" sense primarily to their business clients and to their own fellow practitioners for avoiding any conduct which might cast an ill reflection on the general practice of advertising. Few went so far as to declare that the peculiarly persuasive nature of advertising entailed an added responsibility to the public, but they were generally agreed that, inasmuch as advertising depended entirely on public response, an advertiser who abused the confidence of his public tended to imperil further public response to other advertisers. The public was considered a sort of mining stake in which all advertisers held a claim. An overexuberant or careless advertiser, lest his actions spoil the public domain for the rest, needed to be curbed, and his colleagues should go about curbing him with a sense of professional obligation which would transcend their relations as mere businessmen.

By the close of the first World War the internal regulation of advertising had become a complex operation. Better Business Bureaus, trade associations, and publishers made efforts to enforce standards of behavior against which advertisements might be measured and to encourage those who bought advertisements to respect the interests of their competitors. Where advertising was clearly fraudulent, these institutions and individuals, reinforced by the Federal Trade Commission and by state laws, operated with the nearly unanimous backing of the industry and with effective thoroughness. Where, on the other hand, advertising did not commit fraud but appeared merely to practice deception, offend readers, or annoy but not ruin competitors, internal regulation became a subject of controversy among those whom it served and remained often ineffective. Not, in a general sense, until the 1930's did an aroused public seem capable of threatening sanctions against an advertiser; sanctions at the very least usually required the active support of a discontented competitor. It would be precarious to generalize too readily, however, for the record of regulation and the course it followed reflected the dilemmas inherent in any private institution whose transactions so consistently impinged on the public consciousness.

The California statute which tripped up the mattress maker

and which was re-interpreted to support the professional dignity
of advertising agents was a diluted version of a model statute
which some advertising men proposed in 1911 at the request of
the journal *Printers' Ink*. In that year at a widely publicized convention in Boston, the AACW urged every state to adopt legislation based on the model statute. The statute declared that any
person who placed before the public an advertisement "containing any assertion or statement of fact which is untrue, deceptive
or misleading, shall be guilty of a misdemeanor." [2] No important
advertising association or group, either then or subsequently, objected to it. By 1940 twenty-six states had adopted it; seventeen
others had approved an emasculated version which required the
state to prove that the culprit had deceived the public "knowingly"; five states had taken no action whatever.[3] Prosecutions
under the statute remained few in number, but its principal value
was as a deterrent in the hands of Better Business Bureaus and
other voluntary agencies which sought to dissuade offenders
rather than punish them.[4]

The Better Business Bureaus themselves may be traced in origin
to the work of the AACW and its "National Vigilance Committee," formed in 1907 to help its member associations "curb abuses"
of current business ethics. Subcommittees were soon organized in
a few large cities to act as voluntary policemen, alert to discourage
"unfair" competitive practices of small retailers and to prohibit
grossly deceptive and fraudulent advertising found in local newspapers.[5] The burden of policing soon proved too much for in-

2. The history of its origin and promulgation has been told fully elsewhere. See
P.I. (June 16, 1921), p. 44. H. J. Kenner, *The Fight for Truth in Advertising*
(New York, Round Table Press, Inc., 1936) gives a detailed account of the fight
for the *P.I.* Statute.

3. States with full statute (east to west): R.I., N.Y., N.J., Va., Ala., Ohio, Ky.,
Ind., Mich., Ill., Wsc., Minn., Iowa, Mo., La., Okla., Kans., Nebr., N.D., Colo.,
Wyo., Idaho, Nev., Ore., Wash. States with nominal statute (east to west): Me.,
N.H., Vt., Mass., Conn., Penn., Md., N.C., S.C., Fla., Tenn., Texas, S.D., Mont.,
Utah, Ariz., Calif. Statutes of this sort are regarded as very difficult to enforce.
States with no statute are Del., Ga., Miss., Ark., N.M.

4. *P.I.* (June 16, 1921), p. 44. For the year ending May 1, 1921, local Bureaus
handled 6815 cases, of which 51 ended in outright prosecutions. Bureau officials
frequently employed threats of publicity as an effective means to induce "cooperation."

5. Statement of the Committee, as quoted in Lee, *The Daily Newspaper in
America*, p. 359.

formal voluntary committees, however, and gradually their function was assumed by the full-time professional organizations which became known as Better Business Bureaus, whose operations grew specific and efficient enough to attract the financial and moral support of "respectable" businessmen. By the 1920's the Bureaus were successfully overseeing general business behavior in most of the nation's large cities. Their energies were placed principally at the service of powerful local businessmen who desired above all else to eliminate price cutting and the sale of substandard or defective merchandise, but the Bureaus were additionally effective in encouraging the local press to refuse dishonest retail advertising and to improve the ethical standards of local advertising in general. Behind the Bureaus stood the threat of the *Printers' Ink* statute, though Bureau directors preferred to rely on persuasion and informal pressure.

The effectiveness of the Better Business Bureaus in maintaining a structure of internal control generally depended on two conditions: the power and influence of the groups which backed them had to exceed the power and influence of the offending culprit sufficiently to render certain a measure of compliance and cooperation; and the offense had to be clear-cut and blatant enough to arouse among a powerful majority of business competitors an active and unhesitating disapproval. In their early stages the Bureaus directed their efforts most often against the "little fellows." [6] Reports of Bureau activities emphasized the number of "hole-in-the-wall" businesses, the "marginal" operators, the "petty" chiselers, who seemed to require the constant attention of Bureau officials. As in the case of the California mattress maker, most offenses involved mislabeling, misrepresentation of retail products, untrue price claims, and a number of other practices more characteristic of small retail firms or specialty manufacturers than of the larger merchants with impressive, and consequently valuable, reputations.

But by the beginning of the Depression an increasing number

6. Albert E. Haase, "What Vigilance Work Has Accomplished under the *P.I.* Statute," *P.I.* (June 16, 1921), p. 44. Taeusch, *Policy and Ethics in Business,* pp. 464–70. See also Kenner, *The Fight for Truth in Advertising;* John Richardson, "Business Policing Itself through the Better Business Bureaus," *Harvard Business Review,* 9 (1930), 69.

of large companies now fell under Bureau censure, not for such clearly fraudulent practices as labeling rabbit fur mink or selling goat glands to elderly men, but for a type of advertising practice known euphemistically as a "borderline offense." This form of transgression involved copy claims which could not be considered directly fraudulent or indictable but which were recognized as misleading. A certain make of canned beans, for example, had not in fact been "baked" but, to the distress of manufacturers of genuine baked beans, had been advertised to give the impression that it was a variety of "baked" beans; while advertisements for Lucky Strike cigarettes at one time implied, without directly saying so, that smoking was an effective means for reducing one's weight.[7] Faced with almost countless possibilities of such legal deceptions, most Bureaus in the late 1920's correspondingly broadened their attack on illegal advertising to include borderline practices.[8]

Precisely because advertising men generally disagreed as to which borderline practices ought to be discouraged and which should not, internal sanctions against them proved largely ineffective. No one was prepared to place these practices, no matter how misleading to the public, in the same class with those which involved outright fraud, as, for example, that of a clothing salesman who advertised second-hand garments as new. Least of all were local Bureaus able to impose effective sanctions on powerful national advertisers. They were ineffective in part because national advertisers of established reputation were on the whole less vulnerable than local merchants to charges of open fraud; when they violated standards of practice, these violations were more likely to take the form of borderline deceptions which transgressed no law. To check the accuracy of national display advertising, furthermore, required more resources than were to be found at the disposal of local Bureaus, whose operations were generally confined to passing judgment on copy which had origi-

7. *P.I.* (June 16, 1921), p. 53; (Feb. 23, 1928), p. 89; (Nov. 22, 1928), p. 155. See also below, pp. 62–4.

8. Richardson; *P.I.* (Sept. 30, 1926), p. 109; statement of A. C. Fuller, president of the New York City Bureau, printed in *P.I.* (Mar. 19, 1930), p. 57. See also *P.I.* (Dec. 25, 1930), p. 110; (Mar. 19, 1931), p. 57.

nated with local merchants. But even if it had been possible for a local Bureau to test the validity of national advertisements the Bureau was scarcely capable of effecting a change in them. Against a local merchant, sanctions by a Bureau (supported by other local merchants and perhaps the local newspaper) could and generally did prove a formidable threat; against a large corporation, which sold a product in a national market and advertised it in a nationally circulating magazine, the local Bureau was powerless. Nevertheless, by 1930, to judge by complaints made to Bureaus about advertising, national advertisers had become the worst offenders against canons of advertising ethics.[9]

In consequence of all this, a more powerful organization, the National Better Business Bureau, was formed in 1925 to act as a private policeman for national advertisers.[10] The Bureau operated principally on the theory that the only effective way to eliminate borderline practices was to encourage industry-wide cooperation on matters of advertising behavior. To do this required the voluntary support of the advertisers themselves, for the only weapon of enforcement available to the Bureau was the *P.I.* Statute, which was too blunt an instrument to deter borderline offenders. The crucial problem, as officials of the Bureau saw it, was to eliminate or minimize the condition which made borderline misrepresentation attractive to the advertiser. The condition to which they most often attributed these offenses was unregulated competition, particularly the outbreak of a price war or of an advertising war of competing claims. To discourage such outbreaks the Bureau publicized itself as an umpire in a game which was best played according to accepted rules of fair trade. To persuade advertisers to abide by the umpire's decisions, the Bureau attempted to remind them of the mutual self-destructiveness of trade wars, of the loss, for example, of a general faith in all advertisements which might result from the offensive competitive claims of a few. Hence, as a policeman for business be-

9. Baur, p. 218.

10. *P.I.* (Aug. 20, 1925), p. 44. The National Bureau was incorporated in that year under a charter from the state of Delaware for the purpose of "centralizing and coordinating the Truth-in-Advertising movement." Its technical predecessor had been the National Vigilance Committee of the AACW.

havior the Bureau could claim to bolster public acceptance of business behavior.[11]

For a while the Bureau sought to exercise its power principally in the organization and management of "fair trade practice" conferences, whereby it hoped to obtain agreement among competing businesses on rules of advertising behavior which would help to "stabilize" the industry as a whole. One instance of such a conference will illustrate the nature of the Bureau's role. Early in 1926 the Bureau began an investigation of the advertising and selling practices of correspondence schools. Among the practices particularly questioned were the use of false inducements to enroll and the use of superlatives in advertising copy. In July 1926 the Bureau met with representatives of more than fifty correspondence schools in a conference which aimed, in the language of the Bureau, "to enlarge public confidence in [their] advertising . . . and accordingly increase its value." At the conference the schools agreed to a set of rules and a code of ethics for the conduct of their advertising. Among the prohibitions set for themselves were that none could "guarantee" jobs for clients, that none could claim that the fee was a special offer when in fact it was not, and that no advertisement could state that a school was "largest" or "best" unless the statement was revealed as someone's opinion. Some schools took strong exception to a few of the rules, declaring that they could not operate under such privations, but eventually every school present signed the agreement.[12] Thus the National Bureau attempted to eliminate misleading advertising by gaining the voluntary consent of competing businesses to definitions of unethical behavior which could be made public and against which the behavior of all could be measured. The operations of the Bureau were modeled on the operations of the Federal Trade Commission, and its intention to encourage cooperative fair-trade behavior was not dissimilar from that of the FTC in the late 1920's.

The elimination of borderline advertising, however, proved to be a far more difficult task than the Bureau had evidently antici-

11. *P.I. Monthly* (June 1926), pp. 33-4; *P.I.* (Sept. 30, 1926), p. 33; (Feb. 23, 1928), p. 89.
12. *P.I.* (July 15, 1926), p. 49.

pated. Borderline offenses tended to court censure from advertising men on at least two counts: that by deceiving the public they brought disrepute and moral censure on the entire activity of advertising; that by making unfair and misleading assertions, either on behalf of the product advertised or in disparagement of a rival product, they debased the currency of the competitive market and threatened to damage the reputation of an entire class of products, including the product for which the advertisement had been written. The chances were strong that most advertisements guilty of one count were guilty of the other. Occasionally, however, the Bureau examined appeals which sought beyond a doubt to deceive their readers but which remained circumspectly noncompetitive and consequently provoked no resistance from sensitive rivals, and the Bureau found this merely "public" type of offense far more difficult to curb than the "competitive" offense. In the former case not only was the reading public unable to bring forceful pressure to bear on individual advertisers, but the compelling opposition of an overtly indignant competitor did not exist. The National Bureau, to be sure, attempted at times to create a sense of self interest where justification for it seemed remote or improbable by warning advertisers that their deceptions on the public might easily damage the effectiveness of advertising as a whole. The fact remained that internal sanctions against national advertisers risked almost certain failure except when they reflected the powerful voice of outraged competitors, and even this backing did not always assure success.

Two of the most spectacular instances of "borderline" advertising which the National Bureau felt obliged to oppose aptly illustrate the distinction between the two types of offense, as well as the nearly insurmountable problems inherent in attempting to restrain either one from within the industry. They were, respectively, the use of paid testimonials, and the vigorously competitive advertising which directly "knocked" a rival product. The somewhat dramatic embodiment which both received during the 1920's deserves special consideration here.

Testimonials to products by grateful consumers had thrived for generations and had long provided the staple advertising fare for patent medicines. As long as few except the makers of patent medicines found profit in testimonial copy, however, it was unable to escape the general opprobrium accorded the type of businessmen who used it. Up through the World War many advertising men tended to regard all testimonials, whether genuine or not, as improper and in questionable taste; indeed it was scarcely possible to distinguish a genuine one from a counterfeit. By 1920, however, Lever Brothers (Lux soap), Paramount Pictures, and a few silverware manufacturers had based successful campaigns on the testimonial, making of it an instrument for snob appeal; and comment within the industry began to shift from the question of its moral standing to the problem of how to make it more effective.[13] The paid-for testimonial was not to disappear solely because a number of businessmen found it distasteful. Nevertheless, the demand within the industry for internal sanctions against the paid-for testimonial became insistent and powerful when, in the mid-1920's, there burst forth a wave of testimonials so far-fetched as to arouse the certain suspicion that they were misleading or untrue, and certainly not unsolicited. In 1924 the manufacturers of Pond's Creams, a client of the J. Walter Thompson advertising agency, sponsored a full-page announcement of an interview with Mrs. O. H. P. Belmont on "the care of the skin." [14] Mrs. Belmont herself was not shown; the advertisement featured, instead, an illustration of the library at Beacon Towers, Long Island, where the interview took place. The makers of Pond's Creams at first moved with a degree of caution which would suggest that either they or their agency had serious qualms about the public reception of signed personal testimonials. Mrs. Belmont's statement, however, foreshadowed the appearance of over one hundred distinguished ladies who testified month by month from 1924 through the early years of the Depression to the miraculous properties of a twin elixir of youth, cold cream, and vanishing cream. The format of the advertisement was soon standardized; it included a portrait or photograph (one, for example, was of Marie, Queen of Roumania), embellished with symbols of upper-class elegance, a conspicuous headline ("What the Most

13. *P.I.* (July 21, 1921), p. 65.
14. See *Good Housekeeping*, Feb. 1925.

Beautiful Queen in Europe says about Care of the Skin"), and a garrulous text reminiscent of periodical fiction and sprinkled with direct testimony ("No woman is so highly placed that she can afford to neglect her beauty. Personal appearance is vital to her success—she cannot allow the usual marks of fatigue or exposure to show in her face.").[15] Among others to announce in the next few years that their beauty depended on Pond's Creams were the Duchesse [sic] de Richelieu ("the woman whose life is given not only to Society but to concert singing"), Princess Marie de Bourbon, Gloria Vanderbilt, Lady Diana Manners, and Her Royal Highness Eulalia, Infanta of Spain (who "Discusses Beauty in the Courts of Europe").

Simultaneous with the advertisements for Pond's Creams was a series of advertisements for Fleischmann's Yeast, a product owned by Standard Brands, Inc. Here the testimonial took a technically different form, though its style was no less conspicuous and a good deal more controversial. A long procession of bearded doctors were represented as practicing medicine in obscure European hospitals and research institutes (significantly beyond the effective range of the American Medical Association's sanction against unethical behavior), and testified not that they themselves had consumed yeast but that they had successfully prescribed it for thousands of their patients, who suffered, one gathers, from constipation, skin blemishes, and loss of vitality (carefully unspecified but occasionally illustrated by photographs of women whose apparent age suggested menopause). By 1928 a number of national advertisers had joined the manufacturers of Pond's Creams and Fleischmann's Yeast in the use of testimonials; the most conspicuous were the makers of Simmons Beds (socially prominent men and women endorsed the contribution of a Simmons mattress to their sleep and to the appearance of their bedrooms), as well as Old Gold, Herbert Tareyton, and Lucky Strike cigarettes, of which the last-named offered to opera coluraturas and career women a profitable chance to testify that Luckies kept their bodies slender and agreed with their throats.

An increasing number of advertising men found the practice

15. Ibid., April 1925.

of paying celebrities to endorse a product intensely irritating, and they said so. Though they expressed their fears and doubts frequently and with vigor, their impulse to scold was inhibited by the undeniable evidence of a gratifying public response to testimonial advertising.[16] But in February 1929 the American Tobacco Company, with a single testimonial, shocked a few advertising men into open revolt. A Captain George Fried, in command of the S. S. *America,* had daringly saved some wrecked seamen from the wintry waters of the North Atlantic. Having steamed to their rescue 350 miles by radio compass, he lowered a lifeboat in the charge of Chief Officer Harry Manning and eight crewmen, who, amid a shrieking gale and pounding seas, pulled from a derelict Italian freighter thirty-two members of its crew. Captain Fried sailed into the port of New York a hero; it was the second such occasion in three years, for he had performed a similar feat in 1926. He was described in one account as over fifty, silver-haired, and "very shy." [17] But scarcely had the rescue faded from headlines than there appeared in most newspapers of the nation a large advertisement in which Captain Fried was quoted (totally out of character) as attributing his own cool nerves, the spirits of Chief Officer Manning and his crew, the morale of the survivors, and indeed the heroic quality of the entire venture, to the timely use of Lucky Strike cigarettes. This exploitation by a tobacco company of a calamity at sea seemed to a few advertising men so openly blatant and cynical as to endanger public tolerance of all national advertising. Citing Captain Fried's relationship to Lucky Strikes, Frederick Kendall, editor of *Advertising and Selling,* in March 1929 declared open war on the practice of paid testimonials and invited all who agreed with him to join in a campaign of publicity and pressure against future offenders.[18] The controversy involved several of the most prominent agencies and their executives. Earnest Elmo Calkins,

16. *P.I.* (Apr. 5, 1928), p. 69; (Dec. 13, 1928), p. 49.

17. *Time* (Feb. 14, 1929), p. 14.

18. *P.I.* published the angry views of aroused advertising agents and reported the controversy in full, but was less wholehearted in its convictions. For example, (Apr. 4, 1929), p. 83. See also *Time* (Mar. 11, 1929), p. 54. According to Alva Johnson, who evidently interviewed the crew of rescuers, Fried normally smoked Old Golds, Bosuns' Mate Wilson preferred Camels, while Manning did not smoke at all. *Outlook* (Apr. 1, 1931), pp. 466–7.

Theodore MacManus, and A. W. Erickson, heads of their own agencies, and Paul Hollister, of the Batten, Barton, Durstine, and Osborn agency, denounced paid endorsements with vehemence; some called on publishers to ban paid testimonials and even urged public action by the Federal Trade Commission.[19] These agents advanced three major arguments against paid testimonials: they were likely to contribute to a loss of public faith in the truth of advertising; they made a mockery of genuine (unsolicited) testimonials and were therefore unfair to other advertisers; and they were hypocritical and misleading, for they pretended to represent valid statements of the experiences of those actually using a product or specially qualified to judge of its worth.

With these points Stanley Resor, president of the J. Walter Thompson advertising agency, took issue. His general defense of testimonials afforded a prophetic glimpse of the future of national advertising. Attacks on testimonials by other advertising men, declared Resor, were harmful to the industry and were unfair to the advertisers who had invested money in them.[20] National advertisements must either adopt the techniques of the mass media or fail. Current formulas for mass media stress the human interest story and the personality feature, indeed a deliberately personalized explanation of world problems. The mass market, he suggested, is a tabloid market, and tabloid readers seek to live vicariously; they feed on public personalities which in turn are manufactured to satisfy their appetites. Emulation and hero-worship are not creations of advertising; they are social facts. "People are eternally searching for authority . . . Royalty, aristocracy, feudalism, dominated the world for scores of centuries, instilling in the masses a sense of inferiority and an instinctive veneration for their 'betters'. . . . The public hunger for per-

19. For example, Erickson, *P.I.* (Mar. 7, 1929), p. 3. See also, *P.I.* (Feb. 24, 1927), p. 57; (Sept. 27, 1928), p. 138; (Feb. 28, 1929), p. 110. According to Hower, p. 129, the N. W. Ayer agency considered itself as a bulwark of ethical conservatism in this period and consequently opposed testimonials. The evidence supports Hower's view. Aside from testimonials, the practices to which these individuals particularly objected were the use of pseudoscientific jargon, the unwarranted superlative, and the tabloid-like appeal to "fear" and an interest in sex.

20. *Tide*, Dec. 1928. The J. Walter Thompson agency was responsible for many well-known testimonial advertisements.

sonalities is so great that no successful editor dares to ignore it."
Advertisements compete directly with tabloid features for the
reader's attention. Editors have proved that the public will "relish
personalities" whether in paid space or in free space, and testimonials merely offer the public the sort of personality satisfaction which they crave from their media. The issue of whether
or not the testimonial was paid for, said Resor, is therefore irrelevant, for its popularity with the reading public depends not
on the mechanics of endorsement but on the intrinsic interest of
the advertisement. A paid testimonial might or might not be
truthful, but there was nothing inherently untruthful in paying
for an opinion already formed. Far from bringing discredit on
the advertising industry, paid testimonials may help save it from
public indifference.[21]

To Resor's argument for the practices at which his agency ex-
celled other advertising men added points of their own. Roy
Dickinson, of the staff of *Printers' Ink,* purported to have found
out "what the consumer thinks" about testimonial advertising.
Most of them thought, he said, that it was shady practice, but
that since nobody in his right mind would believe a testimonial,
the practice could do no harm; many thought testimonials made
interesting reading and reported that they looked at them, even
watched for them, "for laughs," but that they would never buy a
product on the strength of them.[22]

Among the major advertising journals *Tide* most firmly supported the practice of paid endorsements. It reminded its readers
that testimonials were overwhelmingly successful in attracting
readership, that they may have lacked "ethical value," but that
it was doubtful whether they discredited advertising. The public,
it asserted, discounted exaggeration in advertising and harbored
no deep feelings about copy practices; consumers tended to complain only when cheated. In any event, *Tide* concluded prag-
matically, the coming years would bring gaudier and more daring
testimonials than ever before.[23] Raymond Rubicam, president of
one of the nation's largest agencies, spoke even more to the point.

21. Reprinted in *P.I.* (Apr. 11, 1929), p. 145.
22. *P.I.* (Mar. 21, 1929), p. 148.
23. *Tide* (Mar. 1929), p. 1.

If some advertising men are opposed to paid testimonials, what do they think they can do about them? To separate paid testimonials from voluntary ones, he asserted, would be meaningless; as an illustration he cited a manufacturer of a children's product who received "hundreds of effusive letters" from mothers who praised the product. "For twenty years it has been his custom to send to the children of these mothers, whose testimonials are used, a Government bond of small denomination as a token of his appreciation." Were the testimonials genuine or not? And who was to decide? Many endorsements were sincere, though paid for; many, though freely given, were untrue. Industry-wide sanctions, he was careful to emphasize, would fail; the only alternative consisted of voluntary action by individual agencies, advertisers, and publishers.[24] Likewise C. B. Larrabee, writing as an editor of *Printers' Ink*, while regretting the use of paid testimonials, fervently disparaged any plans for sanctions. The chief "offenders," he said, would never submit to outside coercion. The only feasible course was moral persuasion and a voluntary review by some authority such as the National Better Business Bureau.[25]

Rubicam and Larrabee seem to have estimated the difficulties correctly. That any action was taken at all was perhaps a tribute to the respectability and influence of the opponents of paid testimonials and the intensity with which they held to their views. Action by the industry itself was perfunctory. In 1929 the National Bureau sent a "questionnaire" to 4050 national advertisers and 640 agencies, seeking information about the use of testimonials and particularly an answer to the following question: "Do you believe that the use of purchased testimonials is *good for advertising in general?*"[26] Of 870 replies, or less than a 20 per cent response, an overwhelming number said "no." But the questionnaire showed that testimonials of any kind undoubtedly produced readers and sales and would obviously continue in use. The Bureau's subsequent action consisted of a warning couched in familiar language: paid testimonials impair the public faith on which the industry depends; when public interest in this new

24. *P.I.* (Mar. 14, 1929), p. 17.
25. *P.I.* (Apr. 4, 1929), p. 83; (Apr. 11, 1929), p. 172.
26. *P.I.* (Mar. 21, 1929), p. 148. Italics mine.

excitement lags, resuscitation will come that much harder. "Advertising is social in its effect. . . . [It] is a consumer's buying guide. When that guide has become permeated with insincerity, it has lost its public use." [27] In a few more years the Bureau's statement might have been taken more seriously, but there is no evidence that it influenced a single advertiser in 1929. Even less consequential were the gestures of the two most powerful advertising associations. After much debate the ANA passed a resolution which declared that its members disapproved of paid testimonials because they reduced public faith in advertising; and the AAAA sponsored a statement disapproving of any practice which "commercializes what has long been held in personal, social, and business relations to be an act of good will." [28]

The matter of commercializing "an act of good will" was not settled by calling it names, and upon the Federal Trade Commission ultimately devolved the responsibility of modifying the practice which the advertising associations were neither able nor particularly willing to curb. Its powers extended to the issuance of cease and desist orders, to the arrangement of trade practice agreements, and to the request for a stipulation against any advertising practice inimical to fair trade or competition. In January 1930 it signed a stipulation with the American Tobacco Company,[29] whereby the latter promised to cease using "unfair" testimonials; specifically the company agreed not to feature an endorser who in fact had never smoked the cigarette endorsed or to attribute to him a statement which he never actually saw. They also promised that where a testimonial had been solicited and paid for, the fact would be published with the advertisement in as conspicuous a manner as the testimonial. In the following year other firms, including Standard Brands (Fleischmann's Yeast), agreed to similar stipulations. But in 1932 the Northam-Warren Company, manufacturers of Cutex nail polish, refused

27. *P.I.* (Apr. 18, 1929), p. 25.

28. *P.I.* (June 6, 1929), p. 73; (July 18, 1929), p. 144.

29. *P.I.* (Jan. 30, 1930), p. 49. *Tide,* Jan. 1932. No technical evidence exists that the company involved was the American Tobacco Co., for the FTC promised anonymity to firms signing a stipulation. But the circumstantial evidence as to the company and the product is overwhelming, and both *P.I.* and *Tide,* among other sources, are agreed that it could have been no other.

to agree to the requirement of a statement concerning payment, and the issue was brought before the courts. In seeking an appeal from the Commission's decision, the Northam-Warren Company denied that money in any way altered the genuineness of the testimonial. The court reversed the Commission's order and upheld the company's contention; it noted that the public was hardly likely to be fooled by such a testimonial and that as a consequence no harm was done.[30]

The problem of paid testimonials was thus resolved in favor of prevailing practices. By this time the editors of *Printers' Ink* had tired of the furor, and Kendall had already announced that *Advertising and Selling* was abandoning its campaign against the advertising behavior of the American Tobacco Company. No agent or publisher, Kendall observed, cared to cut himself off from a share of a $12 million annual "jackpot" which the company offered for its advertising.[31] Within a year *Advertising and Selling* featured an article which defended the payment of money for testimonials as providing the only assurance of obtaining a public figure with a sufficient following to procure a profitable readership; testimonials existed only for publicity; no one should expect them to persuade readers to buy the product anyway.[32] Within a few more years testimonial advertising had settled into a dependable pattern, arranged almost by formula, and the ballyhooed excesses which it had acquired in the 1920's gradually wore off. The fears of the opponents of the paid testimonial were misplaced, if not totally unrealized; and on the other hand those advertising men who regarded such a technique as a liberation from what they maintained were fusty prejudice and outworn taboo could rejoice in the fact that the passage of time and to a certain degree the constancy of public indifference favored their views.

30. *P.I.* (Jan. 7, 1932), p. 105; (June 9, 1932), p. 36. The case was heard on appeal before the U. S. Circuit Court of Appeals, Second District. The decision read in part: "If the testimonials involved here represent honest beliefs of the endorsers there is no misrepresentation concerning the product, and no unfair competition is created." Northam-Warren Corp. *vs.* F.T.C. (59 F. 2d 196).

31. *A.S.* (Mar. 5, 1930), p. 33. Kendall also scored the trade associations as worthless for maintaining standards of practice.

32. *A.S.* (Jan. 7, 1931), p. 20.

It is conceivable that no one would have launched so vehement a crusade against paid testimonials in 1929 had not a still more controversial series of offenses occurred in the same year. Captain Fried, devoted to Luckies, was only one of an endless string of celebrities whose relations to a peculiar world of cold cream, yeast cakes, soap, cigarettes, and mouthwash had been made exceedingly obvious to perusers of magazine advertisements. But Captain Fried had endorsed a product whose makers were in the process of violating one of the most sanctified tenets in the advertising industry: never "knock" another man's product. The American Tobacco Company, led by its skillful and aggressive president, George Washington Hill, was about to engage the manufacturers of candy in a running-fire duel of openly competitive and disparaging claims, a practice which in principle advertising men were almost unanimous in condemning.

Condemnation of disparaging copy was to be found at the very core of those ethical norms by which the advertising industry hoped to govern itself. The norms were never more flagrantly disregarded, however, than during the prolonged market depression of the 1930's, which for some manufacturers had begun even earlier as a noticeable slump in their yearly increase in sales. Confronted with such a threat to his security, the manufacturer was not apt to inquire too closely whether his behavior conformed to the theoretical niceties of advertising codes, and if the pressure to sell were particularly widespread and severe, the manufacturer's views on the sort of advertising he wanted went virtually unchallenged. Codes of behavior in the advertising industry depended essentially upon the operation of a balance of power between agencies, publishers, advertisers, and outside pressure groups. From 1929 through at least 1932 public pressure on advertising had not mounted sufficiently to affect it, and publishers and agents temporarily lost their power to resist the selling tactics of national advertisers. Whatever "professional" dedication to independent ethical standards the agencies may once have possessed now dwindled as advertisers resorted to extreme measures to shore up a sagging market and did not hesitate to drop agents who refused to cooperate with them. By 1930 agencies were fighting bitterly to retain a share of decreased appropriations, and in the extremity of cut-throat warfare even the most conservative of them abandoned, for a while, the luxury of ethical norms. Important clients, then, were able to advertise about as they pleased, and those, like George Washington Hill of the American Tobacco Company, who managed actually to expand their advertising appropriations during a depression in which most firms were reducing them made themselves virtually impregnable to the moderating pressures of agencies.[33]

Hill's spectacular campaign for Lucky Strikes in the fall of 1928 may not have shattered all precedents for competitive advertising, but it unquestionably set some sort of record for notoriety. It began with Lady Grace Drummond Hay, whom the copy described as the first woman to fly the Atlantic from East to West. (She flew on the Graf Zeppelin.) Lady Hay took the opportunity which Lucky Strikes afforded her to confess to her friends, the readers of American newspapers, that the secret of her slender figure lay in her daily consumption of Lucky Strike cigarettes. If that were all she had confessed, her public would not have turned a hair, for comparable claims had become by

33. Hower, p. 148. This view was also confirmed by René Clarke, president of the Calkins and Holden advertising agency, in an interview with the author in May 1952.

The method of agency compensation added to the competitive pressures which overwhelmed the agency in this period. During the prosperity of the 1920's agency income, a fixed percentage of the value of the advertising it placed, was sufficient to permit it to offer expanded "services" at no extra charge in hopes of attracting more clients. But during the Depression the proportion of income to expected services decreased to a point where agencies could no longer make a profit; at the same time many advertisers, feeling equally hard pressed, tried to lighten their own costs by requesting still further uncompensated agency service, and they were in a strong position to get what they wanted. According to one executive (P.I., Nov. 5, 1931, p. 3), the reputation of most small agencies depended so heavily on the prestige of their clients that to antagonize and lose one important client was often worse than to take a temporary loss on servicing his account: the loss of a client might well impair the agency's reputation to a point of preventing the acquisition of new clients. It should be noted at this point that publishers were not in a much better position to resist. Faced with losses of revenue from curtailed advertising and confronted, in the early 1930's, with serious competition from radio, many of them relaxed their standards. Of the role of publishers, more will be said below, pp. 78–84.

that time an industry-wide sport. Had Her Ladyship explained, for example, that what was keeping her trim was the exercise involved in stripping the paper from her Lucky Strike tobacco and sprinkling the tobacco over a morning bowl of Wheaties, she might have attracted little attention. But what she actually said was in fact so eminently logical and plausibly self-evident as virtually to defy challenge. Whenever you crave food, she advised her readers, "reach for a Lucky instead of a sweet," and you might conceivably lose weight.

The candy industry responded instantly. To those who were aware that this industry was itself waging a campaign which stressed that candy was less fattening than heavy desserts ("eat candy instead"), its tone of indignation seemed a little disingenuous.[34] Purporting to be shocked, the candy association accused the American Tobacco Company of engaging in unfair competition, and individual firms in their own advertisements proceeded in turn to slur cigarettes. Jobbers and retailers who handled both products were successfully persuaded in some instances to drop Lucky Strikes, with their low markup, as the price for being permitted to retain the more profitable candy. Rival cigarette firms meanwhile expressed dismay (real or simulated) that one of their number had stooped so low, and neutral observers predicted that George Washington Hill would have to back down.[35]

But Hill was just warming to the fight. The procession of slender celebrities who followed Lady Hay in Lucky Strike advertising continued to repeat her admonition and to testify to the success of her secret; and in a mock gesture of willingness to dilute his original slogan with an adjective, Hill deliberately increased its effectiveness by the insertion of "fattening" before "sweet." This, as one astute observer pointed out, was precisely what "the

34. *A.S.* (Nov. 14, 1928), p. 19. See, for example, the Associated Confectioners' advertisement in the *Saturday Evening Post*, (Oct. 27, 1928), p. 108.

35. See, for various reports on these developments, *P.I.*, Nov. 22, 1928 through Dec. 20, 1928. It can reasonably be inferred, though it is not certain, that until at least Oct. 17, the day after the Graf Zeppelin landed in New York, Lady Hay did not consider herself a smoker. See her comments on the flight in the New York *Times* (Oct. 17), p. 2.

candy industry [had] been trying *not* to say for years."[36] When pressure to retract his advertising continued to mount, Hill disclosed that for 1929 he had planned a $12.3 million advertising campaign whose basic theme would continue unchanged: the advertisements would be directed at women and would urge, as a solution to the problem of overweight, the substitution of cigarettes for rich foods. Testimony from medical authorities, added Hill innocently, supported his view that Americans were eating too much candy. More to the point was the publicity which he then gave to evidence which purported to show that sales of candy, as well as cigarettes, had soared in those areas where his advertising had "hit hardest." The hue and cry, he predicted accurately, would subside as soon as businessmen grasped the principle that a competitive advertising war between two products might just as easily increase as decrease the sales of both. For products which did not really compete with each other, such as candy and cigarettes, public battle and notoriety of claims might even lead the same consumers to buy both.[37] A few months later Hill elaborated these hypotheses in an article which claimed to represent his personal views on the general significance of his campaign: the consumer's dollar is growing, and in it there is plenty of gravy for everybody. "The more the consumer buys, the more he feels the need of having."[38]

36. (Nov. 22, 1928), p. 12. Italics mine. The slogan "Reach for a Lucky instead of a Sweet" was begun in October in local New York newspapers. After two months of "testing," the theme was repeated nationally in magazines. Lady Hay, for example, appeared in local advertising Oct. 24 (see New York *Times*, p. 12), and again in national advertising Dec. 15 (see *Collier's*, p. 41). The word "fattening" to characterize candy was added to her testimony in December.

37. *P.I.* (Dec. 27, 1928), p. 83. See also the *New Republic* (Feb. 13, 1929), p. 343; and the *Nation* (Mar. 13, 1929), p. 305.

38. G. W. Hill, "The New Competition," *World's Work*, June 1929. In an interview (reported in *P.I.*, Dec. 27, 1928, p. 83) which Hill granted the *Confectioners' Journal* he claimed that U. S. Dept. of Commerce statistics demonstrated a marked increase in the sale of cigarettes *and candy* in the New York metropolitan area for October, the place and time of Hill's original newspaper campaign. Hill admitted that he had not originally expected candy sales to increase, whereupon the representative of *Confectioners' Journal* stated that some authorities in the candy trade had predicted that this would happen and in consequence were relatively undisturbed at Hill's competitive copy. A careful investigation of the available data

Hill's arguments failed to sway the federal government, and in January 1930 the American Tobacco Company signed with the Federal Trade Commission a long-anticipated stipulation that henceforth none of its advertising could imply that smoking *per se* would cause slimness or a reduction in weight.[39] By this time Lucky Strike advertising had voluntarily abandoned the overt "anti-sweet" theme in favor of another which served the same ends in a less provocative manner. Picturing slim athletic bodies of men and women engaged in vigorous, youthful activity, the copy writers added to each figure a shadow of middle-age obesity; a slogan warned readers that "coming events cast their shadows before," and the rest of the copy indicated in matter-of-fact tones that readers should avoid overeating and might derive pleasure from smoking Lucky Strikes.

Meanwhile the American Cigar Company, a subsidiary of the American Tobacco Company, burst into print with a series of advertisements for Cremo cigars which intimated that a foul practice

---

leads me to hazard the following evaluation of Hill's assertion. (1) The exact *monthly* figures for the sale of candy in the New York area are no longer available, if indeed they ever were; hence it is difficult now to prove or disprove his assertion directly from his evidence, though the portion of his figures on national sales (from which he made his crucial deduction) do not correspond as they should to existing Dept. of Commerce figures. (2) *Yearly* sales of candy for each state can be determined from available data. They reveal that in 1929 sales of candy registered a "record-breaking" gain over 1928, but that 1928 was a slack year for candy consumption. (3) The Bureau of Foreign and Domestic Commerce has explained the 1929 increase in part as a result of reduced prices, favorable weather, the prosperous condition of business despite the crash, and "extensive advertising" by candy firms. It would be extremely hazardous to attribute any precise effect to one small possible factor in the presence of four large probable ones. (4) There has long existed a considerable body of opinion in the advertising industry that competitive copy of this sort is as apt to help as to hurt sales for the product disparaged. (5) In short, Hill's particular figures in support of his assertion are heavily suspect (and the candy trade questioned his figures at the time); even though there exists no evidence that Hill's slogan hurt candy sales, neither is there any certainty that it boosted sales, however likely a result this may have been. See U. S. Dept. of Commerce, Bureau of the Census, *Surveys of Current Business*, Nos. 87–90 (Nov. 1928–Feb. 1929) for monthly figures of national sales, based on about a 10 per cent sample; Bureau of Foreign and Domestic Commerce, Domestic Commerce Series 31 and 40, *Candy Distribution in the United States* (1930) for *yearly* figures by states and regions based on about a 90 per cent return. I am also indebted to the National Confectioners' Association, Chicago, for further data on the problem.

39. *P.I.* (Jan. 30, 1930), p. 49.

flourished among cigar manufacturers, that of sealing the cigar wrapper with saliva. "Spit is a horrid word," the advertisements announced, "but it is worse on the end of your cigar." Readers were led irresistibly to the conclusion that only those who smoked Cremos could be sure of smoking sanitary cigars.

If Hill were looking for the same sort of outcry as he had provoked from the candy industry he could not have been disappointed. Competitors wrathfully denounced this latest "outrage" and sought disciplinary action from the National Better Business Bureau. The Bureau conducted an investigation and published its findings; it could discover evidence of the "spit-tipping" practice in only a few plants, whose managers were even then eliminating the objectionable condition. Edward L. Greene, president of the Bureau, thereupon accused the American Tobacco Company and Lord and Thomas of a gross violation of advertising ethics and pointedly reminded them of the previous campaign which the Government had forced them to disband.[40] Hill, in reply to Greene, confined himself to asserting that the Bureau's report nevertheless revealed the existence of "spit-tipping," that Cremo cigars were truthfully advertised, and that his exposé of spit-tipping (complete with photographs) ought to be considered a public service. Plainly the American Tobacco Company did not expect the Bureau to take any further action, and in this it was correct. Greene gave the company a verbal dressing-down, declared that the judgment of advertising men had been perverted by the unquestionably imposing budget which such a large firm expended every year for the services of the advertising industry, and warned that a lesser company would not have escaped sanctions.[41]

There is no evidence that direct pressure from within the advertising industry had any noticeable effect on the advertising behavior of the American Tobacco Company. On the contrary, the profitable behavior of American Tobacco was beginning to attract the notice of other advertisers. Resentment of Hill's prac-

40. *P.I.* (Feb. 27, 1930), p. 65.
41. Ibid. Taeusch offers the information, but does not disclose its source, that the Cremo campaign ceased abruptly when the only two examples of "spit-tipping" discovered in "one state" were discovered in Cremo factories. *Policy and Ethics in Business*, p. 469.

tices at first ran high, but not even the dullest businessman could fail to draw an inspiration from Hill's message to his stockholders in 1930. From January to May of that year American Tobacco profits had increased 100 per cent; the company had split its stock two for one and had increased its dividends. *Tide* reported that agencies were beginning to feel pressure from clients to see whether Hill's formula would prove equally successful for them.[42]

For most advertisers, however, the rewards obtained from disparaging other products did not seem to be worth the price. On the contrary, it did not take long to discover how much more profitable it was to scratch a colleague's back than to trample his toes. When in 1934 the J. Walter Thompson agency wrote a series of advertisements for Lever Brothers which stressed the advantages of Lux soap for preventing "cosmetic skin," the cosmetic industry, as represented by the Cosmetic Institute and by the Associated Manufacturers of Toilet Articles, lodged a vigorous protest and charged the agency with having made misleading and derogatory implications about cosmetics. In reply Lever Brothers asserted that cosmetics which were left permanently on the skin were harmful to the skin, that the appeal, far from "knocking" cosmetics, would actually promote their use, and that the Thompson agency was servicing two "cosmetic accounts" and would never knowingly harm one of its clients with the advertising of another. As a partial concession to the cosmetic industry, however, the agency removed the phrase "cosmetic skin" from the headlines of the advertisements for Lux soap, and featured as a theme in the body of the text: *"Use all the cosmetics you wish,* but remove them thoroughly the Hollywood way— guard against ugly Cosmetic Skin." [43] A similar episode took place in August 1931, when an advertisement for Listerine Antiseptic suggested that inasmuch as eggs helped cause "halitosis," anyone who ate eggs ought also to gargle with Listerine. An outraged organization of egg dealers threatened to request the FTC to ban the use of this insinuation. Shortly thereafter, Listerine advertisements featured a photograph of a large number

42. *Tide* (July 1930), p. 4.
43. *P.I.* (May 10, 1934), p. 33.

of eggs with the caption: "Eat more eggs. . . . Buy six dozen with that $3 you save [by buying Listerine toothpaste]." [44]

The variation and uncertainty in the resistance by the advertising industry to "borderline" offenses is readily apparent. Testimonials, for example, did not conspicuously lend themselves to the competitive warfare of disparaging claims and on that account survived to become acceptable. On the other hand, advertising which "knocked" the products of competitors tended either to wither away or to adopt protective coloration under the indignant scrutiny of those agencies of enforcement, such as the National Bureau and the FTC, which were notably responsive to the pleas of competitors.

In all this, did there not exist a curious and instructive irony? Testimonials actually may not have deceived many readers, but as an aid to readers intent on making judgments about a product, testimonials were worthless, if not obstructive; while almost any competitive war of claims for rival products (if the claims were reasonably valid) might conceivably have performed a public service in exposing facts which otherwise would never have been allowed to appear. Did the FTC in fact serve the best interests of the public by insisting that Hill retract his perfectly valid assertion that sweets were fattening, or by cutting off the candy association from retorting (as it might well have done) that nicotine had doubtless ruined the health of more Americans than chocolate drops? It is clear that neither cigarette nor candy manufacturers stood to gain from exposure in the other's advertising, but it is no less clear that the public could learn more from exposure than from a mutual agreement to remain silent.

In short, the border of business morality tended in time to shift to allow some twilight offenses to bask in respectability and to cast others into the darker realm of the illegitimate, and in nearly every case the criterion for deciding where the line was to be drawn was certain to be a private and not a public one. It could hardly have been otherwise. "Advertising," *Tide* reminded its practitioners in 1929 with understandable impatience and refreshing candor, "is not an art. It is a business. The agency man

44. *Tide* (Dec. 1931), p. 13; *P.I.* (Aug. 20, 1936), p. 72.

and the advertiser are emphatically not philanthropists. . . . It is true that advertising men sometimes pose as such . . . and it is regrettable that they themselves are responsible for much of the confusion of thought which applies to an advertising campaign the motives of a Rockefeller Foundation." [45] The National Bureau itself was almost willing to concede the point. In 1928 Edward L. Greene, its president, announced that although "half-truth" advertising was getting worse, publishers and agents alike were so reluctant to view it as a moral or legal problem that few sanctions could be imposed successfully.[46] In patrolling the border, the Bureau in fact had been able to do little more than to scold transgressors, warn them of public disapproval, and attempt to enlist the FTC in curbing unusually flagrant violations of the uncertain rules of fair trade.

The quest for internal regulation of national advertising continued, however, with a change of tactics which was meant to resolve the outstanding dilemma of "borderline" behavior: the determination of what was really permissible and what was not. The National Bureau, with the effective and enthusiastic support of two advertising journals, now undertook to erect both general and specific codes of behavior which trade associations and even an independent authority would enforce on industries and individual firms. The proposal was ambitious, and the tactics were well-intentioned. That they did not succeed was probably not due to a lack of intelligent effort.

The aims of the National Bureau were nowhere more consistently defended than in the pages of *Printers' Ink* and *Advertising and Selling*. A study of either journal for the period 1925–35 reveals a tone intensely troubled by the borderline advertising of prominent national firms. Editorials and articles alike deplored copy which was misleading or pseudoscientific or which contained any sort of disparaging reference to competing products. In 1928, C. B. Larrabee, one of the editors of *Printers' Ink*, even announced a "crusade" against what he designated as "super-advertising." In

45. *Tide* (June 1929), p. 4.
46. *P.I.* (Nov. 22, 1928), p. 152.

this crusade he urged agents, publishers, and other "ethically" minded men to join him in outlawing copy which he feared would ruin "credibility" for the rest of the industry.[47] Larrabee was careful to mute his plea with assurances that no drastic reforms could or should be forced on the industry from anyone "outside" the industry. Agencies and publishers should enunciate their own "internal" standards and should enforce them; if not, he warned, the misdeeds of a few "bad boys" would almost certainly provoke public interference. Such mild remonstrances were not likely to persuade advertisers to abandon borderline offenses; yet the editors of both journals continued with notable persistence to arouse the conscience of their readers and to articulate standards where few had ever before been made articulate.

Printers' Ink was soon to act more boldly. In 1931 it proposed, in conjunction with the National Bureau, that advertisers and agencies be drawn more closely into the Bureau's active "policing." A committee, to consist of an equal number of representatives from the ANA, the AAAA, a group of publishers, and the public (stipulated as "outsiders"), would be authorized to review any cases of advertising deemed "unfair" or "detrimental to the public interest" which the Bureau submitted to it.[48] It was contemplated that the Committee would receive on appeal cases where the offender had defied the power of the Bureau or had disagreed with its rulings. By February 1933 the Review Committee was ready to begin its work. It possessed no power not available to the National Bureau; but the Bureau regarded the Committee chiefly as a means of winning a greater measure of support from businessmen for the Bureau's activities, and, having won such support, it could presumably induce businessmen more easily to comply with the Bureau's decisions. The formation of the Review Committee in part was an effort to forestall two of the principal objections which business firms raised to the operations of the Bureau: that it acted as both judge and jury, and that, because it provided no mechanism for appeal, a disgruntled of-

47. *P.I.* (Jan. 12, 1928), p. 13; (Jan. 19, 1928), p. 41; (Feb. 2, 1928), p. 65; (Nov. 5, 1931), p. 10.
48. *P.I.* (Dec. 17, 1931), p. 80; (May 26, 1932), p. 52.

fender was often stimulated to defy the Bureau on the grounds that its judgment did not reflect the judgment of other business-men.[49]

Integral to the operations of the Review Committee was an elaborate Copy Code to guide its decisions. The code was drawn up in the spring of 1932 and adopted by the ANA, the AAAA, and the AFA; thus, in effect, the three most important associations in the national advertising industry were theoretically committed to the support of the Review Committee and its decisions.[50] The code enumerated seven "practices that are unfair to the public and tend to discredit advertising."

1. False statements or misleading exaggerations.

2. Indirect misrepresentation of a product, or service, through distortion of details, either editorially or pictorially.

3. Statements or suggestions offensive to public decency.

4. Statements which tend to undermine an industry by attributing to its products, generally, faults and weaknesses true only of a few.

5. Price claims that are misleading.

6. Pseudoscientific advertising, including claims insufficiently supported by accepted authority, or that distort the true meaning or application of a statement made by professional or scientific authority.

7. Testimonials which do not reflect the real choice of a competent witness.[51]

Despite its promising start, the Review Committee soon stalled and died.[52] During its first year its services were invoked in but two instances, both at the request of the National Bureau itself; one case inspired an actual review of the facts, but in neither case did the Committee even render a decision.[53] A disillusioned editor

49. Letter to author from Kenneth B. Willson, president of the National Better Business Bureau, Sept. 20, 1955.

50. *P.I.* (May 26, 1932), p. 52; (June 23, 1932), p. 33.

51. *P.I.* (May 26, 1932), p. 52.

52. *P.I.* (Feb. 9, 1933), p. 77; (Apr. 20, 1933), p. 68. No members from "outside" the industry were included; in their place were named two representatives from radio broadcasting companies.

53. *P.I.* (Dec. 14, 1933), p. 20. Letter, Willson to author.

confessed in *Printers' Ink* that it had accomplished nothing; advertisers, he noted, had "flatly refused to discuss with other advertisers their methods." They had objected to being summoned before any ex-officio tribunal and had threatened that if they were forced to abandon media advertising, they would resort to direct mail. Failure to prosecute was scarcely due to lack of evidence: though the Bureau possessed "stacks" of cases, most were beyond reach of the law.[54] Concerning the Copy Code itself, one advertising agency executive, Lawrence Valenstein, was even more precise. "The advertising business," he wrote in 1933, "has probably gone on record more frequently, and in more flowery language, with regard to the importance of a code of ethics than any of the hundreds of industries in this country. . . . Yet the advertising business is as guilty of unfair and misleading practices as almost any industry to which one may point. Its codes of ethics have been little more than scraps of paper."[55]

It was Valenstein's contention that recourse to the more effective coercion of the NRA was the only way to guarantee ethical behavior in the advertising industry, and many others shared his view. In September 1933 twelve prominent agencies proposed to incorporate the Copy Code of the Review Committee into the NRA code for advertising agencies; under this plan the Review Committee would be empowered to notify the Administration of a violation of the Copy Code if the Committee could not obtain prior compliance to it.[56] But the proposal aroused such determined opposition, principally from small agencies, that it was dropped in one month. The most frequent objection to be voiced was that advertisers would apply irresistible pressure on their agencies to violate it; one observer noted that most agents knew they could not possibly obey the Copy Code literally and survive in business.[57] Eventually, codes of "advertising ethics" were included in each of nearly 150 Trade Practice Codes for separate industries

---

54. *P.I.* (Apr. 5, 1934), p. 7.

55. Lawrence Valenstein and E. B. Weiss, *Business under the Recovery Act* (New York, McGraw-Hill Co., 1933), p. 128.

56. *P.I.* (Aug. 31, 1933), p. 25.

57. *P.I.* (Sept. 14, 1933), p. 10; (Oct. 19, 1933), p. 84; (Oct. 26, 1933), p. 85. *Tide* (Sept. 1933), p. 10.

under the NRA, but enforcement was sporadic and generally lax, and in May 1935 the codes disappeared along with the NRA itself. Two years later a survey by *Tide* of national advertising in magazines reported that all seven of the "unfair practices" listed in the Copy Code still flourished, and that a few were widely prevalent.[58]

In retrospect it is difficult to believe that the advertising men who supported the Review Committee and its Copy Code could have entertained very sanguine hopes that either device would become an effective barrier to questionable advertising. In the first place it was well known that similar attempts had almost invariably met with failure. In 1911 the AACW had launched a "Truth-in-Advertising" campaign at a fervent convention in Boston; the impeccable vagueness of its ideal for many years served as an emotional rallying-point for advertising clubs and associations, and the AACW erected in 1914 a "National Commission" which was intended to function as a sort of supreme court on violations of fair trade practice and to arbitrate disputes which arose among advertisers. But the codes of conduct which were to guide the Commission were admittedly only ideals rather than working rules, and few members of the AACW seemed willing to abide by its decisions. As a consequence, the Commission declined during the first World War and soon expired.[59] In 1929, partially as a result of a brief flurry in the United States Senate over a proposal by Senator Smoot to ban all cigarette advertising, the ANA and the AAAA had jointly agreed to sponsor a Copy Committee "to bring about a condition in advertising which would remove any shadow of excuse for Federal censorship." But when Smoot's proposal failed to win votes, the advertising associations, it is reported, "became indifferent and the matter was allowed to drift." [60] The Review Committee itself had an im-

58. *Tide* (July 1, 1937), p. 42. The practices most commonly cited were nos. 1, 4, and 6. It is a significant commentary on the problem of establishing ethical codes in advertising that this survey was conducted by three agency men and three "censors" from publications, but that in 90 cases out of 208 the agents and media censors could not agree on whether the advertisement was permissible or censurable.

59. *P.I.* (June 4, 1936), p. 73, an account of the National Commission by William Ingersoll, one of its presidents. See also Baur, chap. 2.

60. *P.I.* (May 26, 1932), p. 52.

mediate predecessor, endowed with a similar name and possessed of similar powers. It too had failed. It is doubtful whether a new committee could have been expected to fare better unless it were given greater power to enforce its decisions.

Not only was the new Review Committee powerless to coerce advertisers; it had also to judge cases according to a code which, though it held advertisers to a strict and rigorous definition of acceptable advertising, was prefaced with the qualifying statement that, inasmuch as "buying motive is emotional as well as factual," advertising copy could be permitted "imaginative and dramatic leeway." [61] While the Code itself proved to be more of a declaration of ideals, an assertion of things hoped for, than a description of practical rules, its preface expressed what was in fact the operating faith of the industry. This did not mean that codes and review committees served no purpose. Advertising men repeatedly cited the very existence of both as proof that their industry was attempting successfully to regulate its own behavior, that it was determined to protect the interests of business and consumer alike, and that "outside" regulation, particularly from the federal government, was consequently as needless as it was unwelcome. The fact that the Review Committee and its Copy Code focused attention on the work of the National Bureau and bolstered the public image of the advertising industry appeared to compensate in part for their failure to achieve anything else.[62]

The inadequacy of the Review Committee reflected an unwillingness, if not an inability, on the part of business associations to enforce internal sanctions against their members. As in the publicity attendant on the Review Committee, trade associations seemed more concerned with persuading others that internal regulation was strict and effective than they were with actually making it so. The fact was that any private regulatory body would have experienced the utmost difficulty in attempting to prevent an advertiser from engaging in a practice that was "unfair" but not illegal. It was one thing to bring pressure to bear against the small manufacturer or agent for offenses which only a few ever dared practice. It was quite another matter to persuade the mem-

61. Ibid.
62. Letter, Willson to author.

bership of an association to bring pressure to bear on a number of its most powerful members to discourage them from activities which had proven eminently profitable for them. The first type of pressure was a time-honored function of a trade association; indeed it might have been the reason for associating in the first place.[63] But the second type of pressure was almost never exercised except as a grudging response to public or outside opinion, a defense against ill-will, hostile legislation, or a drop in sales.

The most widely publicized example of internal regulation by a trade association was a committee which the Proprietary Manufacturers' Association established in 1934 at the request of a number of prominent manufacturers of dentifrice products and brand-name drugs. The committee was expected to examine the advertising of all members of the Association; if it disapproved of what it found, it had the power to recommend disciplinary action to the Association. The standards which it proposed to uphold were lofty and vague: advertisements were to be truthful and in good taste, and were to contain no assertions or claims 'contrary to reasonable expectation in the use of the product under favorable conditions." [64] Members of the Association could choose to submit their advertisements for inspection prior to publication, and a large number did so.[65] The committee was initially organized to forestall contemporary proposals to amend the Pure Food and Drug Act of 1906, but in this purpose it failed; nor did it prove especially successful in achieving the permanent reform of drug advertising. After nearly three years of work, during which it reviewed over 15,000 advertisements, the committee inspired its supporting Association to comment that though drug advertising had improved considerably in three years the most conspicuous

63. For a discussion of this point see C. A. Pearce, *Trade Association Survey* (TNEC Monograph 18, GPO, 1941), pp. 344–8.

64. *P.I.* (Aug. 16, 1934), p. 24. Kenner, pp. 185–6, lists further criteria for the committee's decisions which the secretary of the Association drew up in 1936: "(1) Preparations should be recommended for the relief of symptoms rather than for cure of an underlying condition. (2) Never refer to serious diseases that should be under the doctor's care. (3) Claims should not be broad—they should be limited and specific. (4) The manufacturer must be prepared to prove his claims by evidence."

65. *Tide,* July 1937.

violations of ethical standards still flourished unchecked and that credit for improvement was due as much to the increasing severity of federal regulation as to the activities of the committee.[66]

Trade associations as a rule were exceedingly reluctant to discipline their members for the conduct of their advertising.[67] Individual advertisements, when merely irritating and not illegal or openly disparaging of other firms within the association, were not regarded as any concern of the group. Trade associations, furthermore, were seldom close-knit institutions. Few of them established restrictions for prospective members any more severe than that the applicant be engaged in the industry and agree verbally to practice good behavior. Not even powerful members had much success in attempting to impose their standards for advertising on lesser ones. As a consequence, internal discipline was confined to those infractions of behavior (such as price-cutting) which most of the association's membership could unite in condemning, and, in general, associations tended to concentrate their efforts on activities which evoked widest agreement. Nearly every member of an association could agree, for example, that activities which served to allay public hostility toward the industry, its products and its behavior, were a desirable and proper function of the association as a whole. Rather than establish effective internal sanctions for this purpose, an association would find it far less controversial to announce codes of behavior, statements of ideals, assertions of good intentions and moral sincerity, and periodic campaigns to "clean house." It was to be hoped that such declarations, whether fulfilled or not, would carry weight; they displayed little more than the fact that their sponsors were aware of mounting demands for responsible business behavior.

66. A.S. (June 3, 1937), p. 17; (May 21, 1936), p. 7. P.I. (Nov. 19, 1936), p. 68; (Dec. 31, 1936), p. 73. Within six weeks after the Association's annual convention of 1937, the FTC persuaded the Bristol Meyers Co.—one of the largest firms in the Association—to sign a stipulation to refrain from "untrue" assertions in its advertisements for Ipana toothpaste and Vitalis hair tonic: A.S. (July 1, 1937), p. 20.

67. See studies and reports by C. B. Larrabee, in P.I. (Aug. 13, 1931), p. 60; (Aug. 20, 1931), p. 60; (Oct. 1, 1931), p. 67; (Jan. 19, 1933), p. 17; (Nov. 24, 1939), p. 11; by George Jaflin, as reported in Milton Handler, "False and Misleading Advertising," Yale Law Journal, 39 (1929), 44; and by Pearce, Trade Association Survey, pp. 344–8.

To the extent that responsible behavior in advertising implied a public obligation, newspaper and magazine publishers were in a more powerful position to enforce internal standards of behavior than the advertiser himself. Many advertising men came to believe, in fact, that the only realistic way to achieve effective regulation was to turn the task over to the publishers. Advertisers as a group had failed repeatedly to apply sanctions against themselves as individuals, and their agents were no more successful. Let publishers, then, assume primary responsibility for the conduct of advertising; advertisers and their agents reasoned that publishers alone held the power to reject advertisements for almost any reason they cared to give. A publisher's ultimate stake in the public acceptability of advertising, advertisers further asserted, was at least as great as that of any agent; hence he could be expected to regulate it with vigilance and care. Did not media of public communication (according to a tradition not easily analyzed) possess obligations to readers which transcended the more doubtful obligations of men who offered merely material products for sale? In ordinary market transactions, it would seem, businessmen could still confess to the spirit, if not the letter, of *caveat emptor,* but it ill became publishers to confess it.

When advertisers and their agents insisted that publishers be apportioned a major share of the responsibility for the internal regulation of advertising, they could depend on support from the FTC. As early as 1921 the Commission had announced that in undertaking to eliminate fraudulent advertising it would hold any "perpetually" offending publisher subject to its "cease and desist" orders.[68] Chief Commissioner W. E. Humphrey later explained this policy by declaring that

> Rightly or wrongly, the public assumes that the publisher has knowledge of the advertiser whom he commends to public confidence and patronage. . . . On that assumption the public pays its money and commits to advertisers, in many instances, things more vital than money. To exercise such power over one's fellows is an extraordinary privilege. It carries with it extraordinary responsibilities. The plea of

68. *P.I.* (July 8, 1926), p. 41.

lack of knowledge is without justification on behalf of the publisher.[69]

In 1928 the FTC sought to enforce its policy by sponsoring a "trade practice" conference of publishers in which it tried to persuade them to agree to a voluntary system of internal control in lieu of compulsory regulation by the Commission itself. The FTC, however, did not obtain the cooperation of major publishers until it had disavowed any intention of altering the publishers' existing legal responsibility for advertisements; eventually the publishers persuaded the FTC to let the Better Business Bureaus assume responsibility instead.[70] But pressure on publishers continued. In 1934 the ANA admitted its own failure to establish effective sanctions on members and called on publishers for help. Three months later it published a report which argued from legal precedent that publishers should be held responsible for advertising under the *P.I.* Statute equally with advertisers or their agents; a publisher's right to refuse to print an advertisement implied an obligation on his part to refuse it if he knew it to be misleading or deceptive.[71]

Publishers in turn resisted the advertisers and vigorously disapproved of the attempts of the FTC to hold them subject to the *P.I.* Statute.[72] Though they were careful to assert that the advertising found in their columns was effectively regulated and required no governmental supervision, they also disclaimed any liability for what an advertiser might say. The ultimate responsibility for an advertisement, they insisted, lay with its sponsor, and the task of ensuring responsibility fell most appropriately to Better Business Bureaus. At most a publisher might agree to maintain more or less rigid standards of copy, a staff of censors, and the acknowledgment of the findings of the Better Business Bureaus and the Federal Trade Commission.

In short, advertisers, agents, and publishers each were firm in

69. *P.I.* (Sept. 23, 1926), p. 125.
70. *P.I.* (June 7, 1928), p. 10; (June 28, 1928), p. 33; (Oct. 11, 1928), p. 28. Also Lee, *The Daily Newspaper*, p. 331.
71. *P.I.* (Sept. 27, 1934), p. 7.
72. See, for example, *P.I.* (June 28, 1934), p. 75.

insisting that the burden of internal regulation fall chiefly on the other.

But if advertising men were not always agreed on how to apportion responsibility for maintaining the mechanism of internal regulation, they were strongly agreed that historically the struggle for regulation had reflected particular credit on the press even though resistance had occasionally been fierce and accomplishments long-delayed. A competent authority on the history of journalism, Alfred M. Lee, has noted that the concept of responsibility to a "public" body of readers did not develop before the era of mass circulation and the penny press: until well into the 19th century newspaper advertising was regarded as a private affair between those who bought and read the paper on the one hand, and those who bought space for purposes of communication on the other hand. Except for a number of editors who periodically eliminated advertisements for patent medicines, newspaper space was sold as private property to be used in any way the purchaser saw fit. Mass circulation, however, brought various forms of public pressure to demand the adoption of controls on what should be printed and what should not.[73] Typically this pressure was indirect; the editor who wished to maintain his large circulation unimpaired had to exercise a precise sensitivity to moral and social taboos: the wider his audience, the less divergence from custom an editor permitted himself in either the substance of his advertising columns or in their tone.

To avoid offending the moral sensibilities of the public did not necessarily imply an effort to shield the public from the deceptions of advertisers, much less to guarantee advertisements accepted for publication. In the 1840's Horace Greeley spoke for most of the important editors in the country when he warned that any *Tribune* readers deceived or otherwise taken in by what they had read "should complain to our advertisers themselves, who are not responsible to us for the style of language (if decent) of their advertisements, nor have we any control over them." [74] To-

73. Lee, pp. 314–15.
74. Quoted in Frank Luther Mott, *American Journalism* (New York, Macmillan, 1941), p. 301.

ward the end of the century a few farm journals began to offer guarantees, of a sort, for fulfillment of what had been promised in their advertising columns, and in 1903 the Scripps-Howard League of Newspapers banned "unethical" advertising from its papers.[75] Neither step, however, was widely copied. The American Newspaper Publishers' Association, in fact, refrained from making any recommendations or stating any policies of censorship, preferring to leave such controversial matters to the discretion of individual publishers.[76] While editors demonstrated a notable concern for the state of morals of their readers in the general practice of prohibiting illustrations of "indecent" subjects such as half-clothed men, and cigarette smokers of either sex, the concern of editors for their readers as consumers was slight. William Allen White was later to recall that as recently as 1900 publishers were known to reject cigarette advertising and retain notices of cancer cures and medicines containing narcotics; and Earnest E. Calkins has stated that in the same period the principle still widely persisted that an advertisement was a paid-for right to say whatever one wished, and that whoever chose to deceive the public through such a right was generally at liberty to try his luck.[77]

The spectacular reform movement which swept through American society during the first years of the 20th century noticeably affected the relations between publishers and their readers. The Progressive Era produced its own peculiar literature, a literature of moral indignation, exposure, and modest sensationalism. Far from merely reflecting current moods and existing changes in social attitudes, however, the writings of the muckrakers often set the pace for reform and were themselves important agents of change. As a consequence the newspapers and magazines which sponsored muckraking expeditions into the world of business and politics and published the results found themselves in a peculiar

75. Ibid. Also Kenner, intro.
76. Edwin Emery, *History of the American Newspaper Publishers' Association* (Minneapolis, University of Minnesota Press, 1950), pp. 40–1.
77. William Allen White, "The Ethics of Advertising," *Atlantic Monthly, 164* (1939), 665. Calkins, *"And Hearing Not,"* p. 230. See also *P.I.,* 28, No. 1, 27; 35, No. 7, 21, for the period 1895–1902.

position.[78] Many of the industrial and business practices which they exposed most effectively and against which they roused the fiercest public opposition were precisely those which were identified with the most lavishly advertised products, such as proprietary drugs, liquor, patent medicines, and preserved foods. Those most aggressive in muckraking often depended least on the advertising from the industries under attack, and the enormous circulation which they gained in response to their muckraking crusades afforded them additional immunity to the powerful pressures of the Proprietary Association and other lobbies. To be sure, the zeal of *Collier's, McClure's,* the *Ladies' Home Journal,* the New York *World,* and the Chicago *Tribune* was unmistakable; but it was not widely imitated. Rural and religious weeklies, for example, found crusading extraordinarily difficult. Their very existence was apt to depend on revenues from drug companies, and when public indignation had become thoroughly aroused they found it harder to reflect this militant opinion and simultaneously retain their advertising.

Calls for reform, however, soon affected the advertising columns of the nation's leading publications. Readers were led to expect greater responsibility alike from business and press, and publishers found it increasingly necessary to make convincing assertions of their dedication to reform.[79] The "Truth-in-advertising movement," launched in 1911 with much of the fervor that characterized Roosevelt's Bull Moose Convention of the following year, led in turn to a convention of newspaper publishers in 1914, at which was approved a general code of ethics; its tone was mild and its influence problematical, but it marked a transition from the frank disclaimers of Horace Greeley to the sweeping codes of a later day. The code stated simply that newspapers were obligated "to protect the honest advertiser and the general newspaper

78. See an account of this in C. C. Regier, *The Era of the Muckrakers,* Chapel Hill, University of North Carolina Press, 1942.

79. A number of press associations opposed passage of pure food laws on the theory that these laws would put an end to food and drug advertising: Lee, p. 331. Between 1894 and 1904 the ANPA consistently urged its members to exert pressure on state legislatures for the defeat of food and drug laws. By 1906 the ANPA itself was officially "neutral" toward the pending federal law, but many of its members were not. Emery, p. 39.

reader, as far as possible, from deceptive or offensive advertising . . . to accept no advertising which is antagonistic to the public welfare." [80] The Curtis Publishing Company, in the meantime, had announced a more drastic code which banned from the pages of its magazines "indecent" or "suggestive" copy, "extravagantly worded" or "superlative" claims,[81] and the unwarranted use of the word "free." Advertisers occasionally exerted pressure on the company's advertising managers to modify their code, but the Curtis publications resisted most pressures and soon ranked as one of the most rigorously policed advertising media in the country.

Others were to follow where Curtis led. By the 1920's the New York *Times* was insisting that inasmuch as its advertisements were "news" and were supposed to present the "facts of business," they were required to conform to the standard of accuracy and taste found in the *Times* news columns.[82] Other publishers soon announced similar standards, and in ten more years every important periodical had evolved a set of at least general principles by which advertisements were to be accepted or rejected. No magazine was more thorough than *Good Housekeeping*, which acquired the services of Harvey Wiley upon his resignation as Chief of the Bureau of Chemistry in 1912. Wiley had fought tirelessly for the Pure Food and Drug Act and had administered it with belligerent zeal, and now *Good Housekeeping* was to give him absolute authority to reject advertisements for drugs and cosmetics which did not meet his standards. Until his death in 1930,

---

80. *Editor & Publisher* (*E.P.*), *14* (1914), 1; Lee, p. 332. The convention was held in Toronto, Canada, as a part of the annual convention of the AACW. The code was drafted by representatives from six large newspapers, including the New York *Times*, and was approved by the membership of the Newspaper Division of the AACW. More representative of publishers' attitudes was the code adopted by newspapers in the state of Kansas in 1910. It stated merely that all advertising ought to be labeled plainly as such, and included a sweeping disclaimer: "We hold that the publisher in no degree be held responsible for the statement of fact or opinion found in an advertisement. . . . Freedom of space should only be restricted by the moral decency of the advertising matter." Published in the *Annals of the American Academy of Political and Social Science,* 101, entitled *The Ethics of the Professions and of Business* (May 1922), p. 179.

81. Hower, p. 427.

82. A.S. (Sept. 3, 1921), p. 9.

Wiley censored advertisements submitted to *Good Housekeeping*, conducted a column of advice on food and drug products, and rejected more than one million dollars' worth of advertising which did not win his approval.[83] The St. Louis *Post-Dispatch*, meanwhile, was to outstrip most newspapers when it placed a ban on borderline cases, citing as an illustration the advertisement of a product harmless in itself but whose use might injure customers by encouraging them to postpone competent medical treatment, and a leading executive of the paper declared that because of the nature and influence of a publisher's role in the community he should be held far more responsible to the public than is an ordinary commercial enterprise.[84]

By the advent of the New Deal, publishers in the United States were able to assert truthfully that for the most part their methods of control were effective enough to spot and eliminate advertising of an unquestionably fraudulent character or of the sort which would directly endanger or hoodwink consumers. In this respect they had gone as far toward protecting the interests of the consumer as had any group in the advertising industry. With respect to the "borderline," however, few publishers had demonstrated a willingness to go as far as the *Post-Dispatch;* the only area of the border which publishers as a whole were willing to police was that near corner wherein flourished "disparaging" copy, a form of advertising equally abhorrent to the rest of the industry.

The resolve to prohibit disparaging advertising was significantly bolstered by the pressure of agencies and by the obvious reluctance of publishers to print any sort of advertisement which, by casting aspersions on other advertisements, might awaken a skepticism toward advertising in general. One of the important

83. *Harvey W. Wiley—An Autobiography* (Indianapolis, Bobbs-Merrill, 1931), pp. 302–305. See also testimony by officials of the Good Housekeeping Institute before the FTC, as reported in the New York *Times* (Feb. 8, 1940), p. 38; (Apr. 20, 1940), p. 22.

84. L. E. Pritchard (Chairman of the Advertising Censorship Board, St. Louis *Post-Dispatch*), "The Newspaper's Responsibility to the Consumer in Advertising Censorship," *Journal of Home Economics*, 30 (1938), 445. Pritchard noted that the *Dispatch* lost over $200,000 advertising revenue each year as a consequence of its censorship, but that it gained more than this as measured in the loyalty of readers.

services which most agencies rendered a client was to guard against, and to seek to eliminate, the publication of any advertisement or information which disparaged the client's product. The N. W. Ayer agency once canceled a client's contracts for tobacco advertising in publications which accepted advertisements for "tobacco cures." Ayer took this action not on the grounds that the tobacco cures were fraudulent but because, as the agency informed the publisher, the competing sales message tended "to destroy the investment which our mutual client is making with you." [85] Another instance of agency pressure was less successful. In 1935, the Quaker Oats Company advertised that one cent's worth of Quaker Oats contained as much vitamin B as three cakes of "fresh yeast." This was an ill-disguised challenge to the prominent (and highly questionable) advertising claims made on behalf of Fleischmann's Yeast, a client of the J. Walter Thompson agency. That agency, in turn, wrote a letter to all newspapers which carried the Quaker Oats advertisements; it deplored this violation of "anti-knocking" ethics, claimed that a number of prominent newspapers had already declined the Quaker Oats advertising because of its unethical tone, and threatened retaliation of a sort which it did not choose to specify. A few newspapers altered the Quaker Oats advertisement, but a large majority called the agency's bluff by refusing to act.[86] An agency's power to suppress "competitive" copy, then, was not unlimited if the competitor were powerful and the copy truthful. The pressure of agencies, however, encouraged publishers to shift the emphasis of their advertising regulations away from the time-honored defense of community "morals" and toward rules which would preserve "fair competition" among business competitors. There was scarcely any danger, to be sure, that publishers would risk permanently offending large classes of readers with flagrant departures from accepted "taste" even under pressure from important advertisers, and there is reliable testimony to indicate that in the early 1930's the printed media lost a number of advertising accounts to radio rather than accept copy which might incur the resentment of readers or adverse action by public regulating

85. Hower, pp. 425–31.
86. *E.P.* (Oct. 5, 1935), p. 36.

bodies.[87] But it was equally certain that no publisher would wish to lose an important advertising account by risking the publication of copy which disparaged its product or questioned its claims.

By the end of the Depression publishers had evolved, haphazardly and by no means uniformly, a structure of safeguards for advertising which seemed entirely adequate to their own needs. They strove to judge advertisements according to the criteria by which the Better Business Bureaus and the FTC judged them, but they refused to interfere with the half-truth, the technically truthful deception.[88] They were willing to assume part of the responsibility for effective regulation, but they were unwilling to assume it all or, except by voluntary agreement, to be held legally liable for the advertisements which they printed.[89] They attempted at all times, by means of market surveys, improvements in printing, and editorial support, to increase the effectiveness of advertising as a technique for selling. For advertising as a whole they were anxious to gain public respect, but on particular copy practices which agents, advertisers, and their associations were unable or reluctant to modify, publishers were equally reluctant to take a stand or to make up singlehandedly for the collective inadequacies of internal regulation.

By these several means, then, the national advertising industry attempted to erect for itself effective and responsible standards of behavior. These efforts were expected to forestall external regulation and to discourage advertising which might injure the success of competing advertisers. They did not necessarily guarantee the consuming public similar protection from injury, and any advantages which accrued to the consumer as a result of internal regulation were incidental to the main purpose. The public, it is

87. *F.T.C. Annual Report for the Fiscal Year Ended June 30, 1934* (GPO, 1934), p. 102.

88. In this respect they were, of course, only echoing a similar disclaimer made repeatedly by the FTC, that "borderline" deception was "comparatively harmless" and that the Commission took no interest in it. Statement by Commissioner W. E. Humphrey, *P.I.* (Sept. 23, 1925), p. 125.

89. See James E. Pollard, "Advertising Copy Requirements of Representative Newspapers," *Journalism Quarterly*, 14 (1937), 259. With the onset of economic recovery, Pollard insists, newspapers became "increasingly aware of their responsibility to the public."

true, could count on both governmental and private authority to protect it from most forms of fraud, but as the process of buying grew more complex and the process of marketing more subtle, the central issue of regulation shifted perceptibly from the problem of fraud to the problem of borderline deceptions. Simultaneously, however, the private internal regulation of advertising tended to center less on the real problem for the consumer, which borderline advertising represented, and concentrated instead on protecting the industry itself from the effects of over-zealous competition. It was exceedingly doubtful whether volunteer internal regulation could ever have offered the public the added protection it sought; yet, on the undesirability of external regulation of any kind, advertising men were in firm agreement.

It was significant and fitting that in the confident years which preceded the Depression no less than two American presidents successively bestowed on the industry messages of good cheer, in which they took pains to assert that nothing further was required to ensure the public interest than to rely on the conscience of the industry itself. Persuaded to appear in person before the 1926 convention of the AAAA, Calvin Coolidge reminded his listeners that their great power to educate and persuade "is always coupled with responsibilities," the chief of which was to tell the truth at all times. After reviewing the early triumphs and the recent growth of the industry, he then stated what his audience particularly wished to hear: no government should interfere with advertising. "The ultimate reformers of business must be the businessmen themselves." [90] In a similar message sent in 1929 to the IAA, Herbert Hoover was less explicit but even more flattering. He was confident, he said, that the advertising industry could handle unaided all matters requiring responsible self-discipline, and he saw no reason to be dissatisfied with things as they were: "The agencies established by the advertisers themselves for checking up the truth of advertising in general, have produced most beneficial results." [91] It was not given to many industries to receive supreme sanction for both its ideals and its existing behavior. Two presidents, like visiting archbishops called to pro-

90. Reprinted in *P.I.* (Nov. 4, 1926), p. 3.
91. Reprinted in *P.I.* (Oct. 24, 1929), p. 82.

nounce benedictions, said only what had been said before and would doubtless be said again, but the mere fact that they said it symbolized a union of business and state which few historians of the period would declare was merely spiritual. It was hoped that such a public assertion of faith would bolster belief in the responsibility of advertising, among its practitioners and elsewhere.

But no public statements possessed value unless the public toward which they were directed believed them. For many years there had been developing a complex opposition to the theories and behavior of the advertising industry. It could hardly be stayed by the mere assertion that advertising was responsible for business prosperity or even by the testimony of two Republican presidents that advertising practices had best be left alone. Indeed, when business prosperity gave way to depression and the Republicans had been voted out of the presidency, neither the assertion nor the testimony could have had quite the impact they might have been expected to have. Gradually a number of interest groups posed a challenge which could no longer be ignored, and they came to demand from the industry an operating concept of public responsibility more comprehensive than advertising men had ever been willing to support.

4

Challenge and Criticism

IN THE DECADE which followed the first World War national advertising had become a weapon of considerable power in the American economy. While it furthered the particular interests of those businessmen who were able and willing to pay for it, there were others whose interests conflicted with the interests of national advertisers, who suggested periodically that the advertising industry be subject to external regulation, and who held that the public should be encouraged to view advertising with at least cautious skepticism. Few who entertained such views were likely to abandon them solely because the advertising industry had disparaged the need for external control or even because the industry had made limited gestures of internal "policing." National agencies, trade associations, owners of media, independent bureaus, and vigilant competitors may be said to have exercised control from within, and national advertisers were quick to contend that the internal control of their industry was so effective as to make external control unnecessary and harmful. But the operation of internal control in national advertising left essentially untouched the issue of responsibility to the public. The very nature of the business relationships and incentives which united advertisers, agents, and media owners in a common attitude toward their public obligations did not and could not satisfy the opposing interests of external groups. Soon a number of outside institutions and individuals confronted the national advertising industry with a more serious challenge to its power than it had yet encountered, a challenge which culminated in the so-called consumer movement of the 1930's.

External pressures on national advertising came from a number of groups who held at least one interest in common: to neutralize or alter the impact and effectiveness of advertising which they found objectionable. Two courses of action were open to them. They might attempt to change what was found objectionable, either by legal coercion or by obtaining the voluntary acquiescence of the advertiser. They might, on the other hand, attempt to induce readers to alter their response to advertising. Save for departments and agencies of government, not many groups sought to exercise legal coercion; the principal weapon employed against national advertisers was the weapon of counterpersuasion, an attempt by publicity and propaganda—through the publication of books, journals, public speeches, and articles in magazines and newspapers—to meet the national advertiser on his own ground, so to speak, and with his own weapons. In the period between the two world wars the most conspicuous interest groups to exert pressure of this sort were governmental agencies, the courts, professional organizations (representing principally doctors and dentists), retailers, and the private individuals and pressure groups who comprised the consumer movement and who provided a critical and an effective public scrutiny of the power of the national advertising industry.

If one were to accept the published views of advertising men, the agencies and branches of the federal government, even before 1933, have bestowed on the advertising industry unvarying abuse and interference. In actuality federal pressures were not as important as other external pressures, but they were more conspicuous, and the industry seldom ceased complaining about them. Federal and state regulatory activities in the United States have generally reflected private interests sufficiently organized to obtain governmental help in delimiting the power of competing interests. Thus, retailers secured the passage of laws unfavorable to the operation of chain stores, while the *P.I.* Statute against fraudulent advertising embodied the desires and fears of well-established businessmen. Similarly with the Pure Food and Drug Act of 1906. Upon the firm prodding of Theodore Roosevelt and in the face of powerful opposition from the Proprietary Association and from patent medicine firms, the Act had finally passed a Congress sensitive to the demands of crusading clubwomen, organized farmers, and a number of individual newspapers and magazines. The law was vigorous in its language, but its subsequent enforcement occasionally lagged as public interest waned and as its original opponents in turn exerted more effective influence on Congress or on the Administration. From 1906 until 1927, in fact, federal action under the Pure Food and Drug Act languished as a result of the failure of the Food and Drug Administration (F. and D. A.), despite earnest pleading, to obtain adequate operating funds from a Congress more impressed with the organized strength of drug companies and their associations than with the dissipated enthusiasm of reformers. In the face of militant opposition from proprietary interests in the 1920's, favorable court decisions enabled the F. and D. A. to combat a greater variety of offenses, particularly deceptive labeling, and the officials of the agency did much to renew interest in more comprehensive federal legislation.[1] In 1930, largely at the insistence of officials from the F. and D. A., Congress approved the McNary-Mapes Amendment to the Act of 1906 which enabled

1. T. Swann Harding, *The Popular Practice of Fraud* (London, Longmans, Green, 1935), pp. 273–5; L. T. Hayes and F. J. Ruff, "The Administration of the Food and Drug Act," *Law and Contemporary Problems*, 1, (1933), 16. In 1924 the Supreme Court ruled that under the terms of the Food and Drug Act of 1906 the government was empowered to prohibit labeling which, even if merely ambiguous and not overtly false, deceived consumers as to the nature of the product (265 U.S. *Reports*, 438–44).

the F. and D. A. to specify standards for canned foods to which all processors must adhere unless they stated otherwise on their labels.[2] An attempt to bring the advertising of "remedials" under the scrutiny of the F. and D. A. failed of Senate passage in 1931, but it marked only the beginning of a long struggle to extend federal regulation of food and drug products to their advertising and to include cosmetics as well. Thus it was shown that even without the continuous support of the public, a department of the federal government could effectively challenge the unrestricted use of advertising in a specialized field and could compel the industry to alter its public standards.

In a similar manner the Federal Trade Commission assumed a central role in the governmental supervision of advertising practices. As initially conceived the FTC had no special warrant to protect general consumers. Through the 1920's it served principally as a referee among competing business interests, and its attention was confined for the most part to violations of fair trade practices, such as deceptive labeling likely to injure the business of a competitor, and promotions of fraudulent financial schemes. Toward consumer advertising it was circumspect; publishers and manufacturers obtained from it the repeated assurance that it did not intend to prevent mere exaggeration or "puffing" in advertising copy, and that doubts as to the legitimacy of a claim should as far as possible be resolved in favor of the advertiser.[3] Yet the FTC in fact was broadening its concern to include the protection of others than the "injured competitor." In its first twenty years of activity two thirds of the three thousand "cease and desist" orders which it issued were attempts to prohibit false or misleading advertising, which was at least as detrimental to consumers as to competitors.[4] In 1928, during its conferences with publishers to discourage the acceptance of misleading advertising copy, the FTC asserted that publishers had an obligation to uphold the right of the otherwise unprotected consumer to be exposed only to honest advertising, and that as a

2. *P.I.* (Jan. 19, 1928), p. 152; *A.S.* (Jan. 22, 1930), p. 36.
3. Statement of Commissioner W. E. Humphrey, reported in *P.I.* (June 3, 1926), p. 133.
4. Harding, p. 297.

consequence of that obligation the FTC was within its rights in compelling publishers to work out some mode of self-regulation.[5] The interest of the FTC in the "public" was made even more explicit in 1932 when one of its staff declared at a meeting of druggists in New York that the Commission regarded itself as an "arbiter" between the business world and the public, and that the Commission "was of the belief that, as advertising affects the health, well-being and economic prosperity of our nation, the public is entitled to protection against false, misleading, and fraudulent representations or inducements in the appeal of the advertiser."[6] The druggists were also reminded that mounting resentment against the unrestricted behavior of national advertisers had already led to proposals for legislation giving the Commission power to prohibit any advertising deceptive to the public.[7] That the increased threat of the Commission's activities appeared to be more than an idle one may be inferred from the mounting resentment toward the Commission in the advertising trade press, which regretted that the agency, begun as an aid to business, had now become an enemy of business in having attempted to interfere with the natural relations between business and the public.[8]

Until 1938 whatever effective power the FTC gained over advertising came as a result of judicial decisions based on the original legislation which had created it in 1914. In 1922 the Supreme Court ruled that the Commission might forbid misrepresentation in interstate commerce primarily deceptive to the public.[9] Nine years later its powers were unexpectedly curtailed as a result of a contrary decision which held that for a practice to come under the purview of the FTC it had to be proven substantially injurious to a competitor as well as to the public.[10] In 1934, how-

5. *P.I.* (Oct. 11, 1928), p. 28. Also, see above, p. 77.

6. *P.I.* (Apr. 21, 1932), p. 94.

7. Ibid. The legislation to which the speaker referred was the Walsh bill, currently before the Senate. It was never passed.

8. *P.I.* (May 5, 1932), p. 5; (Mar. 9, 1933), p. 55. A survey of the increase in the powers of the FTC may be found in Ewald T. Grether, "Marketing Legislation," *Annals of the American Academy of Political and Social Science*, 209 (1940), 172–5. He contends that the courts insisted on this added interpretation of the FTC's function. See also *P.I.* (Nov. 3, 1927), p. 25.

9. *F.T.C. vs. Winsted Hosiery Company* (258 U.S. 483).

10. *F.T.C. vs. Raladam Company* (283 U.S. 643).

ever, the Supreme Court again opened the way for the regulation of noncompetitive practices by declaring that although the Commission was not authorized to issue orders which have "no other purpose than that of relieving merchants from troublesome competition or of censoring the morals of businessmen," nevertheless it could legitimately act against practices designed to "exploit consumers [or] children, who are unable to protect themselves." [11] The FTC was now to seek a fundamental change in the law to permit it to act in a much larger number of cases, such as, for example, those which would involve manufacturers of nostrums, where no legitimate competitor existed. It did not gain what it sought until 1938 when passage of the Wheeler-Lea Act enormously widened the jurisdiction of the Commission by allowing it to prohibit advertising which was deceptive or misleading regardless of whether it could be proved harmful to a competitor. The passage of this act climaxed a bitter struggle between the advertising industry and a large number of public and private interest groups, a struggle which will be discussed in the next chapter.

Until the 1930's advertising regulations and restrictions were passed and enforced very largely by individual states and local communities. From time to time, to be sure, someone in the national Congress was moved to present bills to outlaw misleading advertising in interstate commerce, to levy a national tax on advertising space, to prohibit billboard advertising, or to extend the powers of the Food and Drug Act to include advertising of certain products viewed with particular disfavor by special segments of the voting population.[12] Until 1938, however, no national legislation of this sort passed, and indeed until 1933 only alarmists betrayed any concern that it would; the apparition of local press-supported Congressmen voting to tax newspaper space or to endanger the revenues accruing to local weeklies from cigarette advertising was so remote and implausible that it could hardly have frightened even the conscience-stricken into good behavior.

11. *F.T.C. vs. R. F. Kappel and Bros.* (291 U.S. 304).
12. For examples see *P.I.* (Feb. 26, 1920), p. 125; (May 27, 1920), p. 57; (Apr. 17, 1924), p. 54; (June 13, 1929), p. 65; (June 27, 1929), p. 25.

There was more to fear, however, from states and local communities.

State regulation of advertising varied markedly, but most states had passed statutes which made "false" advertising a misdemeanor, restricted liquor advertisements, regulated the sale of oleomargarine, placed bans on publicity for venereal diseases and the use of contraceptives, imposed strict regulations on political and financial advertisements, defined and proscribed immorality and lasciviousness in any publication, and proposed a variety of rigid rules for the "ethical" conduct of professional classes (doctors, dentists, lawyers, and even barbers) who were forbidden to solicit business by advertising.[13] Many states, on the other hand, gave explicit encouragement and virtually free rein to local and regional publicity: "locate in Cleveland"; "sunny Miami"; "California, land of opportunity." One can summarize the pattern of state regulation by remarking that a number of special interest groups, noticeably uniform from one region of the country to another, exercised a constricting check on the copy writer's imagination even when he wrote for large national firms. Among the groups to exercise such a check, the most conspicuous were farms blocs, religious organizations, Temperance forces or "Drys," and professional persons. Some national advertisers, particularly liquor manufacturers, found it necessary to concoct several variations of individual advertisements in order to conform with state laws, and national advertising agencies were obliged to develop a nice sensitivity to local prejudices and whims.

Another major interest group to impinge directly on the power of national advertising was the medical and dental profession. Its concern over the selling practices of patent medicine companies and dentifrice manufacturers dated from the infancy of modern advertising. Its most powerful component, the American Medical Association, as early as 1911 had sponsored articles which

13. See Bert W. Roper, *State Advertising Legislation* (New York, Printers' Ink, 1945) for a compilation of 2,000 state statutes regulating advertisements. A report published in *P.I.* (Jan. 12, 1939), p. 35, revealed that of the bills related to advertising pending in 42 state legislatures for that year, practically none specifically restricted advertising; they embodied mostly fair trade practices and the taxation of trademarks and out-of-state products.

exposed medical frauds and pseudoscientific claims, and medical journals furnished indispensable ammunition for critics of advertising practices.[14] By 1926, despite bitter opposition from large drug and dentifrice advertisers, publicity by the AMA and similar organizations had driven the most questionable medical advertising out of reputable periodicals and forced it to take refuge in less "respectable" magazines or in direct mail. In its place, however, came pseudoscientific but legally worded phrases which insinuated claims nearly as questionable. The AMA, forced to adopt new tactics, proclaimed its willingness to cooperate with advertisers in an effort to induce moderation in copy and launched at the same time a campaign of publicity both against fraudulent cosmetic advertising, which was then beyond the reach of the Pure Food and Drug Act, and against the misleading claims of a few manufacturers of food products.[15]

The special concern which the AMA exhibited toward food advertising after 1925 coincided with a pervasive fad of advertising nationally distributed brand foods as possessing medicinal value for real or imagined ailments. Fleischmann's Yeast had been sold as medicine with such conspicuous success that its agency, the J. Walter Thompson Company, advertised Velveeta processed cheese in the same way ("for the good of your teeth"). Other advertisers followed suit and began to promote the sale of cereals, fruits, bread, and soft drinks by promises of vitamin quality and other attributes, some wholly imaginary. The AMA had been particularly incensed by Standard Brands' procession of European "doctors" and their testimony for yeast cakes; it viewed Standard's technique, not implausibly, as a ruse for avoiding the American association.[16] Promptly denouncing advertisements which virtu-

14. For a survey of early AMA activities see Arthur J. Cramp, director of the AMA Bureau of Investigation, in *Law and Contemporary Problems*, 1, 51. For journal advertising practices see the *Nation* (Aug. 31, 1927), p. 202; Harding, p. 330.

15. A. J. Cramp, official statement of the AMA, *P.I.* (Mar. 24, 1927), p. 25; Morris Fishbein, *P.I.* (Aug. 19, 1926), p. 3, and *A.S.* (Mar. 21, 1928), p. 22; also Raymond Hertwig, AMA Committee on Foods, in *Law and Contemporary Problems*, 1, 55.

16. See a report on Standard Brands in *Fortune*, Jan. 1936.

ally labeled a product a "health food," the Association sponsored articles and pamphlets on nutritional problems, and to encourage compliance with its standards it announced the bestowal of a "seal of approval" on legitimate products whose advertising was acceptable. The seal of the AMA was not won cheaply; of some five hundred products examined by 1931, less than 15 per cent had won it. Many manufacturers, however, altered their advertising policies to earn the approval of the AMA, which was itself an effective advertising claim; one advertising agency president asserted that in a period of depression no advertiser could afford to ignore the continuous pressure from doctors, health experts, and medical journals for improved standards of copy.[17] Within a few more years the AMA had established and publicized some specific standards for responsible and acceptable advertising: all claims should be clearly stated; they should mean what they say; no advertisement should imply that every essential food value can be found in any one product; claims which relied on "medical" authority were to be rigidly substantiated; implications of danger where none existed in fact (danger from "acidosis," for example) were unethical; "energy" was not to be considered in itself a food value.[18] No one contended that the entire food and drug industries altered their advertising practices in a rush to obtain AMA approval; nor was it clear that the changes which did occur could always be attributed to organizational pressure: claims of vitamin content, for example, may have slacked off because the public was no longer responding to the magic cry of vitamins. Nevertheless, by 1940 normal copy writing had moved closer to the standards of the AMA; and the Food Council of that organization, noting the increasingly effective work of the FTC and the F. and D. A., subsequently reduced its policing activities.

17. *Tide* (July 1931), p. 16; (Oct. 1931), p. 17; (Nov. 1931), p. 17; AMA *Journal* (Oct. 1931), p. 1005; H. E. Lesan, remarks reported in *P.I.* (Apr. 10, 1930), p. 57. The American Dental Association offered a similar "seal of approval" to dentifrice manufacturers. An editor of *Tide* doubted whether "big advertisers" would feel that the seals were worth the price of honest advertising, but several advertisers plainly did think so.

18. Quoted from the AMA in Margaret C. Reid, *Consumers and the Market* (New York, F. S. Crofts, rev. ed. 1942), pp. 372–3.

In opposing the techniques and pretensions of national advertising no group proved more effective or more helpful to the consumer than a few large retail and chain stores. Inasmuch as national advertising had become in part a weapon for control of the market, its continued growth stimulated a considerable amount of opposition among retailers who competed with national manufacturers for that control. When many national firms attempted by advertising, for example, to weaken demand for the so-called "private" brands sponsored by retail chain stores and mail order houses, owners and distributors of these private brands not infrequently retaliated with advertising of their own. Generally, in fact, retail stores employed techniques of persuasion fully as sophisticated as those of a national advertiser and exploited the advertising of well-known brands for their own purposes. Their hostility toward national advertising practices was directed quite obviously not against the institution of advertising but rather against the firms which engaged in it.

More significant than their efforts to deflate the pretensions of national brands were the efforts of a number of important retail and chain stores (in particular Gimbel Brothers, Macy's, Marshall Field, and Sears, Roebuck) to offer the consumer a few of the tools he needed for resisting the blandishments of national advertising copy and for forming his own judgment about the goods he wanted. The most important service which these stores rendered was to make available alternative sources of information and facts, such as grade labeling or the labeling of outside testing bureaus, about a large number of well-advertised products.[19] It did not require a feeling of good will or a sense of moral obligation on the part of a retailer to induce him to satisfy the demands of the growing consumer movement for reliable information. Consumer agitation for more information and less advertising proved a benefit to the retailer who found that the promotion of his own private brands was made easier when positive information had permitted consumers to compare private brands objectively with nationally famous ones. Only the well-informed buyer, for example, was likely to buy a little-known box of aspirin for 16¢ in-

19. See S. P. Kaidanovsky, *Consumer Standards* (TNEC Monograph 24, 1941), pp. 322 ff.

stead of Bayer aspirin, of identical quality, for 59¢.[20] The logical focus for consumer dissatisfaction, furthermore, was apt to be the store from which he obtained the goods, and retailers generally found that well-informed consumers were less prone than were uninformed consumers to buy foolishly and thereby overload the retailers with demands that products be taken back and a refund of money made. That the service which retailers rendered consumers was seldom disinterested did not, of course, lessen its value. Whenever large chain stores such as the A. and P. came under legislative attack from hostile local retailers, they proved anxious to cultivate the good will of every likely consumer group within the locality and often found it useful to pose as the consumer's one trustworthy friend in an otherwise unsympathetic world. The pose in itself guaranteed nothing: many institutions traded cynically on the word "consumer."[21] But time and again consumers found that large retailers backed their demands for more informative advertising and by the very threat of their competitive position encouraged the manufacturers of national brands to exercise greater care in their advertising. They might be said to have offered what John K. Galbraith has recently termed "countervailing power" against the power of large national sellers.[22]

The advertising industry has never lacked critics. Its chief characteristic has been the business of manufacturing verbal stimuli for the purposes of persuasion and salesmanship and forcing those stimuli on the public. These are activities which might arouse criticism at any time. During the 1920's and 1930's, when advertising was intensified to an unprecedented degree, criticism rapidly mounted. In this same period business lost glamour; its fall in prestige, inevitable enough amid the miseries of the Depression,

20. Helen Sorenson, *The Consumer Movement* (New York, Harper, 1941), p. 182.

21. See especially Sorenson, pp. 165–75. A "Consumers' Foundation," founded in 1938, was financed by a number of large chain stores as an experiment in public relations. The national Consumers' Tax Commission was similarly backed. Another organization, the "Consumers' League for Honest Wool Labelling" was described by its secretary, in response to an official query, as "a loose organization of friends of mine from Wyoming."

22. John K. Galbraith, *American Capitalism: the Concept of Countervailing Power* (Boston, Houghton, Mifflin, 1952), p. 136.

was all the greater for its previous assertions of infallibility. National advertising had provided a persistently rosy view of large business enterprise. With little difficulty, critics of the latter became critics of the former, though, contrary to the professed fears of many advertising men, it was perfectly possible for critics to deplore national advertising and approve of large business enterprise, or to deplore some national advertising and approve of the rest. In any case the critics could not be ignored, for even if they did not always reflect widespread popular attitudes, they were frequently in a position to influence and direct them, and a few were skillful and persuasive enough to do so. Some of them spoke directly on behalf of organized consumer groups, and a few others in positions of political and administrative power provided the leadership, the policies, and much of the dedicated enthusiasm which made the consumer movement seem for a few years a formidable threat to businessmen. Some of them demanded of the advertising industry a type of behavior and an ethos which its structure could not provide; others, more realistic, did not attempt to transform the industry, but sought to modify its impact by encouraging consumer education. But all of them represented segments of a public who clearly believed that they had an important stake in advertising behavior and practices and who felt that the prevailing rationale to which advertising men subscribed—not to mention their practice—ignored the claims of responsibility which that stake warranted.

The consumer movement which developed so rapidly in the 1930's had roots in the period just following the first World War. In its predepression manifestations it was scarcely more than a number of local organizations of club women, who lived generally in large cities and who expressed discontent over mounting postwar prices and the rapidly increasing difficulties which they encountered as amateur buyers in an industrial society of unprecedented complexity. These organizations typically conducted investigations of such practices as the sale of food and milk, and inspired occasional boycotts of high-priced goods. Then in 1927 there appeared the first book to offer an articulate and comprehensive statement of a growing consumer interest. Its authors were Stuart Chase and Frederick J. Schlink, an economist and an engineer, and the book, called *Your Money's Worth,* became a Book of the Month selection and a best-seller.[23]

Chase and Schlink directed a searing fire at the entire marketing structure of American business, but they spoke particularly harshly of advertising. They reminded their readers that inefficiency and waste in buying thrived in inverse ratio to the knowledge of products which the buyer could bring to the market. Industrial buyers, government buyers, purchasing agents for large intermediary institutions, and individuals expert in production bought efficiently because they possessed the means to deflate and even disregard the blandishments of advertising. They bought by specification, by impartial testing methods, and according to objectively determinable performance; they sought to test the products themselves. As a consequence men responsible for industrial advertising and for copy which appeared in scientific journals largely avoided the more obvious forms of misrepresentation lest their salesmen be laughed out of the door. But housewives in search of the best vacuum cleaner, engineers in the act of buying toothpaste, or even toothpaste manufacturers perplexed over where to spend a month's vacation, were subject to assault from virtually every technique of one-sided persuasion and frequently had no other source on which to base a rational buying judgment. These "ultimate" consumers, buying as amateurs, would, the authors felt, welcome and eventually demand information from some other sources than advertisements; they were obviously ready to listen to proposals to establish them.

Chase and Schlink did not suggest that general consumers adopt the specific techniques of professional purchasing agents and thereby deprive themselves of the emotional values and the intangible psychic satisfaction of shopping by allure or suggestion or even by illusion. They argued simply that consumers ought to be provided with some system which would place them in a position of power comparable to that of professional buyers in opposition to sellers. Nor did they fear that the rational acquisition of knowledge about consumer products in an industrial society

23. Stuart Chase and F. J. Schlink, *Your Money's Worth: a Study in the Waste of the Consumer's Dollar,* New York, Macmillan, 1927. Over 100,000 copies were sold.

would in any way induce drab conformity of taste or the decay of emotion and romance; it was their view in fact that a little less nonsense and a little more substantial information in advertising might even encourage individuality and imagination in the production of goods. In any case, they were clearly urging the public to disbelieve consumer advertising and salesmanship. The consumer's ignorance of the specialized products which he must buy contributed to economic waste, while most consumer advertising throve on his ignorance and compounded the waste. The consumer, the authors concluded, must find a means to oppose the power of advertising with power of his own—the power of knowledge and the power of skepticism—in order to get exactly what he wants and to know exactly what he is getting. They proposed as a start that governmental, university, and interested private laboratories test and compare brand-name products and publish their conclusions as an alternative to the special pleading of commercial salesmanship.[24]

Of the two authors Chase proved to be relatively less aggressive; he continued to say merely that consumers badly needed education and information in buying, and he emphasized that he had no quarrel with advertising so long as businessmen provided the consumer with facts and treated him as an adult. But Schlink, who condemned even federal testing bureaus as subservient to the interests of big advertisers, acted on his own proposals by founding Consumers' Research, an independent testing agency. Begun in 1928 in White Plains, New York, as a club where members exchanged information about products which they had bought, it grew in two years to national proportions, with a membership of 12,000, a periodical news letter, and a small staff of technicians. By 1931, within one year, the number of its subscribers doubled, and in five more years it had doubled again. An organization whose conceptual framework had been born in conspicuous prosperity was now nourished by the discontents of nationwide economic misery. Not only Consumers' Research, but in large part

24. Advertising journals and conventions devoted a flattering amount of attention to discussing and attacking the book. The following reports occurred in *P.I.* alone: (Oct. 1, 1925), editorial feature; (Aug. 11, 1927), p. 57 (editorial); (Nov. 3, 1927), p. 3 (convention address); Aug. 23, 1928), p. 91 (book review).

the Depression itself provided the consumer movement with an indispensable sense of direction.[25]

The consumer movement was a collection of specialized organizations which sought to rationalize the function of buying and to strengthen the resources and position of the general buyer in a modern industrial economy.[26] Though it flourished primarily as a depression phenomenon, its growth was sustained by a number of deep changes which were revealed in the 1930's in the American marketing system. Generally speaking, it might be said that the abundance of a highly productive economy encouraged the replacement of efficient production with efficient consumption as the primary task of the market. More specifically, however, a substantial decrease in home production necessitated an almost universal dependence on monetary purchases, while a rapid proliferation of consumer goods outpaced the average buyer's skills in judging goods and forced him to rely on published claims and brand names. At the same time sellers developed greater skills in directing and coercing consumer wants, and powerful producers tended to discourage price competition, the major apparatus which could allow buyers to judge products and to assure themselves a "vote" in the market. Finally, the Depression itself intensified the disruptive effect of these changes and created some stresses of its own. Under pressure to reduce costs and maintain profits, manufacturers very often cheapened the quality of their product while maintaining an illusion of brand consistency and value. In consequence of these changes and the frustrations they produced, a number of separate organizations, intent on reforming the market system, soon flourished in an atmosphere of general resentment against the conspicuous decline both in the quality of products and in the reasonableness of advertising. The distinctive characteristic which united these organizations into a consumer "movement" was a driving concern to make practicable on a large scale the exercise of rational intelligence in consumer

25. *P.I.* (Oct. 4, 1928), p. 28; *Scribner's* (Nov. 1937), p. 21; letters, F. J. Schlink to author, Nov. 15, 1957, and Jan. 7, 1958. Consumers' Research was incorporated Dec. 1929. Schlink had had much experience in testing work.

26. Cf. Kenneth Dameron, "The Consumer Movement," *Harvard Business Review*, 17 (1939), 273–6.

buying. At the heart of this purpose was a faith that the spread of "objective" information would enable, and thus persuade, the consumer to exercise his reason and would thereby liberate him from an abject dependence on producers and their salesmanship. It was for the most part a faith of traditional pragmatists in the power and efficacy of factual education.

During the Depression a number of institutions persistently supported consumer "education." The American Home Economics Association, over half of whose 14,000 members were school and college teachers, lobbied for legislation to regulate advertising and labeling and sponsored comparative studies of commercial products. Together with the Stephens College Institute for Consumer Education, the AHEA urged the teaching of courses in "home economics" and recommended standards for such courses. By 1940 more than 250,000 students were enrolled in them and were encouraged, among other things, to discount advertisements and to consume according to rational calculation. The American Association of University Women and the National League of Women Voters, whose combined membership exceeded 100,000, forcefully advocated a stricter Food and Drug Law and federal grading of canned foods; they likewise sponsored exhibits and conferences designed to promote intelligent consumption. Other organizations worked assiduously for similar ends: "consumer" clubs affiliated with churches, labor unions, and farm organizations; welfare agencies; public agencies such as land-grant college extension services, the Bureau of Standards, and the Bureau of Home Economics in the Department of Agriculture; and a small but vigorous consumers' cooperative movement. Cohesion and unity among these diverse institutions were not easily obtained, but during the early 1930's what was conspicuously common to all of them was an abiding concern over the facts of high prices and low purchasing power for the wage-earner. Though this concern had receded somewhat by the late 1930's, consumer organizations did continue to agree on two other more controversial objectives: that reliable information about the quality and price of products be assured either on labels or in advertisements, and that "consumers" be strongly represented in all governmental decisions which affected consumer buying. The consumer movement, in short, sought not merely long-range educational reform: it was proposing immediate alterations in the conduct of advertising.[27]

It remained for the private testing agencies to offer constructive information on which consumers could assess products independently of advertising. The two principal agencies were Consumers' Research, controlled by Schlink, and Consumers' Union, established in 1936 by Arthur Kallet, an associate of Schlink who had broken with him over the labor policies of Consumers' Research. Each organization counted about 70,000 paying members and a readership of their periodicals and syndicated columns estimated at two or three million. They operated on meager budgets, with an income from occasional gifts and modest subscription fees. The core of each organization was a staff of engineers and technicians (some of whom donated their services), and each "tested" and reported on about two thousand products a year.[28]

The task which consumer testing agencies set for themselves by its very nature proved congenial to men with widely differing motives. Committed fundamentally to capitalism, the consumer movement as a whole questioned merely the marketing arrangements of contemporary American business and challenged their practical consequences; yet in several instances during the 1930's this consumer critique was supported and influenced by men who, being closely affiliated with the Communist party, were very probably intent less on saving the consumer or on strengthening his position in a free market than on discrediting or even disrupting the market itself and the capitalism on which it rested. It has been several times asserted, though on inconclusive and conflicting testimony, that Consumers' Union was originally established as a Communist front, that its director, Arthur Kallet, was at the very least a "fellow traveler," and that a number of smaller organizations were similarly controlled by officials hostile to capitalism.

27. Sorenson, pp. 56–109; Reid, pp. 4–9; *P.I.* (Feb. 21, 1935), p. 88; (Feb. 10, 1938), p. 11; (Feb. 17, 1938), p. 81; *A.S.* (Nov. 18, 1937), p. 29. See also, Persia Campbell, *Consumer Representation in the New Deal* (New York, Columbia University Press, 1940), p. 176.

28. For a summary of the operations, history, and methods of Consumers' Research and Consumers' Union, see Sorenson, pp. 32–52. See also, *Newsweek* (Jan. 31, 1938), p. 35; and items cited in n. 25, above.

Accusations have occasionally ranged beyond the testing agencies to implicate individuals in other consumer organizations, but the evidence on which these accusations rest has proved too slender to inspire much confidence in them.[29]

Though it is virtually certain that the leadership of the consumer movement, particularly during the phase of the Popular Front in Communist history in the 1930's, contained a small number of Communists or fellow travelers, it is almost equally certain that they did not dominate more than a fraction of the organizations known collectively as the consumer movement and that the consumer movement would have been significantly the same movement without them. Their influence, if any, has in fact been impossible to isolate or identify as peculiar to their ideology. The fundamental substance of Consumers' Union reports of the 1930's,

29. The principal published source of information, and in some instances the only one, on the relations between consumer organizations and the Communist party, has been the testimony of J. B. Matthews as revealed in Congressional hearings and in his autobiographical *Odyssey of a Fellow Traveler* (New York, Mt. Vernon Publishers, 1938), esp. pp. 257–60. In 1938 Matthews appeared as a witness before the House Special Committee on Un-American Activities and testified unfavorably to the origin, character, and purposes of Consumers' Union (*Hearings*, 75th Cong. 3d Sess., *1*, 868–928; *3*, 2189–2201). In 1939 Matthews became Director of Research for the Committee, and in that capacity he offered further testimony of similar nature both in the process of examining Committee witnesses and in reports bearing the Committee imprint (*Executive Hearings*, *4*, 1737–43; *7*, 3292–3; see also below, pp. 153–4.

Concerning the alleged Communist affiliation of various consumer officials, the testimony of other witnesses as well as Matthews' own testimony was ambiguous and conflicting (Testimony of William Consodine, *Hearings*, supplement to *4*, 3141–53; Howard Rushmore, *Executive Hearings*, *4*, 1737–43; Goodwin Watson, *Executive Hearings*, *7*, 3292–3; Earl Browder, Pt. IX of *Appendix to Hearings*, pp. 658–60). See also Don Wharton, "Arthur Kallet," *Scribner's* (Nov. 1937), pp. 21 ff., as well as the Special Committee's Annual *Report* (House Report 1476), 76th Cong. 3d Sess. (Jan. 1940), p. 9, which lists Communist "front" organizations but does not include Consumers' Union. According to the *New Republic* (Jan. 13, 1940), p. 37, this omission was deliberate. If so, the Committee had again changed its mind by 1944: see Pt. IX of *Appendix to Hearings*, pp. 661–5.

The above-mentioned testimony concerned itself almost exclusively with three consumer organizations: Consumers' Union, Consumers' National Federation, and the League of Women Shoppers. The figures most prominently cited in testimony as having some relation to Communism, on the one hand, and to the consumer movement, on the other hand, were Arthur Kallet, Susan Jenkins, and Harry Bridges. Conspicuous by its absence was any mention of Consumers' Research. For an evaluation of J. B. Matthews' testimony, see below, pp. 155–7.

for example, was for the most part indistinguishable from that which emanated from the reports of Consumers' Research, whose director was openly and militantly anti-Communist. Careful scrutiny of the literature of either agency does not readily reveal any sustained or pronounced ideological commitment save an unexceptionable skepticism of the motives of the average seller when confronted with a buyer. Considering the available evidence, I think it not unreasonable to suggest that the center of gravity for the leadership even of the consumer movement remained solidly within the broad conception of New Deal reform, and, like much of the New Deal, the movement remained responsive somewhat less to the self-contained necessities of an ideology than to the immediate and obvious national needs which accompanied economic catastrophe.

Of all the institutions which comprised the consumer movement the testing agencies were the most radically conceived and provoked the most sustained hostility. Advertising men and other businessmen attacked both their methods and their conclusions with a bitterness displayed on no other occasion. Many commercial media refused to publish their findings. There is no doubt that their opinions of products were often dogmatic and sometimes in serious error; but they reported facts which few consumers could have established for themselves and which had been made public nowhere else. They consequently furnished the consumer movement with a unique foundation of empirical knowledge, an effective counterweight to the prevailing power of advertising judgment. In their efforts to deglamourize advertising by comparing brand-name products and publicizing their conclusions, the independent testing agencies stood almost alone against the commercial structure of publicity and communication in modern society. At no time did any substantial segment of the commercial press deflate claims of prominent national advertisers, nor did any magazine or newspaper which carried an average amount of advertising ever seriously question the fundamental arrangements by which advertising was carried on.[30] As a consequence, con-

---

30. Very few commercial publications in the 1930's exposed deceptive advertising. Most notable was the *Reader's Digest*, which carried no advertising. The Bridgeport *Herald* in 1933 and 1934 featured a series of critical articles on the

sumer agency directors such as Schlink and Kallet did not hesitate
to circumvent the periodical press by resorting to the sensationalism of the muckraking exposé. In 1933, when the two were working together in Consumers' Research, they published a best seller
entitled *100,000,000 Guinea Pigs,* a book which advertising men
found particularly hard to view with indifference. Some of its
material was well known to readers of medical journals; some was
apparently untrue. But in asserting the existence of widespread
fraud and even public danger in the manufacture and advertising
of a number of food and drug products, it conveyed to a wide
audience an important dissent from the pages of countless
periodicals.[31]

Throughout its growth, however, the consumer movement
could count on the *Nation* and the *New Republic.* Supported independently of advertising, these two journals, almost singlehandedly among publishers, offered a relentless and probing skepticism of the business world. Both periodicals published articles
which sought to expose specific untruths in large national advertising.[32] The editors denied that they disliked advertising in principle, but their articles left no doubt that, as they saw it, advertising had become irresponsible, that it helped create the mass man,
that it exalted false standards, stifled effective dissent, and obstructed knowledge, that it specialized in producing glamorous
shows replete with lights and chorus line and soft melodies, and
that behind this façade the business of selling carried on as it

---

advertising and manufacturing of foods, drugs, and cosmetics; it also conducted
a department "Behind the Labels" to answer all queries about products.

31. Published by the Vanguard Press, which followed it in 1937 with *40,000,000
Guinea Pig Children,* by Rachel Palmer and Isadore Alpher, revealing frauds and
dishonest advertising in products for children. Schlink married Mary Phillips, the
author of *Skin Deep,* a best-selling exposé of frauds in the production and
advertising of cosmetics.

Harding, in his comparable but far more reliable study *The Popular Practice of
Fraud,* offered a minute critique of *100,000,000 Guinea Pigs,* exposed its factual
errors, and criticized Schlink's hostility toward the Food and Drug Administration.

32. For two outstanding examples within one month: *New Republic* (Aug. 3,
1927), p. 271; *Nation* (Aug. 31, 1927), p. 202. Prior to its publication as a book,
portions of *Your Money's Worth* had appeared in the *New Republic,* whose editors had originally encouraged the authors to undertake their investigation (conversation with Bruce Bliven, Nov. 1957).

pleased. From the first, therefore, the *Nation* and the *New Republic* championed the consumer movement. They contributed columns for the guidance of buyers, supported the consumer testing agencies, and encouraged federal agencies to increase their control over advertising practice. They were seldom so naive as to insist on radical reform within the industry; rather, they sought to render advertising ineffective by deflating its pretentions.

The influence of the consumer movement is extremely difficult to assess, but advertising men were generally agreed that it could not with safety be ignored. In the years of their greatest strength consumers had won assurances from a few prominent marketing organizations that retailers, at least, would meet some of their demands for informative labeling; as will be seen, they had received formal, if ineffective, recognition from the Administration in Washington and had helped curb advertising by law.[33] The active individuals dedicated to furthering the goals of the consumer movement were few in number, but their influence was considerable. It was true that subscribers to the Consumers' Union testing service, for example, came mostly from professional ranks, with what was reported as a median income of $2,600, and that a survey taken to discover the extent to which the public were aware of a "consumer movement" revealed that three-quarters of them were not.[34] Consumer organizations made vigorous efforts to reach a nation of housewives, wage-earners, and middle-class urban dwellers, but advertising men were seldom so naive as to think that the consumer movement was likely to enlist the active loyalty of everyone whose principal occupation embodied an interest in consumption.[35] Yet there was other evidence to suggest that as many as six million women were making use of the informative material which consumer organizations regularly disseminated.[36] While anxious to derive comfort from the fact that

33. See below, Chap. 5.

34. Results of a Gallup poll, reported by Kenneth Dameron, "Advertising and the Consumer Movement," *Journal of Marketing*, 5 (1941), 234.

35. As an example of the difficulty in trying to define a "consumer" for purposes of the consumer movement, see Saul Nelson, "Representation of the Consumer Interest in the Federal Government," *Law and Contemporary Problems*, 6 (1939), 152.

36. Findings of the Crowell Publishing Co., reported in Dameron, loc. cit.

information to counteract advertising seldom affected directly any large numbers of Americans, advertising men were also aware that those articulate professional groups and teachers whom the consumer movement did not reach controlled a substantial share of national purchasing power and enjoyed a continual access to the public mind.

The challenge which the consumer movement offered to the advertising industry drew much of its strength from a broad current of articulate intellectual skepticism about the appropriateness of advertising in a rational society and the claims which its creators made for it. Criticism ranged in scope and style from the disillusioned confessions of ex-advertising writers to the formal theories of respected economists.[37] Nineteenth-century affirmations of classical economic laws had left little room for the operation of advertising save as an unimportant though distressingly incalculable influence on demand; but this attitude reflected not so much hostility as indifference to advertising. By the 1930's, however, indifference had proved impossible. Text books on economics tended to discuss with equanimity the impact of advertising on the market but seldom avoided opportunities to offer mild moral strictures on its supposed social effects, while both the theoretical and hortatory literature of consumer education generally attributed to advertising a baneful influence.[38] But it remained for the intellectual liberals of the postwar era to articulate for the public a comprehensive and vigorous social indictment. To American advertising they ascribed the coarsest features of Babbittry and commercialism; in it they recognized an abject and frightening servant for the private designs of business enterprise, intent

37. Prominent as examples of the former: Helen Woodward, *It's an Art!* New York, Harcourt, Brace, 1938; James Rorty, *Our Master's Voice: Advertising,* New York, John Day, 1934. Among the latter: Thorstein Veblen, *Absentee Ownership and Business Enterprise in Recent Times,* New York, B. W. Huebsch, 1923; Sumner Slichter, *Modern Economic Society,* New York, Henry Holt, 1934; Stuart Chase, *The Tragedy of Waste,* New York, Macmillan, 1925.

38. See, for example, Warren C. Waite and Ralph Cassady, *The Consumer and the Economic Order,* New York, McGraw-Hill, 1939; Reid, *Consumers and the Market;* Alice Edwards, *Consumer Standards,* TNEC Monograph 24, GPO, 1941; "The Ultimate Consumer," *Annals of the American Academy of Political and Social Science, 173* (May 1934).

on perverting the rational responses of a democratically minded citizenry. One of the most prominent critics of the philosophy and practice of salesmanship was Thorstein Veblen, whose description of a "Leisure Class" in 1899 foreshadowed his pitiless polemic on the business world of absentee ownership two dozen years later. In less savage manner and with varying intensity Walter Lippmann, Sinclair Lewis, Sumner Slichter, Stuart Chase, James T. Adams, Gilbert Seldes, Upton Sinclair, Robert S. Lynd, Henry F. Pringle and others assessed commercial advertising in the spirit and indeed in the intellectual tradition of the Progressive reformers of an earlier decade.[39]

In the forefront of their indictment was the assertion that most advertising was a wasteful and costly wrangling between indistinguishable products. It added nothing to public wealth, despite the high price which the public paid for it. To the individual firm, it was conceded, advertising may not be a waste, for it frequently lowered unit costs; yet there was no guarantee that the savings which resulted would be passed on to the consumer, and advertising had been known to create such loyalty of demand that a firm's prices could be raised without loss of customers. Nor was it ever certain that advertising could take credit for a change in demand. Though advertising men often admitted as much, they tended to capitalize on the probability that once a businessman had begun to advertise, even though he could find no sure way of testing its value or its effect on his business, he seldom if ever risked giving it up. Advances in the skills and techniques of the advertising industry, furthermore, tended to increase both the necessity and the cost of advertising effectively, and in consequence relatively fewer firms could afford effective national advertising. American advertising, according to this view, was gradually reducing Main Street to a row of vending machines and the retailer to a toll collector, for large business enterprise had been able to brandish national advertising as a one-sided weapon against local businessmen and consumers alike.

A second major theme of the reformer's polemic was that modern advertising had encouraged the commercialized degradation

39. For the pertinent writings of some of these "moderate" critics see nn. 37-8, above, and my Bibliography, below.

of American life. Having carved the calendar into Selling Weeks and Mother's Days, it did not hesitate to exploit sentiment for cold cash. It had helped to create a culture of conformity and was acting to erase individuality and distinction from consumer products. It sought to inculcate an excessive materialism by proclaiming ceaselessly that intangible human satisfactions can be bought, and that specific gadgets, whether mouthwash or electric organs, fulfill an absurdly large number of needs. To be feared even more was the capacity of advertising to degrade the press. Neither newspapers nor magazines, said the critics, were free to offer advice contrary to the interests of advertisers; the press could never suggest, for example, that Americans hang on to their old car, that they not wear hats, or that they bake bread at home. In cheapening the price of a newspaper issue, advertising had also cheapened the newspaper. In consequence, advertising carried with it enormous social implications. But businessmen generally admitted that they could not always take into account the social implications of what they did. Was it wise, then, to leave control of such an important educational process to businessmen?

Advertising was challenged most persistently on the grounds of its indifference to ethical values and on the alleged discrepancy between its performance and its avowed aims. Many legally acceptable advertisements were actually dishonest, and dishonest advertising was by no means confined to the "fringe operator" or the fly-by-night "chiseler": large national manufacturers were in an even better position than small ones to benefit from the half-truth and the misleading irrelevancy, and on occasion claims which even conservative advertising men considered ethical were deliberately misleading and deceptive. Still more damaging, ran this view, was the fact that advertising attempted to pervert the rational buying judgments on which the operation of a truly free competitive market must depend. It was commonly claimed that advertising showed the consumer how to obtain added "satisfactions" from his buying, but in fact advertising tended to prevent the consumer from establishing his own criteria for "satisfactions." He might cherish the psychological values which advertising attributed to its products, but advertising was no guarantee that the consumer would get what he thought he paid for; an advertisement might persuade him to make a purchase by arousing in him an intense, momentary desire for something which on cold second thought he might find that he did not want at all. Such tactics obstructed whatever painful progress people were making toward acquiring a rational understanding of the world they lived in and a competence to meet its problems. Advertisers might legitimately seek to affect consumer choice; it was the contention of their critics that in affecting choice they could and should encourage consumers to choose rationally rather than on impulse, whim, or on misleading evidence.

Finally, critics warned that advertising men should not be surprised to find consumers who were dissatisfied enough with advertising to resist it and challenge it. Advertisers who talked of self-correcting measures, internal reforms, and ethical standards were in effect creating a smoke screen behind which the same circus barkers carried on their same old game. The practicing ethics of their business seemed little better in the 1930's than in the previous generation. Few critics seriously expected the advertising man to behave like a public servant, or to be held accountable as one; on the other hand, few doubted that in one way or another the consumer would assure himself of responsible treatment. The consumer was asking, among other things, for accurate, easily available information with which he might judge rationally among products and services in modern society, but national advertising provided no valid way of judging among products. It deliberately attempted, in fact, to thwart such judgments. Was it any wonder, then, that some consumers had rebelled against the monolith of advertising practice and even sought help from state and private agencies?

Thus in the course of two decades did critics of the advertising industry erect an eloquent structure of argument. Though they were by no means united in their challenge, and though their contentions at times were confused and contradictory, these critics were in many ways a less diverse group than the advertising men whom they challenged. They were, in the main, intellectuals, engaged in professional careers not deeply wedded to business: writers, journalists, teachers, economists, technicians, engineers, scientists, and salaried officials of governmental agencies or private pressure organizations. They were most in accord when they professed to be speaking for the "consumer," whom they viewed as inert, apathetic, and easily misled or duped. Conscious of their own position, they occasionally betrayed impatience with the ordinary public at its failure to see what they so clearly considered to have been a massive, deliberate imposition; at times it almost seemed to them as though the public did not want to be saved from advertising, that having grown used to advertising, the public was willing to live with it and like it. It is perhaps at once curious and instructive that the advertising man and his critics alike displayed many of the attributes of reformers intent on constructing the Good Society, convinced in each case that their particular vision of that society depended for its realization on their own dedicated zeal.

To be sure, critics of advertising did not consistently agree among themselves. Some, proposing no solution, seemed merely to be expressing an ill-defined resentment at what they considered were depressing alterations in American society during a period of particularly blatant salesmanship. Others, cynical over the practice rather than the theory of advertising, recommended explicit controls and extensive consumer education. A preponderant number of critics objected to the misrepresentation and the waste in the production of advertisements and to the presumed attempt of the advertising industry to eliminate rational dissent from the responses available to the consumer. Few went so far as to call into question the validity of greater consumption, the principle on which the social role of advertising rested; on the other hand, many found fault with the particular structure of social values which most advertisements transmitted for the purpose of encouraging consumption. Their arguments stood as a worrisome rebuttal to the familiar assertions of advertising men, who rebutted in turn and in kind. Unfortunately, the nature of such debating, like a tennis player's nightmare of an endless set with no scoring limit, precluded agreement between advertising men and their critics, save possibly over the fact that both sides were improving their game.

The debate, in fact, could scarcely be resolved at all, for at least one basic assumption which the consumer critics were apt to make concerning the legitimate function of advertising was at complete odds with a basic assumption of producers and sellers in a modern economy. Critics often assumed that a producer ought first to ascertain what sort of product the consumer preferred, then to make a product which satisfied that preference, and finally offer advertising to announce what the product was, when and where it could be bought, how much it cost, and in as objective a fashion as possible what particular virtues and peculiarities it possessed. Producers, on the other hand, invariably maintained that it was perfectly justifiable and even inevitable to attempt by means of advertising to create or change consumer preference and to persuade consumers by any device short of overt misrepresentation that a given product would meet their preferences. Into the production of such advertisements went increasingly sophisticated techniques of mass persuasion, techniques which enabled advertisers, for example, to ignore actual consumer preferences and concentrate instead on making the consumer believe either that the product as advertised was exactly what he was looking for, or, if the consumer did not think so, that the consumer's judgment, and not the seller's, was at fault. The fact was that techniques for discovering consumer preferences were late in development and haphazard when they did develop, while techniques for manipulating consumer preferences by advertising were, by 1940, well established. Rather than bother to ascertain the consumer's existing preferences, then, producers generally attempted to stimulate in the consumer those responses which would lead him to prefer the products which the producers wished to sell. Advertising men thus hoped to avoid the specific obligations which consumer critics were trying to force on them and sought to win over the consumer in spite of himself.

But the arguments of these critics were to appear and reappear as basic rationalizations of the consumer movement, and they provided a formidable challenge to the national advertising industry. They were important in the sense that all argument is important: they defined the issues on which diverse groups could agree, and they expressed the terms and the nature of such agreements. The challenge to American advertising in the 1930's signified an aroused determination to increase consumer skepticism and distrust, to counteract advertising with information designed to reduce its control over the market, and to regulate advertising by national law.

To this challenge, the national advertising industry offered strong and bitter resistance, and for the first time its assumptions underwent the ordeal to which most democratic societies sooner or later subject the assumptions of their most powerful institutions: they were to be scrutinized and tested in public debate.

5

Public Pressures

In 1933 and for a number of years thereafter the Food and Drug Administration of the United States Department of Agriculture sought from Congress comprehensive legislation which would enable it to eliminate more effectively the sale of harmful and adulterated drugs and food. During the same period the Federal Trade Commission also sought from Congress legislation which would extend its authority to include the prohibition of trade practices deceptive or misleading to the public as well as those detrimental to the interests of a competitor. Each of these agencies proposed that it be given jurisdiction and a degree of regulatory power over the content of advertising which no federal agency had possessed before. The hostile reaction of the advertising industry to these efforts flamed into a lengthy and occasionally bitter controversy which centered in Congress but involved, at one time or another, the interests and passions of publishers, manufacturers, agencies, consumers' organizations, the New Deal Administration, and their spokesmen, lawyers, and advisors. The ensuing struggle to write acceptable legislation did not end until 1938, at which time a new federal Food, Drug, and Cosmetic Act supplanted the earlier Act of 1906 and provided the F. and D. A. with a major part of the new powers it sought (except for the regulation of advertising); while the Wheeler-Lea Amendment (1938) to the Federal Trade Commission Act of 1914 granted to the FTC substantially all of the extension of power which it had requested, particularly over the advertising of food, drugs, and cosmetics.

The four-year contest over these laws brought into clear and open view the latent tensions between the national advertising industry and the public. In the act of resisting governmental regulation and in defending themselves from the attacks of private groups whose interests conflicted with theirs, advertising men restated their tenets of public behavior and reasserted the importance of their service to society. They also attempted to counteract propaganda directed against them with propaganda and publicity of their own. In this chapter and in the one which follows I propose to relate the struggle in which the advertising industry and its clients sought to resist administrative pressures and federal regulation and to win the public to a favorable opinion of advertising in general.

During the first days of June 1933 Senator Royal S. Copeland (Democrat, N.Y.), a physician and former Commissioner of Health for New York City, introduced in the Senate a bill to amend and revise the Pure Food and Drug Act of 1906. The bill had been drafted under the supervision of the F. and D. A., whose director, Walter Campbell, had gained the support of Rexford Tugwell, then Assistant Secretary of Agriculture; and it became known to friend and foe alike as the "Tugwell Bill." The bill empowered the F. and D. A. to prohibit the "false advertising" of any food or drug, and defined any advertisement as false if, "by ambiguity and inference," it "created a misleading impression." In particular, manufacturers of drugs could not advance for their product a claim which was "contrary to the general agreement of medical opinion," nor could they assert a drug to be a "cure" if in truth it were only a "palliative." Any food, drug, or cosmetic falsely advertised was to be deemed misbranded and therefore liable to seizure by the Department of Agriculture. Hearings were held on this bill in December 1933.[1]

At the hearings and just prior to them spokesmen for the F. and D. A. made explicit their reasons for seeking new legislation. In general the Agency sought broad powers as a deterrent to the potential offender (a "club behind the door"). The law was to accomplish what business self-regulation and judicial decision had attempted but had failed to achieve: to ban from publication both fraudulent and *misleading* advertising of food and drugs and to define "misleading advertising" broadly enough to encompass any representations of opinion as well as fact. But legislation, it was expected, might even range beyond prohibition or censorship: the F. and D. A. sought the power to deflate specific claims by shedding "unfavorable publicity," for example, on deceptive advertising or by requiring products advertised as suitable for self-medication to specify in their advertising their exact limitations as well as their effectiveness.

On the other hand the F. and D. A. did not expect to prohibit "puffing": perfume, it conceded, could remain "as glamorous as a night in Spain." It did not propose to waste time in semantic quibbling with an advertiser whose purposes were evidently honest; nor did it seek to curtail "exaggeration" in advertising unless the exaggeration tended to mislead the reader. The principal culprit, rather, would be the advertiser who "asserts his opinion as to a material fact which evidence and authority alike agree to be untrue." The F. and D. A. was concerned not that the intelligent reader would be taken in by *deceptive* hyperbole but that the unintelligent reader might be, and it was largely to this sort of reader that most questionable national advertising was said to be directed.[2]

From the first, the proposals of the F. and D. A. won strong

1. *P.I.* (May 4, 1933), p. 10; (June 8, 1933), p. 10. Senate Commerce Committee, 73d Cong., 2d Sess., *Hearings* on S-1944, Dec. 7–8, 1933 (the bill was numbered S-1944). See also *Law and Contemporary Problems, 1* (1933), "The Protection of the Consumer of Food and Drugs: a Symposium"; and 6 (1939), "The New Food, Drug and Cosmetic Legislation."

2. See esp. testimony and statements of D. F. Cavers (professor of law, Duke University, and an advisor to the FDA), as reported in *P.I.* (Aug. 24, 1933), p. 43; (Nov. 23, 1933), p. 80; (Dec. 21, 1933), p. 68; and statements of Walter Campbell, for publication in *P.I.* (Nov. 20, 1933), p. 6; (Dec. 7, 1933), p. 6; and in *Hearings* on S-5 (Mar. 9, 1935), p. 352.

support. Spokesmen and lobbyists for consumers' organizations, particularly women's clubs, enthusiastically endorsed them, as did the AMA, the *Nation,* the *New Republic,* and *Good House-keeping,* while even *Advertising and Selling* warmly defended many of them. There were also witnesses who felt that the Tugwell bill should be extended in scope and made more rigorous. At the time of its proposal, there had already been suggested to the NRA a plan to require "quality" grade labeling of all canned goods, and even while this plan was pending a large number of witnesses at the Tugwell hearings urged that the F. and D. A. be given the power to enforce such a law.[3] The plan was intended to assure buyers that prices reflected actual quality rather than brand reputation; consequently for at least one major industry it threatened the competitive value of brand names and hence its entire structure of advertising. Consumer organizations were encouraged by the active support which the New Deal Administration seemed willing to give to such proposals and to the consumer movement in general. Within the NRA, for example, there had been established, at the behest of the White House and in direct opposition to the views of General Hugh Johnson, a Consumers' Advisory Board (CAB), the purpose of which was to bring to the formulation of industrial codes a "public" viewpoint, distinct from that of business and labor. The CAB had favored the system of quality grading for canned foods, for which it had gained the open support of the AFL and the General Federation of Women's Clubs, and its recommendations appeared for a brief while to be headed for success.[4]

Opposition to the proposals of the F. and D. A. and the CAB, however, crystallized almost at once, and in the ensuing five years every "consumer-minded" bill was to run a tortuous course of revision, softening, and compromise. Practically the entire food industry, with the exception of the A. and P. chain stores, opposed compulsory grade labeling, while the drug industry fought the Tugwell bill and later revisions of it with unceasing bitterness. The advertising industry and most of the press (including *Print-*

3. At hearings cited above, n. 2. Also at *Hearings* on S-2800 for Feb. 27–Mar. 3, 1934, and *Hearings* on S-5 for Mar. 2–9, 1935. For an account of the activities of the consumer lobbies see Sorenson, p. 13.

4. For a comprehensive study of the CAB see Campbell, *Consumer Representation,* pp. 10 ff., 168, 173 ff.; *P.I.* (Feb. 15, 1934), p. 25.

ers' Ink) condemned the original bill and tended to support mod-
ifications of it only when it became evident that new legislation
of some sort was practically inevitable. In May 1933 a number of
publishers and advertising groups had supported a Senate bill
expressly designed to forestall a "worse" censorship of advertising.
Introduced by Senator Capper, a publisher, it sought merely to
enact the *P.I.* Statute into national law.[5] When Congress shelved
the Capper bill in favor of the Tugwell bill, most of the witnesses
who represented manufacturers, publishers, and advertisers at the
subsequent Committee hearings urged that the Tugwell bill be
rendered as innocuous as possible. Through persistent lobbying,
a number of the original recommendations were modified or eliminated; and when the Tugwell bill died in committee in June 1934
with the termination of the Seventy-second Congress, the subsequent bills to replace it, in 1935 and 1937, were each milder than
their predecessors.

First to be changed (and advertising men considered this
change of paramount importance) was the definition of "false"
advertising, which was narrowed by substituting the phrase "misleading in a material respect" for the phrase "create a misleading
impression." No copy writer, it was argued, could be expected to
foresee what sort of impression his advertising might make on irrational or unintelligent readers. Of equal importance was the
elimination of the provision that a manfacturer of a drug which
was merely a "palliative" had to add the phrase "not a cure" to
his advertisements: the F. and D. A. was considered to have
stepped beyond the limits of reason by requesting that, for the
sake of the consumer, the manufacturer of a drug be forced to
announce the limitations of his product. The drug lobby, in fact,
won a further concession when in 1934 the bill was amended to
say that no advertisement could be judged false if its assertions
were "supported by substantial medical opinion or by demonstra-
ble scientific facts."[6] In the final legislation passed in 1938, however, the original request of the F. and D. A. was in part regained,
for it was there specified that in deciding whether an advertisement was true or false the FTC should consider the extent to

5. *P.I.* (May 11, 1933), pp. 3 ff. The AFA approved of the Capper bill on
condition that it should not prevent a "reasonable persuasive advertising appeal."
For comment on the *P.I.* Statute see above, p. 46.

6. *P.I.* (Jan. 11, 1934), p. 24.

which the advertisement failed to reveal relevant facts as to performance and *consequences*.

The drug industry, meanwhile, had also managed to remove from the Tugwell bill the stipulation that if an advertisement for a drug "misled" a consumer into endangering his health, the drug could be considered "adulterated" and thereupon could be seized. Their principal objection was that the question as to whether an advertisement was misleading involved merely "matters of opinion, thought, fancy, and taste" which could not be determined objectively. To seize and confiscate a product actually dangerous to health was unexceptionable; to do so because of its advertising or labeling was to subject manufacturers to an intolerable censorship.[7] Eventually provision was made for the Government to seize articles which endangered public health by being "misbranded," though no advertisement could be considered to constitute "misbranding" unless "falsely or grossly misleading in a material respect."[8]

The proposal to institute a triple-grading system for canned food products fared no better. Initially offered as a compulsory feature of the NRA codes, it had failed largely because of the failure of the Consumers' Advisory Board to wield any substantial power in the code-making process. In contrast to the influential representations of industry and labor, which governmental agencies were bound to respect, the CAB actually represented no interest capable of effective political definition. Its predicament was perhaps most concisely symbolized in the scornful skepticism which Hugh Johnson, the Code Administrator, revealed in his oft-repeated remark, "Who is the consumer? Show me a consumer."[9] The members of the CAB were dedicated liberals, but they were hardly naive about their chances of success, and perhaps only their talent for shrewd administrative wire-pulling and infighting (a talent which dedicated liberals are traditionally supposed to lack) enabled the Board to operate at all.[10] Their fight for a

7. See testimony of J. R. Hoge, counsel for the Proprietary Association, reported in *P.I.* (Jan. 10, 1935), p. 110.

8. *P.I.* (Jan. 14, 1937), p. 12.

9. Quoted in Campbell, p. 31.

10. The full members of the Consumers' Advisory Board in the year 1933–35

grading system represented only a small portion of their total program, but their failure to achieve it was symptomatic of the more general problem of achieving special national legislation for the "consumer." Representatives not only of the canners but of publishers and advertising agencies argued against grading at the Code hearings; the latter professed to fear that eventually any new labeling requirements would be extended all too easily to advertising, and no one denied that quality labels would possess what could be called a "deflationary" effect on the advertising of all canned goods. Advertisers, in fact, countered the CAB proposal with a voluntary plan for "descriptive" labeling, which the Code Authority rejected as insufficient to protect the consumer.[11] In turn the code which the canners finally submitted contained no provisions for grading, and the issue remained thus at deadlock until both the NRA and the canning code expired in May 1935. The persistent opposition of the canning industry had meanwhile managed to stall with equal effectiveness an effort to adopt the grading system into the F. and D. A., and in this instance also did publishing and advertising men provide the canners with significant and perhaps decisive reinforcement for their testimony.[12]

The most drastic modification of the Tugwell bill and its successors, however, was yet to be made, for the F. and D. A. was ultimately to be deprived of all its proposed jurisdiction over advertising (as distinct from labeling) and the jurisdiction lodged instead with the Federal Trade Commission. It was a change which reflected a compromise among a number of groups whose views of the authority of the F. and D. A. to regulate advertising were all but irreconcilable and some of whom assumed that regu-

---

were as follows: Mrs. Mary Rumsey (chairman), William F. Ogden (executive director), Mrs. Emily Newell Blair, Dr. Frank Graham, Miss Belle Sherwin (President of the National League of Women Voters), Willard Thorp, Louis Bean, Dexter M. Keezer, Corwin Edwards, Thomas C. Blaisdell. Among the consulting members were Frederick C. Howe, Gardiner C. Means, Robert Lynd, George Stocking, Walton Hamilton, Paul H. Douglas, Huston Thompson, Stacy May.

11. Campbell, p. 176.

12. *P.I.* (Dec. 14, 1933), p. 6; (Dec. 21, 1933), p. 6; (Nov. 11, 1935), p. 91. Since 1930, however, the Food and Drug Act has been amended to permit the F. and D. A. to operate a "single-standard" grading system.

lation by the FTC would prove abortive.[13] By March 1935 most members of the advertising industry had indicated satisfaction with the amendments so far proposed and were willing to have the Tugwell bill enacted. In general, food processors and distributors, the advertising industry, and most of the mass-circulation magazines had urged adoption of Senate bill S-5 (successor to the Tugwell bill) as the best way to ward off demands for stronger legislation. But proprietary and drug manufacturers consistently resisted legislation of any kind.[14] The drug industry had organized its forces at an early stage to bring pressure on Congress and had used their heavy patronage of small local newspapers as a lever to induce both heavy editorial support for themselves and a campaign of unfavorable publicity against the F. and D. A. and its bill. The industry also maintained a powerful lobby in Congress and attempted particularly to sway the votes of Congressmen already susceptible to their advances.[15] Represented by the Proprietary Association and the United Medicine Manufacturers of America, drug manufacturers argued that the FTC should retain sole responsibility for eliminating questionable advertising claims.[16] Their position was shrewdly calculated to delay consideration of the entire issue, for they were capitalizing on the fact that the FTC, counting on more friends and influence in Congress than could the F. and D. A., seemed anxious to obtain for itself the very authority which the F. and D. A. had requested. Among many representatives from rural constituencies, moreover, the Department of Agriculture (in which the F. and D. A. resided) was in current disfavor.[17]

13. It was generally known that the FTC had often failed to proceed against advertising claims which the F. and D. A. had banned from the labels of the same products: D. F. Cavers, "The Food, Drug and Cosmetic Act of 1938," *Law and Contemporary Problems*, 6 (1939), 14.

14. *New Republic* (May 1, 1935), p. 328. *Tide*, May 1, 1935. The E. R. Squibb (drug) Company proved a notable exception to this statement by supporting the F. and D. A.

15. *New Republic* (Nov. 8, 1933), p. 353, corroborated both by *E.P.* (July 27, 1935), p. 40, and by the industry's own publication, *Drug Trade News*, Sept. 18, 1933. It was well known, for example, that Senator Clark (Democrat, Mo.) was alert to the interests of the Lambert Pharmacal Co., St. Louis (Listerine), as was Senator Bailey (Democrat, N.C.) to Vick Chemical Co., Greensboro, N.C.

16. *P.I.* (Mar. 7, 1935), p. 34; (Mar. 14, 1935), p. 27. *Hearings* on S-5 (Mar. 2, 1935), p. 84.

17. *Ibid.* The chairman of the FTC had testified before the Senate Committee

In its fight to substitute the FTC for the F. and D. A. the drug industry at first stood largely alone. The chief reason for its support of the FTC was the expectation that regulation by the FTC would prove somehow timid and ineffectual, but this expectation was also, of course, one of the principal reasons why the American Medical Association and most consumer organizations were opposed to the substitution. Even the trade journal *Advertising and Selling* supported the F. and D. A. and warned that if the drug industry had its way on this issue its current advertising policies would go unreformed.[18] Most of the opposition to the drug industry, however, was stimulated by the fear that the FTC would prove not too weak but too strong, that the added authority which the drug industry proposed for the FTC would make of it a tyrant over the entire world of business. Manufacturers and publishers alike betrayed a deep-rooted uneasiness toward the FTC. In the Raladam Case the courts had ruled that the FTC could not prohibit a firm from engaging in a deceptive trade practice unless a competitor had been injured by it. It was now feared that the proposed legislation would enable the FTC to intervene on behalf of an ordinary consumer as well. The Commission, protested one publisher, "will be in a position to establish its own ethical standards, whatever they may be, for all business conduct. . . . The Commission should not be set up as a final authority on matters which relate to differences of opinion." [19]

By the summer of 1936 it appeared as though all hopes and

---

considering the Tugwell bill, that the FTC should be given the proposed increase in power over advertising and that the F. and D. A. should be given greater power only to prohibit the sale of harmful products. This incipient jurisdictional dispute between two agencies was undoubtedly aggravated by the publication, in 1936, of a muckraking account of a large number of food and drug products: *American Chamber of Horrors* by Ruth Lamb of the Department of Agriculture. In it she inferentially scored the FTC for laxness in its regulation of advertising. *Tide*, May 1, 1936.

18. *A.S.* (June 17, 1937), p. 34. According to William Allen White, *A.S.* (July 29, 1937), p. 23, drug manufacturers had boasted openly of what the FTC would do to protect their interests.

19. *P.I.* (Feb. 20, 1936), p. 15; (Mar. 26, 1936), p. 7. The ANPA, at first as stubbornly opposed as was the drug industry to any new legislation, apparently considered the FTC a greater menace to advertising than the F. and D. A. and eventually supported efforts at finding a compromise proposal: *P.I.* (Feb. 21, 1935), p. 12; *E.P.* (July 27, 1935), p. 40.

fears would prove equally groundless when the projected bill, having passed the Senate, was "killed" in a deadlock with the House over the issue of which agency should be vested with its authority. On all other points agreement had finally been reached. The drug industry could not have delayed action more effectively.

But further postponement of legislation was becoming more difficult. By the following spring organized consumer pressure on the succeeding Congress had all but forced the passage of two bills, one bestowing on the FTC powers to regulate all advertising in the public interest, and the other granting to the F. and D. A. similar broad powers with respect to the sale and labeling (but not the advertising) of foods, drugs, and cosmetics.[20] Finally, in the fall of that year there broke in headlines over the nation a tragedy of shocking and decisive import. Dr. Samuel Massengill, a prominent druggist of Bristol, Tennessee, had been informed by salesmen (according to the reports of federal investigators for the F. and D. A.) that as a result of widespread publicity recently given a new "wonder" drug, sulfanilamide, a demand had been created for it which might prove highly profitable to the enterprising soul who could package it in some convenient form, such as a liquid. Having found that diethylene glycol would dissolve sulfanilamide, Massengill bottled up nearly five hundred gallons of the mixture and proceeded to sell it as a patent medicine called Elixir Sulfanilamide. He had not bothered to test its effect even on animals. Within a few weeks of his first sales sixty people had died from it, and ultimately it was to account for seventy-three deaths in seven states. The entire inspector's staff of the F. and D. A. was required to track down the dispersed product before what remained of it was finally recovered and impounded. Under the existing law of 1906, however, the F. and D. A. was unable to hold Massengill responsible, nor could the Government have legally seized the drug had it not been for a technicality: an "elixir" by law had to contain alcohol, and by sheer chance Massengill's Elixir did not. The F. and D. A. consequently was permitted to act, and ultimately Massengill was fined $200 for having misbranded a drug product.[21] The gruesome incident seemed to

20. *P.I.* (Jan. 21, 1937), p. 12; (Feb. 18, 1937), p. 12; (Mar. 4, 1937), pp. 12, 124; (Mar. 11, 1937), p. 12.
21. A convenient summary of the facts in the case is to be found in *A.S.*

speak for itself. By the end of the year all opposition from drug manufacturers to a revision of the law collapsed, and Congress delayed no longer in passing the acts in question, which took effect in June 1938.

The five-year controversy over the terms of governmental regulation of advertising revealed a fundamental divergence of views between, on the one hand, commercial advertisers and, on the other, the proponents of broad regulatory powers over certain practices of mass persuasion. Viewed casually, the disagreement did not appear basic, for much of it turned on a question of the degree of power to be vested in an administrative agency; to some extent it resembled classic constitutional disputes over loose or strict construction. On one side, a government agency or commission attempted to widen its "enabling" legislation to include powers which were liable to misuse if the agency's officials were injudicious but which the officials asserted would in fact not be misused; in effect, the publicly responsible authorities argued that their intentions of enforcement were both clear and moderate, but that if the law which enabled them to operate were narrowed to the precise limits of their intended operations, effective enforcement would prove impossible (a fact which experience had amply borne out). In opposing this view businessmen tended to insist that the legal limitations on the powers of a public agency should be narrow enough to assure all private interests that the behavior of the agency be moderate and that businessmen be enabled to know where they stood in relation to the law. It was maintained, for example, that should the F. and D. A. be empowered to penalize an advertiser because his claims were merely misleading or deceptive, it could theoretically penalize anyone who advertised at all, for to a "bureaucratic mind" which did not allow for hyperbole or exaggeration, nine-tenths of all advertising could be so classed.[22] Although F. and D. A. officials had promised not to take such a quibbling position, a large number of advertisers preferred not to have to rely upon their promise.

(Nov. 18, 1937), p. 11; (June 1939), p. 39. See also *Time* (Nov. 1, 1937), p. 61; (Dec. 20, 1937), p. 48.

22. See, in particular, *P.I.* (May 25, 1933), p. 40, statement by Lee Bristol, of Bristol-Meyers Co.

But the issue of broad or narrow construction betrayed a deeper cleavage which the mere passage of the legislation under question did not bridge. Having come to view the increase of governmental power over their advertising as a threat to long-established selling practices, businessmen tended in self-defense to support the theory that a governmental agency should conduct itself like a civil court—that is, to act merely as a referee between competing private interests and thus to maintain a position of impartial neutrality between the advertiser and the consumer, who were considered under such a theory to be equal and independent bargainers in a free market. When, on the other hand, the Department of Agriculture and its F. and D. A. engaged in propaganda and publicity on behalf of a stronger law, or, worse, when they attempted to counteract commercial advertising with derogatory information about certain foods or drugs, businessmen felt outraged and resentful that governmental agencies were thus "taking sides" with consumers against advertisers and manufacturers. The original Tugwell bill had authorized the F. and D. A. to publish "such information regarding any food, drug, or cosmetic as [it] deems necessary in the interests of public health and for the protection of the consumer." Manufacturers saw in this provision an effort to "authorize the 'legal blackmail' by which the Department of Agriculture distributes at public expense and all over the country reports and bulletins which are frequently very damaging to the products named."[23] In other words, behavior which a private business could engage in as "good public relations" or even advertising was considered an unfair example of "shameless" pandering to public emotion when undertaken by a governmental agency.[24] The Government, it was felt, had no more justification for intervening on behalf of consumers than it had for intervening on behalf of any other private interest.

23. *P.I.* (June 8, 1933), p. 10; (Nov. 23, 1933), p. 6.
24. *P.I.* (Dec. 28, 1933), p. 41. The F. and D. A. engaged in some imaginative publicity to emphasize the need for further legislation: for example, a display of poisonous, adulterated, or worthless products, all misbranded, which had been available in the commercial market but which could not be seized under the existing law. Its prize exhibit was, according to an official of the F. and D. A., "a series of testimonal letters endorsing a fake tuberculosis cure, each letter matched with the death certificate of its author." Quoted in *A.S.* (June 1939), p. 38.

In its interference with advertising, furthermore, the Government was in effect damaging the property of individual businesses without due process of law, for at the heart of modern advertising lay the intangible equity of a brand name, carried not infrequently as an asset on the books of the company. For an executive agency to possess the power to cast public aspersions on a firm's advertising was to mock the ideal of governmental impartiality.[25]

Even more threatening to the activities of an advertiser, as he might view it, was the fact that the Government tended to blur the distinction, long a cardinal tenet in advertising, between mere emotional exaggeration and openly deceptive claims. The F. and D. A., for instance, initially sought to classify the inferential conclusions which one *might* draw from an advertisement in the same category as direct statements of fact. The advertising industry professed to welcome governmental assistance in eliminating the false fact but resisted the implication that the optional inference, even if misleading, was qualitatively similar. Hence the advertiser sought refuge in the argument that facts offered as opinions are not answerable to the requirement of truth but are merely hypotheses to be tested and argued for; under this assumption a string of facts could be judged only on their own test of truth, not on their cumulative effect or on their emotional overtones. In order to put this policy into effect the drug industry had requested that the operative definition of advertising which was liable to investigation be limited to exclude "statements which involve matters of opinion where there is no exact standard of absolute truth"; advertising could be deemed false only if "in any particular, representations of fact are untrue." [26] Other advertising men took a similar view of the question. They wished to draw from the Government an assurance that "colorful" advertising language would not be considered subject to the same criteria of truth, as for example, labels on bottles; they argued from the premise that advertising had to "use emotional and imaginative appeals that cannot be literally construed," and contended that to prohibit verbal color was to deprive business of

25. *P.I.* (Dec. 21, 1933), p. 6.
26. Quoted in *Commonweal, 19* (Mar. 2, 1934), 491, from the text of the so-called "Black Bill," introduced in 1934, but never brought to a vote.

an essential tool of marketing.[27] A label could well be considered
as a cold recital of facts for the benefit of a consumer who had
already bought the product which bore the label; but an advertisement had to be given a chance to sell, persuade, or cajole.
If it were composed like a label it would sell nothing; but its job
was to sell, a job essential to prosperity and a free press. To do a
proper job, an advertisement had to put the best possible face
on things, for "in some cases [the advertiser] knows what the consumer wants better than does the consumer himself." [28] In short,
the advertising industry attributed to its own functions a critical
role in purveying public information, a role which, because of
the relativity of all truth, could not be regulated according to
normal criteria of truth without destroying the power of advertising itself.

The new powers which the FTC could exercise under the
Wheeler-Lea Act were soon tested in a major action brought not
against an advertiser but against a publisher, and in the course
of this action there was revealed another significant conflict of
principle, a conflict with respect to the obligation of a publisher
who accepts advertising. The occasion was an investigation of the
magazine *Good Housekeeping*. In August 1939 the Commission
lodged a complaint against the publishers of that magazine for
having engaged in "misleading and deceptive practices in the issuance of Guarantys, Seals of Approval, and the publication in its
advertising pages of grossly exaggerated and false claims for
products advertised therein." The publishers refused to agree to
the charges and insisted on a series of hearings, which took place
in late 1939 and early 1940 before a trial examiner.[29]

At the hearings the attorney for the Commission sought to
demonstrate, first, that consumers were being misled by the
stated terms of the *Good Housekeeping* Guaranty and Seal of

27. John Benson, representing the AAAA, *Hearings* on S-5 (Mar. 2, 1935), p. 59.
28. Testimony by John Benson and C. C Parlin, *Hearings* on S-2800, Feb. 27,
1934; and statement by Lee Bristol, of the Bristol-Myers Co., quoted in *P.I.*
(Dec. 14, 1933), p. 92.
29. 32 FTC 1440–54, May 13, 1941; New York *Times* (Aug. 21, 1939), p. 20;
P.I. (Nov. 3, 1939), p. 18; (Nov. 17, 1939), p. 40. The Commission simultaneously
brought charges of deceptive advertising against fifteen advertisers responsible
for the alleged deceptions.

Approval, and second, that a number of products (mostly cosmetics) were falsely advertised in its pages. The attorney for *Good Housekeeping* in turn attempted to demonstrate that the Seal of Approval had not been unfairly bestowed, that the Guaranty was not likely to deceive the average reader, and that the claims in the advertisements under question were either correct or at least had not definitely been proven false. The defense also developed at length two other contentions which were not strictly at issue but which were expected to bolster the position of the publishers. One was that since 1920 the magazine had tested all of its advertised products with great care and effectiveness and had rejected a large quantity of advertising offered for publication. The second was that the present action of the Commission placed an unconstitutional restraint on the freedom of the press.[30]

The decision of the Commission, announced in 1941, supported its original charges. It stated that a number of advertisements which had appeared in *Good Housekeeping* were false and misleading, that the various seals and guarantees of the magazine tended to make the public think that all products were guaranteed when such was not the case, and that a few of the products which *Good Housekeeping* had guaranteed "as advertised" could not possibly have been so guaranteed within any acceptable meaning of the word. The Commission thereupon ordered the publishers to "cease and desist" from the practices with which it had been charged. It did not challenge or deny the efficacy of the publisher's testing service but insisted that recommendations of products be worded unambiguously and be based on the actual tests undertaken to establish them.[31]

The decision of the Commission said nothing explicitly on the

30. New York *Times* (Sept. 20, 1939), p. 49; (Oct. 6, 1939), p. 38; (Nov. 2, 1939), p. 32; (Dec. 12, 1939), p. 50; (Dec. 13, 1939), p. 42; (Dec. 14, 1939), p. 42; (Dec. 15, 1939), p. 47; (Dec. 16, 1939), p. 24; (Feb. 8, 1940), p. 38; (Apr. 9, 1940), p. 34; (Apr. 10, 1940), p. 37; (Apr. 11, 1940), p. 38; (Apr. 12, 1940), p. 42; (Apr. 17, 1940), p. 34; (Apr. 20, 1940), p. 22; (May 9, 1940), p. 42; (May 10, 1940), p. 41. *P.I.* (Dec. 8, 1939), p. 43; (Dec. 22, 1939), p. 15; (Feb. 16, 1940), p. 15; (Apr. 19, 1940), p. 67; (Apr. 26, 1940), p. 23; (May 10, 1940), p. 20; (May 17, 1940), p. 23. Coverage of the hearings elsewhere in the press was small. Both the New York *Times* and *Printers' Ink* tended to give greater publicity to the brief for *Good Housekeeping* than to the brief for the Commission.
31. 32 FTC 1454–63, May 13, 1941.

issue of freedom of the press, but by implication both its action and its findings against *Good Housekeeping* challenged the validity of an important contention of publishers concerning their freedom as owners of media for commercial advertising. This freedom was declared to consist of two propositions. One, advanced by counsel for *Good Housekeeping*, stated that whenever differences of "scientific" opinion exist as to the validity of a claim in advertising, the interests of truth and free speech are best served if the contending claims are allowed to flourish. Expert witnesses for the magazine disagreed, for example, with the expert witnesses for the Commission as to whether a cold cream could supply the body with Vitamin D directly through the skin as had been advertised. "In such cases," argued I. W. Digges, counsel for the magazine and speaking also on behalf of the Association of National Advertisers, "it is our strong view that the Commission, composed of non-technical men, should not attempt to elect as between two honest but differing schools of opinion . . . that it not penalize initiative, forestall scientific inquiry, [or] take sides between scientific bodies of opinion." [32]

The second proposition was related to the first and was entered as a petition to the Commission by the ANPA, the most powerful national spokesman for publishers, on behalf of *Good Housekeeping*. It spoke of the "freedom" of an advertiser and a publisher to determine for themselves standards of behavior in advertising; it declared that in censuring the press for the advertisements which it printed, the Commission had violated the First Amendment; the FTC had no right to restrict the "dissemination of information" in advertising or to set itself up as judge of what was truthful in advertisements. The publisher alone possessed that right and was exercising it satisfactorily. The publisher had the right to publish what he pleased; if an injury was thereby done a reader, the injured party had recourse to the courts. Advertising offered information and opinions to people who were free to accept or reject them as they chose. [33]

32. *P.I.* (May 31, 1940), p. 93. See also the judgment of dismissal entered by Commissioner Freer in the complaint against the Lambert Pharmacal Company, 38 FTC 726–53, May 3, 1944.

33. *P.I.* (May 31, 1940), p. 93. The petition was filed by Mr. Elisha Hanson, as *amicus curiae*.

In finding adversely against *Good Housekeeping* the Commission implicitly and of necessity sanctioned the view that the mere existence of a difference of opinion over a factual claim was an insufficient reason for allowing a claim to be advertised if the preponderant weight of scientific opinion opposed it. Nor, said the Commission in effect, by way of answering the ANPA, was the right to persuade by advertising sanctified by any special constitutional guarantee offered the press, particularly if the advertisement were guaranteed by the press. In undertaking such a guarantee the publisher became as responsible as the advertiser for false claims or deceptions. In an instance of this kind the power of a federal agency to prohibit a commercial practice extended equally to the press whenever the press assumed a share of the responsibility for the consequences of that practice.

By now, public debate over the control of advertising had come temporarily to an end, but the issues it had raised were perhaps never to be fully resolved. The passage of the Wheeler-Lea Act, and to a lesser extent the passage of the Food, Drug, and Cosmetic Act, confronted advertising men with a new set of minimum legal conditions within which they must carry on their trade, but the minimum was less than the Government had hoped for, and advertising men could reasonably expect that in the long run the bulk of national consumer advertisements would not be greatly affected by it.[34] Shortly after the passage of the act, the trade journal *Advertising and Selling* accurately predicted the response to be expected in the advertising industry. Some advertisers, the editorial unhesitantly prophesied, would resort to dodges, verbal subterfuges, and legal quibbles to continue to say what would now be forbidden. Others, more conscientious, would acquire a "safe Washington way" of writing copy, to imply proof or suggest a fact without stating it. But the journal's editor expressed a hope that many advertisers would devote greater efforts to studies of their products in order to supply consumers with facts which would sell products on their actual merits.[35]

34. The Food, Drug, and Cosmetic Act of 1938 only indirectly pertained to advertisements.
35. A.S. (Oct. 1938), p. 29.

Trade journals and lawyers for the industry were quick to urge compliance with at least the letter of the law, to make no assertion of fact unless it could be substantiated, and to become circumspect even in venturing an "opinion." [36] The distinction between fact and opinion was, of course, a matter of some importance to copy writers, who were required henceforth to exercise greater care in their use of facts. A "cease and desist" order was not to be taken lightly—though, as Printers' Ink observed in 1940, the far more common "stipulations" may not have proved overly burdensome to their signers. Nor was it uncommon to find advertisers who leaped from one offense to another, pausing only long enough with each to gain a profit and obediently giving up the offending practice when requested.[37]

Most advertising agencies inevitably were inspired to perfect techniques of copy writing which would comply with the law and yet serve the purposes of techniques now rendered illegal. It was obvious that a pictorial illustration could frequently pass muster where a verbal presentation would not, that a promise of reward as a result of purchasing the product could often be enhanced by being left unspecified and thereby innocent of legal transgression.[38] One advertiser, speaking anonymously, confessed to a representative of Printers' Ink: "Advertising has little or no social conscience. We are not concerned with the broad economic significance of individual campaigns or merchandising policies. With one eye on the FTC we compose our advertisements, edging right up to the line and frequently over it. We judge a copy writer's skill by his ability gracefully to skate on thin ice." [39]

In the eighteen months following the passage of the Act, warnings or stipulations by the Commission induced a good deal of graceful skating where the ice was thin. Fleischmann's Yeast, forbidden to be advertised as moving bowels or removing pimples, was abruptly promoted as a source of vitamin nourishment. Vivadou Talcum could no longer be advertised as making one

36. See, for example, Charles Dunn, *P.I.* (Apr. 14, 1938), p. 19.
37. *P.I.* (Mar. 1, 1940), p. 21.
38. *P.I.* (Aug. 25, 1938), p. 11.
39. *P.I.* (June 14, 1940), p. 11. For a supporting comment, see Henry Eckhardt in *A.S.* (June 1938), p. 11.

"utterly safe" from giving off offensive odors or as making one perspire less, but it was allowed instead to be sold as having a cooling quality. On the other hand, Djer-Kiss Talc was considered misrepresented in claims that it reduced body temperature; its copy writers consequently sought refuge in an illustration of a French beauty bathing coolly in strawberries. Most stipulations resulted in more prosaic changes, some of them so trivial as to allow one to infer from the Commission's acceptance of them a rather captious and overly literal spirit in insisting on the change in the first place. One could no longer say, for example, that Devoe Paint was "definitely durable," but rather "durable"; it "outlasts average paints" but does not outlast "other paints." The claim that Smith and Corona typewriters "will help any student," drew a protest from the FTC, but an illustration of a pupil giving his teacher beautifully neat and handsomely typed schoolwork was permissible.[40]

It is difficult, then, to assess explicitly the impact of the Wheeler-Lea Act on the ethical performance of advertising. While it seems clear that during the ten-year period from 1929 to 1939 there occurred a noticeable decrease in the frequency of national advertisements whose claims were highly questionable, a careful examination of the advertisements themselves suggests that little fundamental change took place in the shorter period 1937–39, during which the Wheeler-Lea Act was passed. A check of the national advertising in 1929 in three magazines and one newspaper, for example, revealed an average per issue of twenty

40. Between 1938 and 1940 a number of heavily advertised products were the subject of FTC action, among them Lifebuoy and Lux soaps (could not enhance skin color, bestow youth, or remove odors), Ipana Toothpaste (could not cure "pink tooth brush"), and Sani-Flush (could not kill germs). See *P.I.* (July 7, 1938), p. 52; (Aug. 4, 1938), p. 26; (Sept. 15, 1938), p. 23. *A.S.* (Jan. 1940), pp. 25 ff.; (Apr. 1940), p. 48. In this same period the FTC found that about 10 per cent of the advertisements regularly reviewed in nearly 1,000 magazines and newspapers violated the law in some way; by far the largest single class of offender was the drug manufacturer. Approximately 1,000 violators were "warned" each year, half of whom agreed to sign stipulations that the offending practice would cease; an additional quarter required a "cease and desist" order before complying. Only ten suits were brought to court for violation of a "cease and desist" order, of which five resulted in fines averaging $2,000: *A.S.* (May 1940), pp. 22 ff.

claims which were conceivably open to at least some question of validity; a check of a similar series for 1937, 1938, and 1939 revealed that the average had decreased to about nine; but from January 1937 to December 1939 the numbers per issue decreased imperceptibly, except toward the latter months of 1939, nearly eighteen months after the new legislation was adopted.[41] The claims were apt to involve principally face creams, soap, yeast, toothpaste, toiletries, cigarettes, and sundry drugs and remedies. An additional investigation revealed that most of the questionable advertisements between 1929 and 1939 became noticeably less specific and more noncommittal in their verbal claims, which were conveyed with increasing glamour and indirect assertion; but, again, this development had taken place largely before 1938.

Analysis of the advertisements for Listerine as found in popular magazines from 1937 through 1939 provides striking confirmation of the impressions I have just set forth. Listerine advertising fell into three distinct categories: those which claimed that Listerine could eliminate "bad breath," those which announced that it would "cure" dandruff, and those which insisted that it would aid in "fighting" colds and sore throats.[42]

The "halitosis" theme was set forth as a double argument: "Listerine halts fermentation in the mouth, the major cause of odors" could be considered the primary assertion; the secondary assertion suggested that Listerine brings personal and social rewards

41. These figures are the result of an analysis which I made of the national advertisements found in the following periodical issues: *Woman's Home Companion*, May 1928; Feb., Mar., May, Sept., Dec., 1929; alternate months (beginning in Feb.) for 1937 and 1938; Feb., Mar., July, Sept., Oct. 1939. *Ladies' Home Journal*, June 1928; Jan., June, Sept., Oct. 1929. *Good Housekeeping*, Jan., Apr., Nov. 1929; Aug. 1937–Jan. 1940 (consecutively). *Saturday Evening Post*, alternate months (beginning in Feb.), the second and third week in each month for 1929; every ninth issue in 1937, 1938, 1939. New York *Times*, the Sunday issues for Jan., Mar. 1929; Jan., Apr. 1937; June, Oct. 1938; Oct. 1939. For a criterion of what was "questionable" I resorted for the most part to rulings or judgments of the FTC, the F. and D. A., and the AMA. In a few cases I relied on information or comment found in advertising journals.

42. For the period 1937–39 I made a special analysis of the magazine advertisements for Listerine as found in *Good Housekeeping* and in the *Saturday Evening Post*; the specific aim was to detect any significant differences in copy appeal between advertisements in the year prior to July 1938 and the year subsequent to it which in any plausible fashion could be attributed to the Wheeler-Lea Act.

denied those whose breath is unpleasant. Only the primary assertion could be tested or challenged for veracity; the secondary assertion, which was the more significant, by itself could be neither proved nor disproved, though if the primary assertion were not true the secondary assertion would have been meaningless. By 1937 the primary assertion had already been modified from a previous and untenable claim that Listerine halted the fermentation of food; in the next two years it was made so subordinate to the secondary assertion as to exist scarcely at all, but remained rather as an implicit, unstated assumption and therefore invulnerable to legal action. The secondary assertion ("social rewards") carried, then, the major burden of the advertising, which generally consisted of a large photograph with an explanation: a lonely, unwanted person, a failure at attracting a mate or winning business promotions or finding "happiness" in marriage is revealed as having failed because of foul-smelling breath. ("Will he gradually grow indifferent as so many husbands do?") Further explanation was often confined to the word "halitosis" and the name of the product.[43]

The "dandruff" theme, on the other hand, remained virtually unchanged from 1937 to 1940, in which year the FTC banned it as being unfounded in fact. The untenable statements which had prevailed in 1929 were dropped (such as that a person could "catch a case of dandruff that may lead to baldness"); in their place in 1937 came the following revelation: "Laboratory and clinic show how Listerine kills the germ Pityrosporum Ovale and achieved amazing results against dandruff. . . . Pityrosporum Ovale causes dandruff . . . a germ disease requiring persistent and systematic treatment." In 1938 there followed photographs and a description of "scientists" inoculating rabbits with the "dandruff germ" and applying Listerine to half of the fur of each rabbit; the conclusion was that "Listerine actually cures dandruff." Subsequent advertisements offered signed testimonials such as "Listerine cured my daughter's dandruff in ten days." [44] During a

43. The "halitosis" theme occurred in the following monthly series: July, Aug. 1937; Feb., June, July, Aug., Oct. 1938; Apr., May, Aug., Sept. 1939.
44. The dandruff theme was presented in Oct., Nov. 1937; Apr., May, Sept., Oct. 1938; Mar., Apr., June, July, Sept., Oct. 1939.

lengthy hearing before the Commission, it was established that the discovery of the vaunted germ had been an error, that its eradication would not guarantee the disappearance of dandruff, and that the efficacy of Listerine to "get rid of" dandruff was in all likelihood due principally to its washing effect, something which had nothing to do with its antiseptic qualities, which water could do equally well, and which would no more "permanently" remove dandruff than a bath would "permanently" remove dirt.[45]

In the third major appeal for Listerine, as a relief for colds and sore throats, there was a noticeable alteration and softening of claims between 1937 and 1940. As in the "halitosis" theme, the major qualifications in claims had taken place by 1937, and thereafter inference, innuendo, and pictures increasingly replaced outright assertion of fact. In 1932 the advertising for Listerine had become untenable: "Use only Listerine to relieve Sore Throat. . . . Heals tissue while it kills germs." By 1937 and 1938 the claims, however questionable, had been made far more circumspect: "The prompt use of Listerine may often head off a cold. At such times this wonderful antiseptic seems to give Nature the helping hand it needs in fighting germs. [It] reaches far down into the throat and kills millions of germs associated with colds and simple sore throat." In January 1939 the argument had become still more subtle: "Do not think for a moment that Listerine will always prevent or check a cold." (By warning a reader not to think about something, one has surely established the probability that the reader will think about it seriously.) "We do say, however, that the best clinical evidence indicates that if you gargle with Listerine your chances of avoiding serious colds are excellent." By the end of the year, apprehensive over possible action by the FTC, the Lambert Pharmacal Company had altered its copy to assert merely that Listerine was a mild antiseptic and would kill certain germs, while a series of captioned photographs revealed the quick relief which an agonized cough-and-cold-wracked gargler was obtaining from Listerine.[46] Through 1942,

45. 29 FTC (*Decisions*) 1446–7 (July 28, 1939). See also T. B. Clark, *The Advertising Smokescreen* (New York, Harper, 1944), pp. 84–93; A.S. (Sept. 9, 1937), p. 22.

46. The "cold and sore throat" theme occurred in Nov., Dec. 1937; Jan., Mar., Nov. 1938; Jan., Dec. 1939.

at least, the ambiguous but technically safe insinuation that Listerine could relieve some of the symptoms of a cold survived legal challenge when the Commission in 1944, having taken 7,500 pages of testimony in three years, dismissed a second complaint against the Lambert Pharmacal Company for its advertising of Listerine.[47]

What may one conclude from these findings? While it is always precarious to generalize from partial evidence, one conclusion particularly suggests itself: the increase in the powers and in the regulatory activity of the FTC which occurred in the summer of 1938 was in all probability only the culmination of a larger sequence of factors which, over the course of the previous decade, had tended to encourage greater honesty and accuracy in a large number of national advertisements. Consumer agitation and public pressure for regulation stressed most heavily the advertising transgressions of the drug and cosmetic manufacturers, for example, and both the agitation and the pressure were most in evidence in the period 1932–36, which coincided with what appears on close examination to have been the period of greatest "improvement" in the advertising of drugs and cosmetics. The Wheeler-Lea Act, in other words, took effect when the worst abuses of public confidence had begun to abate; further abatement was discernible only after the Act had been in force for many months, and though the Act undoubtedly had some effect in bringing this about, it would be hazardous without exhaustive investigation to say how much.

47. Clark, pp. 146–51. 38 FTC 726–53. A lone vote against dismissal was cast by Commissioner Ayres, who took the unusual course of writing a dissenting opinion.

6

Defense and Reaffirmation

PASSAGE of a federal law to regulate advertising climaxed a
lengthy struggle between the advertising industry and a number
of diverse groups, including organizations of consumers. At the
close of the struggle it was difficult to say what had been won. The
consumer gained a new standard for responsible behavior in national marketing, but the standard he gained was a minimum
which left the major goals of the consumer movement unattained.
In practice the law affected only a small portion of the nation's
advertising, and almost no political sentiment of any size or
consequence existed for more radical or more comprehensive
action.

For this the national advertising industry could by no means
take full credit, but it is fair to point out that in the course of a
struggle which had been waged intermittently for three decades,
advertising men had not been idle. They had tried out, in fact,

a variety of powerful weapons with which to allay or neutralize public sentiment and mitigate the influence of unfriendly critics. They sponsored in the commercial press advertisements on behalf of advertising, and with persistent and skillful publicity they attempted to "educate" the public to like advertising, to approve of it, and to defend it from censure. To this end they sought to influence the curricula and the textbooks of public schools; a few of them made efforts to discredit consumers' organizations; and they endeavored to construct intellectually persuasive and politically respectable arguments by which to explain and thereby justify their purposes and their actual behavior. I wish here to consider the way in which advertising men, individually and collectively, struggled to improve their relations with the public and to render less urgent the necessity of responding to the pressures of critics for the reform of their conduct.

Before 1916 no advertising man had thought that the reputation of advertising mattered enough to warrant a campaign to advertise advertising. The campaign of that year, which the AACW sponsored and for which publishers donated space, was undertaken to encourage more businessmen to use advertising, to dissuade state and national legislatures from taxing it, and to "put advertising on a more substantial foundation in the public mind, making the facts clear that advertising is an economic benefit, in that it does not increase the cost of the article advertised." [1] The campaign ended in 1918, but the problem did not. "The mass of the people, from whom our legislators are drawn," reported an editor of *Printers' Ink* that year, "have not yet realized . . . [that] advertising is justified and is even demanded by sound economics. . . . Congress has shown and is showing a disposition to regard advertising as a waste." [2] Some in the industry attributed this apparent popular suspicion to ignorant and radical agitators, socialists, politicians, school teachers, and economists.[3] There were

1. Baur, *Voluntary Control in the Advertising Industry*, p. 90, quoting a statement released to the trade press by the AACW.
2. *P.I.* (July 18, 1918), p. 108. An editor of *A.S.* expressed almost the same view (Mar. 1, 1919), p. 4.
3. *P.I.* (Apr. 22, 1920), p. 49, statement by the ANA secretary John Sullivan.

those, on the other hand, who plainly agreed with Stanley Resor and Gilbert Kinney, of the J. Walter Thompson agency, that a business which could attract a considerable number of college graduates, even Yale men, had become respectable and secure, and had in fact arrived.[4] Nevertheless, the conviction grew that hostility toward advertising was widespread. "In Congress, in state legislatures, in schools and colleges, and in public and private discussions," warned Paul Cherington, a research investigator in 1920, "advertising is on the defensive." [5] Legislators, both state and national, impressed with the lavishness and scale of advertising expenditures, tended, unfortunately, to regard these expenditures as likely sources of tax revenue. Billboard advertising was particularly vulnerable because of its blatant conspicuousness in an urban society whose memories and esthetic values were rooted largely in a rural environment. In a few years bills to tax advertising reached what the ANA described as "an insidious flood," and advertising associations made earnest attempts to close the floodgates with lobbying and other less overt pressures.[6]

Efforts to advertise advertising proceeded slowly and sporadically until the 1930's. Among advertising men one might have expected partiality to the use of paid advertisements as a device for propaganda, yet publicity of this sort was infrequent. Few agencies could afford to sponsor what was at best a device of indeterminate influence; though agencies planned and wrote them, the media in which they appeared paid for them. In 1921 the New York *American,* for example, bought from a number of agencies a series of "canned" editorials to be run in Hearst papers throughout the country. They were, in effect, advertisements to urge the public to buy only nationally branded (i.e. heavily advertised) products and to consider unadvertised brands as unreliable and worthless.[7] In the following year the AAAA prepared a series of fifty-two advertisements to be distributed without cost to any newspaper or magazine who wished to run them; directed

4. *P.I.* (Nov. 15, 1923), p. 105; (Nov. 29, 1923), p. 105.
5. *P.I.* (Oct. 28, 1920), p. 154.
6. *P.I.* (July 1, 1926), p. 17. For further instances of and comments on "tax advertising" bills see *P.I.* (Nov. 29, 1923), p. 105; (Jan. 15, 1925), p. 25; (Feb. 5, 1925), p. 10; (May 27, 1926), p. 3; (Jan. 6, 1927), p. 65.
7. *A.S.* (Mar. 12, 1921), p. 16.

at businessmen as well as the general public, they attempted to demonstrate the indispensability of advertising to business prosperity.[8] In like manner the N. W. Ayer agency composed a series that ran through the entire interwar period; eventually over 1600 newspapers were to publish them. Designed, in the words of the agency, "to develop a national consumer-consciousness of the tremendous value of advertising," they conveyed to the general reader month after month the fundamental rationale of the industry: advertising saves money, serves the community, and makes friends for the businessman; it promotes sound business ethics and maintains consumer demand at the high level which a leisure society requires; some advertising is dishonest, for some businessmen are so; but the fair-trading, progressive businessman advertises honestly in order to serve the American family; to censor, or to restrict his advertising was to endanger the American way of life.[9]

By 1938 publicity of this sort had become commonplace. In the Hearst magazines there appeared advertisements which attempted to discredit the so-called debunking literature" (such as *100,000,000 Guinea Pigs*) by asking "Who's a guinea pig?" and by answering "Those who buy unadvertised or private brands." [10] Simultaneously, advertisements sponsored by the *Ladies' Home Journal* debunked the consumer movement by arguing that the only authentic friends of the consumer were the publishers of women's magazines, while the Crowell Publishing Company ran an illustrated series depicting a "consumer" (nearly always a career woman, a teacher, or a housewife) interviewing a "businessman" (a prosperous-looking fruit rancher, standing in a grove of orange trees, or a sales executive sitting in a conspicuously elegant office), who is asked "Does advertising help anyone but the advertiser"? and who answers with enthusiasm that advertis-

8. *The Advertising Yearbook for 1922* (Doubleday, 1922), p. 208.
9. A.S. (July 9, 1921), p. 3. This description is derived from an examination which I made of forty advertisements in the series. These advertisements are not to be confused with the so-called "house ads" which the Ayer agency occasionally sponsored in the same media. Normally, "house ads" publicize the advertising firm and attempt to win customers for it. The Ayer "house ads" stressed not only the competence of Ayer but that of advertising in general.
10. See, for example, *Cosmopolitan* (Nov. 1938), p. 103.

ing helps everybody. ("Fact of the matter is, Mrs. Rogers, the advertiser is the *last* one to benefit from advertising. Take oranges, for example . . .") [11] Noticeably more subtle was a cartoon sequence which the G. Lynn Sumner agency created for the AAAA and which was published in national magazines. It depicted two businessmen named Od and Ad. Od was the unenlightened producer who tried to market his wares without advertising: he earned no profit, exhausted himself, and was a failure in his community. But Ad became a national advertiser, reduced his costs of distribution, undersold his competitor Od, grew wealthy and respectable in his community, and derived satisfaction from having offered mankind a reliable, standardized product. [12]

Though it was not uncommon for advertising men to "remind" publishers of their stake in the loyalty and docility of those who read advertisements, [13] publishers of mass media generally required no outside persuasion to win friends for advertising. Articles or editorial items commenting favorably on advertising appeared with regularity in nearly every leading commercial magazine and in countless newspapers. Many featured the writings of advertising men who sought to persuade the general reader of the benefits and reliability of the advertising industry, its role in modern society, and the competent sense of responsibility which most of its members could be counted on to display toward the American consumer. Even the more obvious foibles of the advertising world, the glamour of its inhabitants, and the occasional absurdities of their behavior were turned to shrewd account in indulgent satire which served the dual purpose of publicizing the industry and turning aside the skeptic. [14]

11. *Woman's Home Companion* (Oct. 1939), p. 116.
12. For data on the Od and Ad series see *A.S.* (May 1938), p. 36.
13. For example, *E.P.* (Nov. 26, 1938), p. 10; (Dec. 17, 1938), pp. 25–52.
14. Fully representative of such journalistic publicity are the following: E. E. Calkins: "Does It Pay to Advertise?" *Century* (Apr. 1924), p. 851; article by Kenneth Collins in the *Elks Magazine*, reprinted in *P.I.* (Nov. 8, 1923), p. 145; article in the *Saturday Evening Post* (Apr. 8, 1922), p. 27; article by Bruce Barton in *Liberty*, Feb. 1925; article by James Webb Young for the fiftieth anniversary issue of *Good Housekeeping*, May 1935. From 1921 to 1940 these and similar magazines carried (according to the *Reader's Guide to Periodical Literature*) over 200 articles on advertising. A large sampling of these articles reveals that they were overwhelmingly favorable in tone.

OUT OF THE BACKGROUND

EVERY morning, millions of people take their automobiles, their telephones or their market-baskets, and do their own shopping. Name after name leaps to their lips without hesitation. This brand of shoes. That brand of flour. This tire. That soap. This ginger ale. That stocking. Names correctly and clearly spoken. Given with the ease of long familiarity. Recognized instantly by clerks, these names of products that are accepted by the buyers without inspection and without question.

These people who are asking for known merchandise in thousands of stores today are *buying*. They are not *being sold*. More and more each year, such people are insisting on their own preferences. And retail business everywhere is feeling the influence of their trade. One of the shrewdest retailers in New York recently said that "the merchant now tries to buy what the consumer wants. For these consumers, with advertisements, catalogs and bulletins, have developed an exactness in taste and an expertness in buying that are changing merchandising conditions. Manufacturer, wholesaler, retailer — all must observe the buying habits and listen to the demands of the consumer."

Many manufacturers long ago sought the aid of advertising to make their products known and trusted; demanded by consumers and consequently by retailers and wholesalers. Today the names of their products stand out in bold relief against the hazy background of the public mind. Familiar names . . . accepted names . . . advertised names. Placed definitely on the Nation's shopping list with the help of the printed page. And to such manufacturers it is a commonplace to say that any article of real merit can be sold in greater volume, and in less time, with the aid of advertising.

Many other manufacturers of more recent advertising experience are steadily increasing their sales and widening their market. Year after year, keeping everlastingly at it, advertising is helping their products to emerge from the background of the public mind. They are getting into jobbers' stocks. They are finding a place on retailers' shelves. Salesmen are taking them a little farther afield each year . . . Growing . . . Growing . . . until finally everyone will say, whenever their names are mentioned . . . . "Oh, yes."

N. W. AYER & SON

ADVERTISING HEADQUARTERS, PHILADELPHIA

NEW YORK   BOSTON   CHICAGO   SAN FRANCISCO

5. One of a series of advertisements on behalf of advertising run by the N. W. Ayer agency in general magazines (September 1926).

While the press, in advertisement and article, furnished a continual flow of propaganda on behalf of advertising, other organizations sponsored a variety of promotional activities to the same end. Within the industry itself, there emerged, toward the end of the 1920's, a major nationwide association, formed in part to establish better relations between the advertising industry and the public. Called the Advertising Federation of America (AFA), its membership consisted both of local and of regional clubs and professional organizations, such as the AAAA. It was intended to replace the International Advertising Association (IAA), a loose coalition of local clubs with neither a budget nor an organization effective enough for the task of publicity. "The public is clamoring for more information in advertising," announced Walter Strong, Chairman of the Board of Governors of the IAA by way of explaining this task. "That it needs a better understanding of advertising must be obvious to anyone." [15] The AFA was to provide the answer. Theoretical control of the Federation continued as before in the hands of member organizations, but the practical power of the central office was increased to permit greater activity in public relations.[16] Its aims were soon embodied in a "Code" which, like many codes, revealed little of the way in which the organization operated but reflected unwittingly the unspoken concerns of its members. The Code somewhat vaguely pledged the AFA to work for truth in advertising, to discourage "unfair" competitive practices, to encourage market research, and to disseminate "the truth about advertising" in order to stimulate "an increasing acceptance of its value." [17] Commenting on these objectives of the Association, Walter Strong, who had now been named chairman of its governing board, emphasized that the interest in public relations would be comprehensive but dis-

15. *P.I.* (May 24, 1928), p. 150.
16. Ibid. See also, *P.I.* (Sept. 29, 1927), p. 33; Baur, pp. 168–201; Lee, pp. 359–65. In 1926 the Better Business Bureaus had withdrawn from the IAA, depriving that organization of over half its income. The decision to form the AFA was undertaken largely to permit the American members to concentrate their resources on their own increasing problems, one of the most important of which was a growing criticism of advertising. Letter, C. James Proud (president of the AFA) to author, Dec. 23, 1957.
17. *P.I.* (May 23, 1929), p. 65.

creet. "I want it clearly understood," he warned, "that the bally-hoo principle is to be entirely eliminated, that our promotional education shall be sensibly identified with our fact-finding work. . . . We must convince . . . the public that our effort is based on scientific principle . . . [We must convince] the consumer . . . of the honesty of our purpose and values." [18] This was not to say that the AFA was concerned only with the public opinion of advertising. It would be more true to say that its leading members regarded the need for more research, for more effective advertising procedures, and for greater immunity from legislation as specific facets of the more general problem of gaining widespread public approval which this large federation of advertising clubs had been explicitly constructed to solve.

Meeting year by year in convention, members of the AFA reminded themselves of the growing urgency of their task. They tended to assume that criticism of advertising stemmed both from a failure of the public to understand its operations and from an apparent impression that advertising was wasteful and inefficient. One need only reduce the waste and "explain" the operations, and the criticism would disappear. Year after year the AFA resolved to "strengthen its educational work" in schools and colleges and in the mass media, and to demonstrate that advertising men possessed high standards of ethics and therefore could be counted on to regulate themselves. They were ready to admit that "advertising is distinguished by its public power and responsibility, and consequently must be operated with greater efficiency and greater freedom from abuse than other business methods." [19] Yet they were just as quick to insist that "educational" activities and public relations work take precedence over policies of self-regulation, and in point of fact their annual conventions served in large part to bolster the faith of the membership in the need for and the efficacy of favorable relations.[20] The 1936 convention was it-

18. *P.I.* (May 24, 1928), p. 150.

19. Report of the Annual Convention in June 1934: *P.I.* (June 28, 1934), p. 46.

20. See, for example, Report of the Second Annual Convention, May 1930: *A.S.* (May 28, 1930), p. 82. Report of the Seventh Convention: *P.I.* (June 20, 1935), p. 28. For specific evidence that members of the AFA overwhelmingly preferred publicity to "policing" see *E.P.* (Dec. 22, 1934), p. 36.

self conceived and run as a gigantic promotional celebration on behalf of the entire industry. Designated as a "silver jubilee" to honor the founding of the Truth-in-Advertising Movement in 1911, those assembled at the convention invoked the past by publishing an official "history" of "Truth" in advertising, heralded the future as one of continued but ultimately victorious struggle to eliminate offensive and misleading copy, and consecrated the present with a resolution that the public should be vigorously persuaded of certain "self-evident truths":

> The great bulk of advertising is honestly conceived, is reliable in statement, fair to competition, useful to the reader, and soundly economic. . . .
>
> The American people like advertising and respond to it. They like its emotional appeal. It suits their temperament, is cheerful and optimistic. It gives to common things of the market a subjective value which goes beyond mere use. It helps people to enjoy life. . . .
>
> Advertising is the voice of commerce. . . .
>
> But it has a higher responsibility than private trading or individual conduct because it is a public pledge made in a public medium and disseminates to millions of people information and impressions which affect their daily lives.
>
> Advertising has become a vital social and economic force in maintaining a widely circulated and independent press and other public media . . . indispensable to democratic self-government.[21]

The AFA did not spend all its efforts in self-examination. It printed booklets on advertising and distributed them to businesses, schools, women's clubs, and the press. It sponsored short weekly radio talks and sent speakers on nationwide tours to address public audiences. Everywhere the AFA denounced private brands, excoriated the consumer's research agencies, and urged

21. Reported in *P.I.* (July 9, 1936), p. 44. The official "history," entitled *The Fight for Truth in Advertising,* was written by H. J. Kenner, an official of the AFA, formerly of the National Better Business Bureau. It offered a resounding argument for the effectiveness of self-regulation, a major theme of the convention.

citizens to express to their Congressmen disapproval of impending regulation of food and drugs.

Nor did the members and affiliates of the AFA remain idle. An organization closely associated with the AFA and known somewhat euphemistically as the National Advisory Council of Consumers and Producers attempted (with a notable lack of success) to set up forty "local councils" of consumers to counteract and head off the influence of the more "legitimate" consumers' organizations.[22] Representing, as it did, a large number of local units, the AFA was continually called on to assist individual clubs in conducting "forums," consumer "clinics," and other devices for furthering good will between local advertising men and ordinary citizens. In the late 1930's, when the Tugwell proposals became law, these activities proliferated. The "Advertising Women" of New York City held a "consumer conference" in 1940 at which representatives from several hundred women's clubs in New York State gathered to discuss the benefits of national advertising and learn of the unreliability of professional consumer agitators.[23] In Chicago the Advertising Club installed a Speaker's Committee, conducted a local radio program, and set up a Bureau of Buyer Information, which consumers were urged to consult in the place of consumers' research organizations.[24] On the West Coast the Pacific Advertising Clubs once sponsored an "entirely unrehearsed" quiz show on which a panel of advertising men urged eighteen "housewives" to state their opinions of advertising, their recollection of brand names, and their preferences as to national brands or private brands; the panel professed to conclude from the show that there existed little animosity toward advertising as such, but that advertising, nevertheless, needed to be made more subtly effective if it were to remain secure.[25]

22. *A.S.* (Apr. 11, 1935), p. 40; *P.I.* (June 20, 1935), p. 28; *Tide* (May 1935), p. 19. This deceptive use of the word "consumer" was repeated by the "Consumer-Advertiser Council," established in 1938 as an adjunct of the AAAA to further the "education of the public to the value of advertising": *E.P.* (Apr. 30, 1938), p. 99; (Nov. 26, 1938), p. 10.

23. *P.I.* (Mar. 1, 1940), p. 50.

24. *P.I.* (Mar. 8, 1940), p. 14.

25. *P.I.* (July 7, 1939), p. 51. *A.S.* observed (Jan. 1938), p. 40, that many advertising organizations and clubs were planning "to do considerable evangelization" for national brand advertising at the New York World's Fair in 1939.

Like a tidal current, carrying the institutions and devices of publicity for American advertising, there ran through the 1920's and 1930's a distinct rationale which countless numbers of advertising men helped to articulate and to which they themselves professed to subscribe. This rationale consisted both of statements of principle and of arguments, occasionally defensive in tone, and endlessly repeated in the literature and rhetoric of the trade. The arguments were expected to permit advertising men to find meaning and value in their own trade and to enhance public respect for it. They actually helped to define an area of general agreement within the industry concerning its function and its economic role. In attempting to show that the current behavior of the industry was even more responsible than the public was insisting it should be, the arguments unwittingly revealed the advertising man's concept of how he ought to behave. These arguments took four principal forms.[26]

26. The following characterization of advertising rationale is based on a close study of the literature of the advertising industry from 1924 to 1942. Though derived from the sources listed below, it is representative also of a much larger number of writings and comments by many other individuals.

a. Agents and advertisers in formal addresses: Stanley Resor, to the N. Y. Graduates Club of the Harvard Business School, 1925, *P.I.* (Dec. 17, 1925), p. 41; Earnest Elmo Calkins, to the annual convention of the ANA, 1927, *P.I.* (Nov. 10, 1927), p. 33; Bruce Barton, to the convention of the AAAA, 1927, *P.I.* (Nov. 3, 1927), p. 3; Bruce Barton, to the National Chain Store Assn., 1929, *P.I.* (Oct. 3, 1929), p. 3; John Benson (president of the AAAA), to a student forum, City College of New York, 1929, *P.I.* (Nov. 28, 1929), p. 152; John Benson, to the Chicago Federated Advertising Club, 1937, *P.I.* (June 10, 1937), p. 53; John Benson, to the Institute for Consumer Education, 1939, *P.I.* (Apr. 13, 1939), p. 76; Ralph Starr Butler, to the Northwestern University forum, 1930, in *The Ethical Problems of Modern Advertising*, Ronald Press, 1931; Allyn McIntire (president of the ANA), to a convention of the AAAA, 1934, *P.I.* (May 31, 1934), p. 64; Roy Durstine, to the U. S. Chamber of Commerce, 1935, *P.I.* (May 9, 1935), p. 76; Albert Lasker, to a convention of the AFA, 1935, *P.I.* (June 13, 1935), p. 7; William L. Day, to the AAAA, 1936, *A.S.* (May 7, 1936), p. 33; Raymond Rubicam, to a BBB conference, 1940, *P.I.* (May 24, 1940), p. 13.

b. Publishers and editors: Marco Morrow, *P.I.* (Aug. 15, 1928), p. 41; Frank Crowninshield, to the AFA, 1934, *P.I.* (May 31, 1934), p. 7; Anna S. Richardson, to the AFA, 1934, *P.I.* (June 21, 1934), p. 7; Gilbert Hodges, to the AHEA, 1934, *P.I.* (July 5, 1934), p. 60.

c. Economists and academic commentators: Daniel Starch, *Principles of Advertising*, A. W. Shaw, 1923; Fred E. Clark and G. B. Hotchkiss, to the American Economics Assn., 1924, *Am. Econ. Rev. Suppl.*, 15, Mar. 1925; Glen Frank, *P.I.* (Apr. 14, 1927), p. 81; Carl F. Taeusch, *Policy and Ethics in Business*, McGraw-Hill, 1931; Virgil Jordan, to the AFA, 1932, *P.I.* (June 23, 1932), p. 64; Howe

The most basic contention of the advertising man about his trade was an assertion of its economic and social value. For the manufacturer, it was repeatedly argued, advertising had shown itself to be a selling device of unrivaled efficiency for gaining a mass market. Inasmuch as a mass market generally meant a savings in cost greater than the investment in advertising, it could be said that advertising really cost no one anything. For the consumer, advertisements were tolerably reliable guides to new products and sources of information about the market in which he bought them. The increase which advertising added to price was usually infinitesimal, and in return the consumer of nationally advertised brands was assured a standardized product of known repute and value. (Crackers used to be scooped from a grocer's dirty barrel; now they came cellophaned and branded.) At times, advertising also assured the consumer a tangible value in resale, exchange, or psychic use. (It was possibly less important to smoke than to smoke Camels.) Producers, furthermore, were encouraged to live up to the promises they and their competitors made in their advertising, assuring the public, thereby, a high quality and a large range of products. Finally, by stimulating the masses to buy, advertising was making possible an economy of leisure, abundance, and progress.

While admitting that the performance of some advertising was deplorable, advertising men contended that the weaknesses of their trade reflected the business world which it served and the public to which it catered. Those who produced it were no more or less prey to human weakness than those who paid for it; a dishonest advertiser was no worse than a dishonest doctor or clergyman. Advertising merely reflected the permanent propensity of men to sell themselves. ("The world's first successful salesman

Martyn, *P.I.* (Dec. 28, 1933), p. 61; G. B. Hotchkiss, *P.I.* (Jan. 7, 1937), p. 6; Neil F. Borden, *The Economic Effects of Advertising*, Chicago, Irwin, 1942.

d. *Editorial and other comment in trade journals: P.I.:* (Jan. 15, 1925), p. 25; (Feb. 5, 1925), p. 10; (Apr. 30, 1925), p. 3; (Oct. 1, 1925), p. 3; (June 2, 1927), p. 125; (June 30, 1927), p. 121; (July 28, 1927), p. 3; (Aug. 11, 1927), p. 57; (Apr. 30, 1930), p. 10; (July 24, 1930), p. 41; (Aug. 5, 1931), p. 17; (Jan. 14, 1932), p. 34; (Jan. 11, 1934), p. 10; (Feb. 1, 1934), p. 37; (Aug. 18, 1939), p. 49. *P.I. Monthly* (Apr. 1928), p. 40. A.S. (Oct. 8, 1930), p. 36; (Sept. 15, 1932), p. 13. *Tide* (Sept. 1927), p. 3; (Apr. 1930), p. 6.

was the serpent; Eve was the second.") Did it preach materialism? Americans were a material people, a hustling, exuberant and
competitive people. Did it peddle dreams? Americans were idealists, who lived by more than their bread. Did advertisements exploit sex? In this activity they lagged behind the mass media and
even serious literature. Did they tend to exaggerate? Exaggeration
was an accepted convention of modern speech, part of the folk
talk of a nation. The "tall story," it was argued, never hurt anyone,
and the public enjoyed a tall story. Advertising, in short, reflected
popular taste. To perform its function, even to survive, it had to
give the people what they wanted.

From this argument, another readily followed. Advertising was
primarily a business and only incidentally a public service. It
existed frankly to induce consumers to buy goods and services,
and those who produced advertising should cease yearning for
professional status if a consciousness of that status should ever
lead them to place non-monetary considerations ahead of their
fundamental purpose of selling. An advertising agent, like a law-
yer or doctor, could refuse a dubious client or a harmful product;
once he accepted a product, however, he was obliged to do his
utmost to sell it. The advertising man, then, was responsible primarily to his client and only secondarily to his competitors or his
public. It was possible to feel needlessly tender toward the public.
The public was really many separate publics, each with a distinct
attitude toward the advertising it read. Some were sophisticated
and discriminating; some were repelled by ballyhoo but were persuaded to buy in spite of themselves; others were overtly hostile.
In all cases the criterion for acceptable advertisements should be
nothing less than the limit of public tolerance, and only the various publics could determine this limit for themselves; excessive
criticism of advertising by its own practitioners would only discredit it in public eyes. Perhaps, suggested some advertising men,
the fetish of Truth-in-Advertising, honored in every code and at
every convention, was even misleading and harmful. The public
should not be led to expect truth from advertising. Truth occurred
nowhere else in life, and the problem in advertising as in life itself
was not truth but credibility. An advertisement which convinced
its readers that it was true was usually preferable to one which

was merely true but unconvincing. In short, the purists in advertising who attempted to write large on the industry their own moral and esthetic predilections were out of place in business.

The fourth major argument asserted that advertising deserved to remain free from all external coercion or controls. Because its messages invariably revealed their sponsors, advertising was the most honest form of persuasion; nor had any other business gone so far to protect the public. The internal policemen of the industry, it was argued, were quick to spot the fraudulent and unethical advertisers and could be counted on to eliminate them. A fraud might occasionally go unpunished, but the public could never be permanently fooled. Even as the best check on a fraudulent claim was the claim of a competing firm, so the best check on any advertisement was the common-sense skepticism of the average reader. The industry, then, needed no external regulation. More than that, however, it *ought* to be left free. Advertising was a neutral commercial technique available to anyone who could pay for it. Censorship of advertising, many warned, would mean a fatal impairment of the freedom of ideas to gain a hearing. No one, it was said, possessed a monopoly of Truth. Who was to say whether an advertisement was true or not? Experts had often been wrong. What were once thought lies turned out to be truths. To censor claims in advertising on the basis of known truth was to stifle the process of establishing future truth. Since truth was indeterminate, let persuasion flourish. To censor advertising, on the other hand, was to repudiate the democratic principle that the public should be allowed to choose as freely between alternative ideas as they did between alternative products in a competitive market. Let the public decide. To restrict public choice was political tyranny. Against political tyranny stood the freedom of ideas and the freedom of the press. They depended on commercial advertising. Were restrictions to be imposed from without, freedom would perish.

Pervading both the substance and the rhetoric of the industry-wide publicity which erupted in the 1930's was the assumption that advertising was the object of a conspiracy, the target of a host of unfriendly and scheming opponents, tiny in number but possessed of an insidious influence among consumers who would otherwise be disposed to accept and like advertising. Critics of advertising, according to this view, were of three types. Most to be feared were those economists, professors, political idealists, and consumer agitators who knowingly condemned the basic structure of advertising and its institutional arrangements. Their attitude was inimical to the success of the capitalist system; their aim, not to improve advertising but to overthrow it. Few of them, it was said, knew first hand anything about business; seldom had they ever met a payroll. Bent on exploiting popular grievances, their tactics were opportunistic, sensational, and destructive of established values. Some of them were socialists, Communists, or fellow travelers. Some, employed in the federal government, were attempting to destroy advertising. They should be fought tooth and nail. A second type was observed to be the dedicated home-economics teachers and the intellectual career women. They tended to demand that advertising be impartial and factual. They cried for grade labeling and "thread counts," and they opposed emotional appeals and hyperbole in advertising. They claimed to represent consumers, but in fact they represented no one but themselves, and advertisers were scarcely obliged to heed them. Third were the moral fundamentalists. They considered most advertisements offensive and spiritually degrading. Opposed to the encouragement of materialism and social success, their standards were archaic and they had lost touch with the masses. All three types of critics were wrong, but only the last two could generally be ignored or placated with minor concessions. The first type, on the other hand, was a distinct danger to the advertising industry, indeed to society itself.[27]

The apparent ability to attribute a substantial part of one's difficulties to the presence of deliberate conspirators made it easier for an organization such as the AFA to propose a plan of action. The assumption that hostility to advertising reflected a subversive attitude toward American institutions had by now been accorded the status of a formal principle approved and adopted in June 1939 at the annual convention:

27. This characterization of the advertising industry's view of the articulate consumer derives from the writings and editorial comment of a multitude of individuals in the advertising industry. See, explicitly, *P.I.* (Aug. 18, 1939), p. 49.

Advertising is the mouthpiece of free enterprise in this country. . . . It is therefore naturally the target for all those who
prefer collectivism and regimentation by political force. It is
being attacked insidiously by radical elements both in and
out of our Government which are aiming, consciously or
otherwise, to subvert the present order and convert the American way into ways of alien and sinister origin.[28]

One month later, A. T. Falk, the research director of the AFA, distributed to all of the local affiliates of the Association a pamphlet
in which he urged that advertising clubs investigate their local
schools in order to uncover and eliminate textbooks or teaching
unfriendly to the advertising industry. What Falk explicitly had
in mind was a social science textbook by Harold J. Rugg in which
Rugg had noted that manufacturers tended to pass the cost of
selling goods on to the consumer, "thereby increasing the cost
both of selling and of buying goods. . . . Perhaps you may ask
then 'Is advertising necessary?' " A few pages later Rugg had an-
swered his own question: "It is impossible to carry on our economic life today without advertising. . . . We note the very
important role played by advertising in our lives. That we cannot
do without it is clear." [29] Falk, ignoring Rugg's answer to his own
question, attacked him as a "subversive" opponent of advertising,
and added: "His own mind is evidently made up. It seems he
wants the student to conclude that advertising is an economic
waste and perhaps ought to be abolished." If any advertising man
should discover that Rugg's book was being used in his schools,
Falk warned, "your local school board should be asked whether
they approve the teaching of this kind of stuff. If this book is not
used then see what books there are." [30] Falk's proposal did not by
itself produce any nationwide action, but it was partly responsible
for at least one statewide investigation of textbooks, and school
boards in some cities subsequently barred Rugg's book from circulation.[31] Falk's excited warnings, however, left most national

28. Reported in *P.I.* (June 29, 1939), p. 67.
29. Harold J. Rugg, *An Introduction to the Problems of American Culture*
(Boston, Ginn, 1931), pp. 455–76.
30. Quoted in Sorenson, pp. 160–1.
31. *E.P.* (Aug. 17, 1940), p. 8. The Arkansas Press Association in 1940 made a

advertising men unruffled. In 1941 the AFA again felt it necessary to call for a "counter-offensive against opponents of advertising" and again recommended local censorship of any textbooks or classroom teaching which presented "unfair and untrue descriptions of American business, industry, and advertising." [32]

Meanwhile, dramatic publicity from another quarter had temporarily refurbished the "conspiracy" theory of opposition. Coinciding with the patriotic vigilance of the AFA and following closely on the first hearings which the FTC had scheduled for its complaint against *Good Housekeeping* magazine, there was released to the press, on December 10, 1939, a report bearing the imprint of the Dies Special Congressional Committee on Un-American Activities. The report described in detail an alleged relationship between the consumer movement and the ideology of Communism. It was the particular work of J. B. Matthews, publicist, ex-official of Consumers' Research, ex-debunker of advertising, and self-styled "ex-fellow-traveler," who had broken with his Communist affiliations by 1936 and since 1938 had been assisting the Dies Committee as a Director of Research in its efforts to expose subversion in the United States. [33]

In his report, Matthews asserted that the Communist party had infiltrated and was controlling a number of consumer organizations and public school systems, that many leaders of the consumer movement were fellow-travelers or "dupes" of Communism, and that the Communist party had been given special orders

---

survey showing that textbooks in the state school system were unfriendly to advertising and that many teachers had subscribed to the Consumers' Union reports. Strong pressure was consequently brought to bear on school officials to have the textbooks "revised" (ibid.).

32. *A.S.* (Feb. 1941), p. 6. For evidence of the effect of Falk's proposals see *P.I.* (Apr. 12, 1940), p. 11; (May 10, 1940), p. 15. In 1942 the Pacific Advertising Clubs reported having raised over $30,000 for the purpose of halting the sale and distribution in local communities of thirty-six books considered "detrimental to the advancement of business." Examples included Stuart Chase, *The Economy of Abundance;* Robert and Helen Lynd, *Middletown* and *Middletown in Transition;* and Rugg's book (*Publishers' Weekly*, Feb. 14, 1942, p. 765).

33. N. Y. *Times* (Dec. 11, 1939), pp. 1, 14; *P.I.* (Dec. 15, 1939), p. 15. The report is missing from the official records and publications of the Congressional Committee (see below). I have depended on the lengthy excerpts quoted from it in the N. Y. *Times* and in *P.I.* On J. B. Matthews, see his *Odyssey of a Fellow Traveler*, pp. 257–60.

to foment a consumer rebellion against the American advertising industry. "Communists believe," wrote Matthews, "that to sabotage and destroy advertising, and through its destruction . . . the capitalist system of free enterprise, is a revolutionary tactic worthy of a great deal of attention." [34] Singled out as being particularly under the influence of Communist dogma on advertising was the Consumers' Union, its director, Arthur Kallet (whose writings, Matthews declared, followed the party line), and the Consumers' National Federation, whose "active" membership included Donald Montgomery, an official of the Department of Agriculture. Matthews concluded his report with a carefully worded insinuation whose point advertising men could scarcely have missed in 1939:

> The Committee is in possession of evidence which shows that a great part of the current popular and official attack upon advertising is the direct result of Communist propaganda in the field of consumer organizations. . . . This is borne out by the recent action of a Government official in the Department of Agriculture who undertook an investigation of national advertising in *Good Housekeeping*. . . . While there is no record of the findings of the investigation being used as a basis for action against the magazine, it may be assumed that such was the intention. This is evidenced by the close affiliation of the Government official in question with the heads of the Consumers' National Foundation and Consumers' Union. . . . The publications of these [organizations] make it clear that some of the current Government procedures against advertising and advertising media have been instigated and are being aided by those consumer organizations which are under the control of the Communists. [35]

Though it was evident that the Matthews Report would not win its author friends among some of his ex-associates in the consumer movement, the mixed reception which it drew from responsible periodicals and even from the advertising industry was considerably less enthusiastic than its author had probably any

34. *P.I.* (Dec. 15, 1939), p. 15.
35. Ibid.

reason to expect. To the surprise of no one, Richard Berlin, a vice-president of the Hearst Magazine Corporation, declared triumphantly that the report demonstrated clearly that the action of the FTC against *Good Housekeeping* was Communist inspired,[36] but most other commentators felt that the report had gone too far. The editor of *Printers' Ink*, in fact, denounced the whole episode as a witch hunt inspired by a few publishers and advertising men in defensive retaliation against the general pressures of the consumer movement and the specific investigation of *Good Housekeeping* by the FTC.[37]

The editor may have been right. Involved in the report were three notable peculiarities that almost instantly inspired a general skepticism of its motives. The first and least conspicuous was the evasive nature of its accusations, particularly with respect to the question of actual Communist party influence, and the deviousness with which it made clear a set of specific charges accompanied by virtually nothing that could reasonably be designated as supporting evidence. What began as a statement that the consumer movement was a front for Communists ended with a well-hedged insinuation that the federal case against *Good Housekeeping* was being conducted by subversives. Although the charges of "fellow traveling" which Matthews leveled against some individuals in the consumer movement were substantially correct, the basis for only a few of the charges was made apparent, while with respect to the principal and more general contention that the consumer movement was inspired largely by Communist ideology, the report simply inferred that such was the case from the well-established fact that the consumer movement and the Communist party shared a hostility to advertising.[38]

The second peculiarity of the report was the highly irregular circumstance of its release. Seemingly a Committee report, it had in fact been submitted to Chairman Martin Dies acting in the capacity of a one-man subcommittee at a "hearing" which included

36. Ibid.

37. *P.I.* (Dec. 24, 1939), p. 11. See also N. Y. *Times* (Dec. 16, 1939), pp. 16, 24; *Business Week* (Dec. 16, 1939), p. 17.

38. See above, p. 104, n. 29. Consumers' Research was excluded from censure in the Matthews report.

only Dies and Matthews. It was thereupon announced that it had been placed in the records of the full Committee, although some members of the Committee had not even known of its existence until its release to the press. Two members of the Committee vigorously protested its release, and the report was never made a part of the Committee record. No hearings on the findings of the report were ever held, none of the accused was ever called to testify in his own defense, and the annual report of the Dies Committee, published within a month of the release of the Matthews report, virtually denied its validity by failing to acknowledge that it had ever existed.[39] In short, one is compelled to infer that the report was intended largely to satisfy purposes of publicity which required that it appear to have received official endorsement when it had not and when to have received such endorsement would have fatally exposed it to the scrutiny of an official hearing.

The third and major peculiarity of the report was to be found in a suspicious array of circumstances which surrounded its origins. In the first place, testifying merely as a witness during the previous year, Matthews had already made public several hundred pages of personal recollection and opinion concerning the "popular front" activities of the Communist party. In the course of that testimony he had revealed essentially what he knew of the fellow-traveling connections of his ex-associates (particularly Kallet) in the consumer movement but had revealed it in such a manner as to make it fairly plain that within the context of the total activities of the "popular front" he did not attribute to the consumer movement critique of advertising anything like the importance, the danger, or the subtlety he was now, suddenly, one year later, to accuse it of possessing. While his testimony in 1938 concerning the role of Communism in the consumer movement scarcely mentioned advertising at all, his report of 1939, based essentially on the same set of facts, concerned itself with little

39. N. Y. *Times* (Dec. 11, 1939), p. 1; (Dec. 12, 1939), p. 22; U. S. Congress, *House Report* 1476 (76th Cong. 3d Sess.), Special Committee on Un-American Activities, *Annual Report* (Jan. 3, 1940), p. 9; *New Republic* (Jan. 13, 1940), p. 37; letter, Jerry Voorhis to author, Apr. 5, 1957. See also, Jerry Voorhis, *Confessions of a Congressman* (New York, Doubleday, 1948), pp. 211–13. Voorhis (Democrat, Calif.) was a member of the Dies Committee.

else.[40] In the second place, a fairly direct relationship appears to have existed between Matthews' suddenly renewed interest (with its altered emphasis on advertising) in the consumer movement, and the growing concern of advertisers and publishers over both the mounting criticism of advertising by the consumer movement and the invigorated policing of the FTC. This relationship hinged on the way in which much of the substance of the Matthews report had been disseminated and conceivably influenced in advance of its release in December 1939. As early as August, Richard Berlin, by way of replying to the announcement of the charges made by the FTC against his magazine, stated that he was even then in receipt of "information" that much of the criticism of advertising was Communist-inspired.[41] Two months later, in October, Stanley High, a free-lance journalist, had publicized what was to prove virtually the substance and conclusions of the forthcoming report in an article entitled "Guinea Pigs, Left March!" which appeared simultaneously in *Forum, Reader's Digest,* and a special pamphlet printed and circulated by *Good Housekeeping.*[42]

Thus not only the form and the conclusions of the report itself but the timing of its substance and the revelations of its contents in advance of official release (undertaken in a highly irregular manner) strongly suggested the characteristics of a "smear," an attempt to discredit or nullify the action of the FTC against the advertising practices of *Good Housekeeping* by the tactic of casting discredit on the consumer movement.[43] In condemning the re-

40. Cf. above, p. 104, n. 29; also, Matthews, *Odyssey.*

41. N. Y. *Times* (Aug. 21, 1939), p. 20.

42. *New Republic* (Jan. 1, 1940), pp. 10 ff. See *Reader's Digest* (Oct. 1939), and *Forum* (Oct. 1939) for High's article. It warned readers that Communists were perverting the consumer movement and were inducing school children to be skeptical of advertising. See also the N. Y. *Times* (Dec. 16, 1939), p. 24. A few weeks later, Dies informed reporters at a luncheon of grocery manufacturers which he was addressing that his Committee was about to make a search for Communist party influence in the consumer movement: *Business Week* (Nov. 11, 1939), p. 44; N. Y. *Times* (Dec. 17, 1939), p. E2.

43. A widely publicized assertion by Drew Pearson ("Washington Merry-Go-Round" for Dec. 22, 1939) that Matthews had discussed the report in advance of its release with certain interested individuals has been denied by those concerned. Letter, John A. Clements (Hearst Magazines) to author, Nov. 19, 1957.

port, neither advertising men nor liberal critics of the episode denied that some of Matthews' earlier testimony about certain individuals in the consumer movement was probably valid. What bothered them in part was that Matthews had pushed his new conclusions far beyond the reach of his evidence in implying that an attack on advertising ought normally to be regarded as a likely sign of Communism. In addition, some advertising men feared that the episode would serve only to intensify existing distrust of the advertising industry. Many recommended that henceforth the industry concern itself less with exposing consumer "subversion" and dedicate itself instead to publicity and advertising policies of a more constructive sort.[44]

On the subject of the consumer and the relations of the advertising industry to him, many voices from within had long urged moderation. A noted authority on the consumer movement observed, in 1942, that "consumers have discovered no defects in advertising that have not been widely discussed among advertisers." [45] Even before there could be said to have been a consumer movement, a small number of advertising men, generally a few agents, a few officials of advertising associations, and often the editors of advertising journals, could be numbered among the sharpest critics of advertising behavior. Their adverse comment, freighted with moral indignation, soon became standard fare at conventions and in the trade press. Admitting much that the critics of advertising had asserted, they left it uncertain whether, by confessing in public the weaknesses and transgressions of their own and their colleagues' behavior, they were merely seeking the absolution of a confessional for themselves and, vicariously, for their audience, or whether, convinced of their own honesty, they were angered and frightened lest the dishonesty of others be attributed to all. "Long ago," lamented an editorial in *Printers' Ink* in 1938, "the ardent followers of dishonest and misleading advertising demonstrated that they care not how much they are attacked so long as they get the dough." It was they who nullified

44. Revealed in virtually every issue of *P.I.* and *A.S.*, Jan.–Mar. 1940. See also the N. Y. *Times* (Dec. 16, 1939), p. 24, a statement by Paul S. Willis, president of the Associated Grocery Manufacturers.

45. Reid, p. 6.

the efforts of "the honest and decent reformers within the business to clean up advertising. . . . There are in the business many people who are exceedingly uncomfortable at the ballyhoo, bombast, and lying of their colleagues . . ." [46] Whatever the motives that led these critics to risk the opprobrium generally accorded Cassandras and Jeremiahs, they repeatedly admonished their hearers to save the advertising industry by putting an end to its irresponsibilities and by coming to terms with its opponents. Advertising men, suggested one industrialist succinctly in 1932, "should give [the consumer] credit for being something more than a sheep who can read." [47] Edward Greene of the National Better Business Bureau declared that the "responsibility of advertisers" was to help "make national advertising worthy of consumer confidence." [48] Throughout the fight over federal legislation the editors of both leading trade journals lashed out at those who would counter the consumer's demand for better advertising with merely larger doses of publicity and propaganda. "The consumer," said one editor, "has just entered the American business picture. If his first request is a demand for quality standards, that must be accepted as prima facie evidence of advertising's failure to fulfill its primary obligation—to tell facts about merchandise." [49] Still more explicit was the statement of Malcolm McNair of the Harvard Business School to the ANA in 1935: "The right to advertise imposes obligations—the obligation to reduce the cost of distribution, the obligation to improve advertising standards, the obligation to understand the social significance of advertising. . . . You are going to have to do some pretty fast thinking to protect your right to advertise. You can no longer take it for granted, you are going to have to justify it." [50]

46. P.I. (Nov. 3, 1938), p. 76.

47. W. H. Hodge, chairman, American Gas Association, quoted in P.I. (Oct. 10, 1932), p. 57.

48. P.I. (Mar. 29, 1934), p. 45.

49. A.S. (Feb. 1, 1934), p. 13. See also A.S. (July 16, 1936), p. 5; and P.I. (May 24, 1934), p. 25; (Jan. 3, 1935), p. 82; (Jan. 24, 1935), p. 48; (June 16, 1938), p. 65.

50. P.I. (Nov. 7, 1935), p. 21. Several others conveyed similar warnings in this period. See also John Benson, president of the AAAA, P.I. (June 10, 1937), p. 53.

Convinced that the advertiser ought to meet the consumer at least half way, the journals further sought to uncover for their readers exactly what the organized consumer wanted and to what extent his demands could be met. While the trade associations remained content merely to sponsor the appearance of an occasional consumer spokesman at their conventions, the editor of *Printers' Ink,* for example, attended conferences of consumers and reported at length on their proceedings, while other staff writers and outside authorities on the consumer movement analyzed its aims and assessed its power.[51] They urged advertisers to note that the "rank and file" of teachers and consumer educators were in no sense opposed to capitalism or to private enterprise as such and that businessmen tend to alienate them by assuming falsely that they were. Advertisers were reminded that their own failure to aid and contribute to a legitimate, impartial process of consumer education was in part responsible for inducing others— retailers, testing agencies, federal officials, even radicals—to befriend the consumer instead. Consumers, it was suggested, were not easily satisfied. Some sought facts on which to make reliable comparisons among products without actual purchase, others desired grade labeling and specification of standards for each product, and still others expected advertisements to furnish them with candid statements of the product's limitations, unretouched photographs of the product in use, and reliable reports of the results of impartial testing. These demands, in the opinion of those who reported them, were at times impractical, at times excessive, but they were nevertheless genuine and ought not to be dismissed out of hand.[52]

The earnest admonitions bore little fruit. Despite mounting evidence of what the consumer movement wanted advertising to be, almost no corresponding change in the character of adver-

51. For trade association see *P.I.* (May 31, 1934), p. 44; (Nov. 7, 1935), p. 74; *A.S.* (Dec. 1939), p. 2.

52. *P.I.* (May 13, 1937), p. 16; (Feb. 10, 1938), p. 11; (Feb. 17, 1938), p. 81; (Apr. 7, 1938), p. 21; (May 4, 1939), p. 62; (Feb. 23, 1940), p. 25; (Mar. 29, 1940), p. 13; (Apr. 12, 1940), p. 11; (May 10, 1940), p. 15. *A.S.* (Nov. 18, 1937), p. 29. See also Kenneth Dameron, "The Consumer Movement," *Harvard Business Review, 17* (1939), 271. See Borden, appendix, for a survey made of consumer attitudes toward advertising.

tising took place. Even those who, it may be presumed, had strong hopes of finding a change could detect none. In 1939 the National Better Business Bureau held what it called a joint Business-Consumer Relations Conference in Buffalo at which consumer and businessman alike concluded that few advertisers had made any notable effort to understand and respond to the needs of consumers to become more intelligent buyers; some businessmen, it was further concluded, still preferred to regard most consumer criticism of advertising as having been inspired by political subversives.[53] In 1940 *Printers' Ink* sent a questionnaire about the consumer movement to a large number of national advertisers and agents, of whom 172 responded. One of the questions read as follows: "Has your company developed any definite program in connection with the consumer movement?" The answers indicated that 39 definitely had not; an additional 105, by leaving the question unanswered, suggested strongly that they had not; 26 reported that they had merely increased their efforts at public relations, such as to provide publicity material for schools and consumer groups. In but two or three instances out of 172 had any effort been made to adopt a new advertising policy.[54] A more reliable investigation of the actual degree of response to demands for information in advertisements was undertaken in 1940 and 1941 by the Committee on Consumer Relations in Advertising, a special body sponsored by, and answerable to, the AAAA and a number of leading national media. The Committee made a survey of the national advertising which appeared in *McCall's, Ladies' Home Journal,* and *American Home* for 1939 and 1940; the advertisements were rated according to their informational content, the criterion being a list of items most often sought by consumer groups. The Committee reported that only one type of product (heavy appliances such as refrigerators and washing machines) was advertised with anything like the amount of relevant information or the degree of rationality which consumers were requesting. Rated lowest were cosmetic advertisements, a phenomenon which led the Committee to observe that the Wheeler-Lea Act had unwittingly led many copy writers for cosmetic firms deliberately

53. *P.I.* (June 8, 1939), p. 82.
54. *P.I.* (June 28, 1940), p. 15.

to avoid information and to seek refuge in ambiguities and inference. "Objective product information is the kind of information
consumers want (or *say* they want)," concluded the Committee,
"and it is chiefly this kind of information which magazine advertising fails to provide." [55]

Yet the plea to accommodate the consumer was not a barren
one. Businessmen were now less apt to assume that if they merely
fired a barrage of propaganda in the direction of the consumer
movement it would disintegrate, and for perhaps the first time
they made a serious attempt to discover what the consumer movement was after. They were as determined as ever to argue consumer leaders out of their tenacious convictions as to what advertising ought properly to be, and it was demonstrably true that
their advertisements, except to become more persuasive, had
changed scarcely at all, but concessions to the consumer's apparent interest in rational information were, in fact, taking place in
small but significant ways. Manufacturers could and did resort
more readily to studies of consumer preferences before embarking
on design and production, and if their advertisements remained
innocent of useful information, their products were more apt to
come padded with booklets of advice about their use and care and
occasionally with information of as technical a nature as the most
enthusiastic consumer expert could wish. Aid of this sort as a
rule did not begin to operate until the consumer had bought the
product, but as the numbers of middle-class consumers grew,
there gradually seeped through the society a body of specific information about products which was beginning to strengthen the
competence of individuals to judge products independently of
advertising appeals.

The advertising industry itself, in fact, had already made at
least two partial concessions to the consumer. One consisted of
the so-called Fact Booklets which the Better Business Bureaus
issued free of charge to consumers, offering them competent advice about consumer problems and information on a wide variety
of products. Though they were careful not to call into question

55. The report, entitled "Information in Advertising" was summarized by
Kenneth Dameron, director of the CCRA, in the *Harvard Business Review, 20*
(1942), 482 ff.

the fundamental adequacy of advertising, they often revealed information which advertisements could seldom be depended on to disclose; and because they were designed to instruct the public in what to look for when buying certain goods, consumer organizations regarded them with respect.[56]

The Committee on Consumer Relations in Advertising could be considered, in a roundabout fashion, as a second concession to the consumer movement, but the ultimate failure of this organization to transcend the rather standard functions of publicity and propaganda makes of it less a symbol of concession than a harbinger of resistance. Established as an agency to analyze consumer preferences toward advertising and to recommend to the industry policies for improving its relations with consumers, it soon published a small journal (the *Consumer News Digest*) of factual advice for consumers and explicitly promised to become a "two-way street," public relations jargon for the double task of talking both consumers and advertisers into making concessions to each other.[57] On this "two-way street," however, the traffic of advice to the advertiser soon dwindled, while the flow of publicity to the consumer grew in size and effectiveness, a development perhaps due less to the obligations which the Committee may have owed its sponsor than to the fact that the outbound lane was apparently producing results in the form of a less intractable consumer leadership, while the inbound lane was producing nothing at all in the way of changed advertisements. Before long the Committee was engaged in a full program of "education" which aimed to influence the image which consumers held of national advertising.[58] The journal deliberately wove publicity on behalf of advertising into its columns of factual advice even as the advice became the bait to attract consumer readers.[59] The Committee directed its weapons particularly at teachers on the explicit theory that it was important to train future generations to accept and support the pre-

56. Sorenson, p. 199.
57. Unpublished records of the CCRA in AAAA files; especially, "A Report on the C.C.R.A., Inc. Feb. 1, 1950," pp. 1–7. See also the *Consumer News Digest* (privately published by the CCRA) and its Consumer-Buyer Booklets. Also, for the origins of the CCRA, *P.I.* (Jan. 19, 1940), p. 81.
58. CCRA "Report," pp. 9–15, 70 ff.
59. Ibid., pp. 26–7.

vailing system of distribution and marketing. Scarcely less important in its own eyes were the Committee's efforts to persuade authors and publishers of textbooks to present modern advertising and marketing in a more favorable light and to explain more fully and persuasively the rationale of the competitive economic system and its immediate benefits to the consumer.[60]

By the time the Committee disbanded in 1950 it was able to point to an impressive record of consumer "relations." A dozen textbooks had used its publications, and a few had altered their judgments on marketing and advertising. The Committee had encouraged the outside publication of articles favorable to advertising and had succeeded in funneling material to the public through the editors of women's pages in newspapers. The relatively "low-pressure" salesmanship of the Committee's journal and its consumer booklets had enabled it to influence countless teachers, school boards, and colleges.[61] If the Committee had not succeeded in persuading businessmen to make advertisements more informative (and it had tried to do so), it had been notably successful in conveying to consumers the arguments that advertising was in practice more informative than consumers would admit, that advertising was under no necessity to become more informative if that information were made available elsewhere in the marketing system. The Committee denied that its mission was propagandistic either in nature or in intent and explicitly described its work as that of "educating" the public with objective facts about the national advertising industry.[62] Though the validity of this contention, like most arguments over words, will perhaps never be satisfactorily resolved, it is clear that the work of the Committee had educated consumers more effectively than it had educated the advertising industry. If for a moment in the recent history of American advertising the road between con-

60. Ibid., pp. 9–10; 57–8; 61 ff.

61. Ibid.; also pp. 26–7; 58–60; and "Exhibit F," Appendix. The Committee was terminated in part because the promotional work of other organizations such as the AFA had developed to a point which made the CCRA superfluous (letter from Richard L. Scheidker, Vice-President of the AAAA, to the author, Sept. 23, 1955).

62. Ibid., p. 8. For a survey which concluded that the Committee had influenced consumers see A.S. (Feb. 13, 1941), p. 150.

sumer and advertiser had been opened to permit a two-way flow of ideas, the traffic, nevertheless, remained as it had before— largely one way.

What may be said, then, of the response of the advertising industry to its challengers in the 1930's? It had attempted, quite naturally, to defend itself through its principal trade associations by political pressure, by argument, by a prodigious dedication to "public relations." A few extremists had proposed censorship and witch hunts. Their influence was difficult to assess, but there is no doubt that the bulk of their colleagues did not actively, at least, follow in their path. By the 1940's, most of the more thoughtful advertising men in the nation were willing to subscribe to a more moderate course of reasoning on the subject of the consumer movement and their relations to it. Their views were most ably and candidly expressed in an exhaustive study of advertising published in 1942 under the joint auspices of the Advertising Research Foundation (which drew its support from leading advertisers and agencies) and the Harvard Graduate School of Business Administration. Entitled *The Economic Effects of Advertising*, the project was directed and the study written by Neil Borden.[63] It combined an impressively impartial analysis of the subject with a judicious display of the principal attitudes of the national advertising industry which had become current by the close of the 1930's. The advertising industry, this study declared, must assume the existence of "a society in which consumers are free to determine their patterns of consumption and sellers are free to use influence . . . so long as ethical dictates are observed." [64] Consequently,

> In a free society consumers need to be equipped to look out for themselves and should be trained to be wary in their buying. . . . In certain product fields appeals which the advertisers use are so strong that they are particularly effective in attracting consumers who are not well informed regarding merchandising qualities. In short, the evidence indicates that there is need of consumer education regarding products be-

63. Borden, *Economic Effects of Advertising*.
64. Ibid., p. 643.

yond that attainable from the persuasive messages of advertisers.[65]

The study concluded that the best guarantee of security for the
consumer was that, rather than seek to regulate and restrict advertising or insist on changes in its practices, he seek instead to become a self-reliant, rational and intelligent buyer, dependent not
on the good graces of others but on his own sophistication.[66]

Thus in a scholarly study that was itself possibly the most sophisticated work of public relations that advertising men had
ever supported, the advertising industry was declared to be justified in its customary practice of holding the public to a sort of
nonlegal application of the principle of *caveat emptor* and in
attempting to dissuade the public from trying to upset this relationship. For many years the industry had undertaken programs
of publicity and propaganda to strengthen its position in the
economy and its relations with the public. The consumer was told
that what was best for the advertiser and the advertising industry
was best for him, and that the proposals of many who professed
to champion him were neither good for him nor good for the
advertiser. Meanwhile, advertising men had yielded little to the
consumer; their concern over the nature and scope of consumer
demands on advertising seemed more like the concern of a wary
combatant assessing his foe. It could be argued, of course, that
publicity had proven insufficient as a weapon to prevent federal
legislation from strengthening the position of the "wary buyer,"
nor had public relations prevented a few of the more articulate
consumer intellectuals from continuing to encourage rational
skepticism of advertising. But the setbacks in these engagements
were minor. Advertising men had meanwhile devised other weapons with which to resist the challenge to their power. The war was
by no means lost.

65. Ibid., p. 873.
66. Ibid., p. 875.

7

The Weapons of Persuasion

IN THE TWENTY YEARS which preceded the second World War the national advertising industry drew upon itself both sustained criticism and hostile action. It was accused of failure to evolve safeguards for the unwary and unsophisticated consumer, and so ineffective were its own efforts to curb the misrepresentations and deceptions which a few advertisers habitually practiced that private pressure groups soon attempted to do so through state and federal regulation. To this criticism and pressure advertising men responded in a number of ways. They tried to devise standards of internal regulation and to enforce those standards. They constructed propaganda to discourage their opponents, to dissuade the public from its criticism, and to create the impression that the advertising industry was acting with careful consideration for the consuming public. At times they merely ignored the criticism and resisted the pressure. But no matter what form their response to opposition took, advertising men were primarily concerned with strengthening their ability to influence the consumer in spite of himself, and during the second of the two interwar decades the remarkable advances in this ability comprised the principal achievement and the distinguishing characteristic of the national advertising industry. It was an advance which a general refinement and a sophistication in the techniques of advertising made possible and which, in turn, depended ultimately on a growing interest in the findings of psychological and marketing research and the techniques of journalism.

The significance of these developments for the influence of advertising in modern society was enormous. They enabled the industry to emerge from a period of opposition more impregnable than it had been in its entire history. The Federal Trade Commission, for example, could assert in 1940 that advertising copy was subject to more exacting requirements of responsible utterance than ever before; but copy writers were meanwhile perfecting techniques by which those claims, now prohibited from being made explicit, could be made implicit and thereby immune from official censure. Leaders of the consumer movement by 1940 were able to view with some satisfaction their efforts to educate their following to resist printed blandishments, to question claims, to discount hyperbole; but none of them was foolish enough to assert that the consumer movement had seriously impaired the operations or effectiveness of the national advertising agencies which specialized in increasingly refined and irresistible techniques of propaganda and which not infrequently hired professionally trained psychologists to advise them. Publishers of important newspapers and national magazines could maintain that by 1940 they were guarding their columns with great care lest discreditable advertisements or press agentry enter them; but it could also be maintained that by 1940 publishers had evolved habits of thought and patterns of journalism congenial and even similar to the paid messages of businessmen: not only did each borrow techniques from the other, but each found it commercially expedient to encourage a climate of opinion favorable to the acceptance of the other's message, and this was generally done without benefit of conspiracy. Advertising men themselves occasionally deprecated the notion that they could ever mislead the public —or even want to mislead it—against its own best interests; but by 1940 they were also proclaiming their business to be a proven tool for the mass communication of ideas, and they had, in fact, helped to make techniques of mass persuasion readily available to anyone desirous of influencing public opinion and wealthy enough to pay for it. In short, developments in the scope and techniques of advertising enabled the industry to resist the challenge which public and private interest groups offered it and provided reason to hope that it could allay future challenge by its greater resources for inducing public consent.

Nothing in the development of American advertising since 1930 has exceeded in importance the enthusiasm which advertising men have come to exhibit toward psychological research. During the Depression the industry began to encourage occasional systematic investigations of the techniques of persuasion and the psychological principles which underlay them, and as a consequence, advertising promised to become a reasonably precise and effective instrument. Historically, most advertising research had been empirical and haphazard; advertisers preferred to eschew principles in favor of a single pragmatic measure: which appeals had in fact most effectively increased sales? Sales could generally be determined with some assurance and objectivity, but to establish a connection between sale and appeal in order to derive from the connection a general rule applicable to other cases were tasks which advertising men had tended to solve largely by the guesswork hunches which they sometimes spoke of as common sense or "intuition." Their decisions were as likely as not the result of a process of thought inscrutable to an outsider and seldom capable of generalization. Past habit or tradition, the chance specialties of one's copy writers, an overly rational tendency to assume that most of one's readers resembled oneself, a well-developed sensitivity to the technical demands of the law: these and a score of other influences were apt to make any choice of appeals so unpredictable as to suggest, perhaps, that "intuition," for lack of a more exact word, was as valid a description as any to apply to the process by which advertisements were produced. It was not until the

1920's that agencies and publishers occasionally made studies of "market" conditions to seek data on the numbers of potential customers for a product, where they might be found, and how much money they would be likely to spend. Still more time was to elapse before advertisers were willing to make serious efforts to discover habits of readership and to determine the relative effectiveness of various advertising appeals. This latter preoccupation became known as "copy testing," and it rapidly absorbed most of the energy and attention of advertising research staffs.

The application of formal psychological research to advertising became widespread only with the Depression. It is unclear whether the Depression contributed to it or whether it was due solely to the increasing reputation and effectiveness of psychological studies. It is not unlikely that when the deepening economic paralysis heightened the concern of advertisers over the question of why people buy and the problem of how to make them buy, advertisers found the operations of applied psychology increasingly useful and attractive. At the same time the investigations of applied psychologists themselves, whether deliberately or not, tended to reflect a growing preoccupation with the problems of advertising and persuasion. By 1940 the advertising industry had become one of the most important paying customers for applied psychological research and was an ever likely field for the employment of psychologists with advanced degrees. The industry, indeed, had come a long way from the early 1920's, when its interest in psychology of any sort had been meager and its attitude toward the theoretical investigations of academic psychologists indifferent or skeptical. The example which the J. Walter Thompson agency set in 1920 when it acquired the full-time services of John B. Watson, ex-university professor and pioneer "behaviorist," was rare enough to have become celebrated, but in the following two decades many other large agencies were to employ trained researchers to supplement their extensive use of independent research agencies and the psychology departments of a few universities.[1]

1. For general observations on the relations between psychology and advertising in the 1920's and 1930's see H. E. Burtt, *The Psychology of Advertising*, Boston, Houghton, Mifflin, 1938; M. P. McNair and H. T. Lewis, eds., *Business and*

The influence of psychology on the advertising industry was almost limitless in scope, and without doubt much of it defies precise analysis, but one influence in particular is significant enough for the question of responsibility in advertising as to warrant mention at this point. That was the contribution which some psychologists could never refrain from making to the question of the relationship of factual accuracy to persuasiveness in ad-

---

Modern Society, Cambridge, Harvard University Press, 1938; Hower, History of an Advertising Agency; Borden, Economic Effects of Advertising; and Printers' Ink: Fifty Years. I am particularly indebted to a private conversation on the subject with Warren Rebell, Research Director, Calkins and Holden advertising agency, and to an unpublished report by John Burnham of Stanford University of an interview with John B. Watson, July 23, 1955. It was Watson's recollection that until the 1940's advertising agencies and their clients remained singularly impervious to the suggestions of psychologists and tended to restrict their influence on the production of advertisements. For a recent account of Watson and his own influence see Lucille C. Birnbaum, "Behaviorism in the 1920's," American Quarterly (Spring 1955), pp. 15–30.

The interest of advertising men in psychology did not develop without some earnest and extensive proselytizing on the part of independent organizations of psychologists. A large part of the public record of such a group as the Psychological Corporation, for example, was a continuous effort to persuade advertisers and other businessmen to buy its research. See the Journal of Applied Psychology, 6 (1922), 213; 23 (1939), 310; 24 (1940), 109; 25 (1941), 213; and, particularly, the "apologia" by Paul S. Achilles, director of the Psychological Corporation, to the effect that "the Corporation frankly endeavors to furnish business firms, big and little, with evidence that the services of psychologists are of economic value": Psychological Bulletin, 35 (1938), 548.

The Psychological Corporation, it is true, admitted frankly that it was a commercial company bent on making a profit for its stockholders, who were professional psychologists, and that it considered applied psychology of greater importance than theoretical psychology; yet it is ironical that although some psychologists thus felt they had to argue advertisers into exploiting psychological research, it is almost certain that the advertising industry profited far more from this burgeoning relationship than did the science of psychology itself. It has been convincingly argued, in fact, that the applied psychological research which the advertising industry inspired or bought contributed little or nothing to the advancement of psychology as a science or to any fundamental knowledge of human behavior. A pungent and lucid critique by a social psychologist on the professional implications and conduct of Link, Achilles, and their corporation of psychologists is to be found in Leonard W. Doob, "An 'Experimental' Study of the Psychological Corporation," Psychological Bulletin, 35 (1938), 220 ff.

It must be pointed out that since 1940 the advertising industry has become sufficiently concerned over its failure to plan for general research in psychology that it has established the Advertising Research Foundation, a nonprofit institution to administer research of a general nature of interest to the industry as a whole.

vertising. An elementary principle of persuasion in advertising was to convince the consumer that the product would satisfy his needs. Once an advertiser had determined what the consumer needed, or thought he needed, and had discovered the most effective appeal to use on him, the advertiser tended to view his principal task as that of establishing a plausible connection between the appeal and the product. The requirement of plausibility has always stood as a forceful check on the more far-ranging imaginations and unscrupulous spirits among advertisers, but this requirement itself has varied according to the product offered and the type of need for which it is likely to be sold. A man seeking relief from pain, a cure for "bad breath," or freedom from some intangible and emotional frustration is apt to accept as plausible a great many assertions about aspirin, Listerine, and Camel cigarettes which would strike a man in search of a hammer or a garden rake as ridiculous. In any case, the criterion was not the accuracy of a claim but its plausibility. For a few products, a claim, to be plausible, had to be accurate; for many others, it did not, though it usually has had to appear so.

In his endless search for more persuasive appeals, then, the advertising man was urged, and indeed himself found it occasionally necessary, to forego one of the more significant, yet unhonored, theories of his "profession," the theory that the persuasiveness of an appeal was proportional to its truthfulness. The rhetoric of the industry was well-stocked with such observations as "truth will out," "in the long run only honesty pays," and the earnest warning that no customer can be permanently fooled. Advertising practices, however, tended to be derived from the rough observations of experience, and experience, though often deceptive and unreliable as a guide to effective advertising, was likely to suggest that at times truth was not only unrelated to persuasiveness but incompatible with it. Faced with such a set of alternatives, the practical responsibility of the advertising man seemed only too clear: "truth" could be, and perhaps ought to be, occasionally dispensed with, but persuasiveness could not. The advertising man would, of course, prefer to find an appeal which possessed both qualities. Finding, for example, that the assertion, "Campbell's Consomme is made from nourishing beef and is good for children," however truthful, lacked persuasiveness in sweltering summer months, he would be more than satisfied to be able to substitute for it an appeal that was both accurate and more likely to sell soup, such as the assertion, "Campbell's Chilled Consomme is cool in hot weather." Decisions of this caliber have probably been more common in the recent history of advertising than its critics have supposed. The history of advertising, however, is also studded with decisions based on the rather different principle that the discovery of an appeal which seemed certain to sell a product automatically made irrelevant the question of its truthfulness. Thus, a generation ago, an organization of metal bed frame manufacturers, having conducted an investigation (which it characterized as an "exhaustive inquiry") to determine the most effective advertising appeal for their product, discovered it to lie in the assertion that metal frames were more sanitary than wooden frames. Without pausing to consider whether the appeal was valid, the organization employed it in their advertising, and *Printers' Ink* reported their action as a commendable example of the use of consumer research to determine an appeal.[2] The manufacturers of a leading mineral oil, disappointed in the results of advertising which stressed the benefits of the oil to one's health, learned from a study of consumer attitudes that sales of the oil would in all probability rise if it were advertised as being capable of endowing men and women with "strength," "vitality," and a "clear head." Though these claims were invalid, the manufacturers used them and achieved satisfactory results.[3] In similar fashion the makers of a prominent yeast found that sales for their product increased when they changed its dominant appeal from a reasonable promise of vitamin content to the more blatant assertion that yeast eliminated "intestinal fatigue."[4] The practice in each instance was for the advertising industry a popular and uncomplicated one: having found out what consumers would like to think the product could do for them, one had only to persuade them, within the limits of plausibility and without reference to the facts, that the product could indeed do it.

2. *P.I.* (Feb. 21, 1918), p. 38.
3. *P.I.* (July 14, 1921), p. 101.
4. *P.I.* (Nov. 19, 1931), p. 104.

Advertising men in all probability were perfectly capable of constructing this principle by themselves, but had they not done so there existed psychologists who almost certainly would have persuaded them to adopt it and who in fact did urge it as a most satisfactory and profitable theory on which to base advertising behavior. The most prominent psychologist of this sort was Henry C. Link of the Psychological Corporation who was ever ready with suggestions for more effective advertising. An applied psychologist, who in 1932 developed an improved method to measure the effect of brand-name advertising on consumers, Link repeatedly cited his own findings to demonstrate that the most successful advertising was the sort which associated an immediate fulfillment of a need felt in the reader's mind with the product advertised.[5] Link explicitly disclaimed any wish to judge an advertising appeal on its veracity; in fact he made it clear that as a psychologist he felt that he had no business to allow questions of veracity to affect his recommendations: psychology, he insisted, was merely "the science of measuring behavior in order that it may be more effectively dealt with." [6] His disclaimer was needless, for the examples of advertising appeal which he particularly commended as fulfilling his requirements for effective advertising happened to be questionable or misleading: the assertion that Lux soap "stopped runs" in silk stockings he found, on investigation, was widely successful at a time when the quality of silk stockings was poor, while the assertion that Ipana toothpaste reduced "bleeding gums" he discovered was commendably effective because many people's gums bled "habitually," and the claim was thus likely to find a ready reception.[7] Truthfulness and "sincerity," advised Link at another time while addressing a gathering of advertising men, were in any case merely intellectual concepts and should not be permitted to hinder the work of an advertisement; it was his opinion that when people responded more effectively to the "calliope, the circus, the brass band" than to the presentation of intellectual argument, an advertiser would

5. Henry C. Link, article in *P.I.* (Jan. 26, 1933), p. 76; article in *Journal of Applied Psychology, 18* (1934), 1. See also his *New Psychology of Selling and Advertising*, New York, Macmillan, 1932.

6. *P.I.* (Jan. 26, 1933), p. 76.

7. Ibid.

be foolish indeed to impose an artificial handicap, in the form of a fetish for truth, on his own actions.[8] Link's recommendations, in short, coincided with the most articulate sentiments in the national advertising business. Successful advertising did not require the quality of factualness, reason, or logic but the quality of "credibility." One assertion scrupulously and literally truthful might fail to convince readers of its truth, while another might sound credible or plausible and be a tissue of lies.[9] Plainly the dilemma of attempting to be both honest and an advertiser was, it appeared, not unlike the dilemma which struck Mark Twain when he once observed that truth was stranger than fiction because "Fiction is obliged to stick to possibilities; truth isn't." [10]

Yet credibility itself was observed to depend on a rational process of the intellect, and by 1940 a major goal of those who feared the possibility of increasing public skepticism was to develop advertising to the point where, according to advertising theorists, it could circumvent conscious reasoning processes by seizing hold directly on the reader's emotions. To arouse one's reason or to stimulate one's intellectual comprehension of the appeal was to risk the possibility of resistance to it and resentment of it. The chief problem of the copy writer, then, was to avoid arousing the consumer's mind; he should strive for an immediate emotional impact, the presentation of a stimulus which might be apprehended without reflection.[11] As one prominent agency executive put it, copy writers would do well to take as their model the French novelist de Maupassant, whose concern for the reader's

8. *P.I.* (June 21, 1934), p. 48.

9. The issue of credibility gained particular prominence by 1941. See *A.S.* (Aug. 1941), p. 13; (Sept. 1941), p. 12. Most writers on the psychology of advertising from 1920 to the present have considered the distinction between truth and credibility of the utmost significance. For a recent view see Melvin Hattwick, *How to Use Psychology for Better Advertising* (New York, Prentice-Hall, 1950), pp. 337–49.

10. From "Pudd'nhead Wilson's New Calendar," in *Following the Equator.*

11. *P.I.* (Jan. 31, 1935), p. 65; (Oct. 29, 1936), p. 63; (Nov. 5, 1936), p. 94; (Apr. 7, 1938), p. 11. These references reveal that the current agitation for federal copy regulation made the matter seem urgent to advertising men. Dr. Louis Bisch, a psychiatrist, volunteered the opinion to a *P.I.* editor in 1938 that advertising which was based on fundamental emotional drives was less apt to irritate the average reader, who resented hypocrisy and trickery: *P.I.* (Jan. 6, 1938), p. 11.

mind, he said, was "secondary." "Primarily he aimed at the emotions. His only appeal to intellect was to *lull its suspicions and
thereby establish veracity.*" [12] Still more explicit and to the point
was the conviction voiced by a number of advertisers at a convention of the ANA in 1941 that advertisers should not worry
about credibility but instead develop psychological techniques
of persuasion so emotionally powerful and subtle that they could
induce a determined opponent of advertising to buy the product
even if he disbelieved the claims advertised for it.[13]

In the development of so-called "reason-why" advertising, one
is afforded a striking illustration of the way in which this theory of
persuasion came gradually to affect advertising practice in the
1930's. Intended to appear as a rational approach to the consumer, "reason-why" copy was in truth only a moderate pre-
cursor of later and more pronounced practices of emotional persuasion. The publicity which the consumer movement shed on
advertising, together with the greater caution which the Depression encouraged consumers to exercise when buying had forced
advertising men to alter some of their tactics. Critics of the industry, assailing advertisements for a disregard of facts and for
exploiting public ignorance were urging ordinary buyers to seek
factual statements and to ignore emotional hyperbole. Under such
pressure, advertising men preserved their principles by shifting
their method of attack. If readers were to be led to seek "factual"
copy and rational arguments, it was easy enough to bathe the
nonrational appeals in a fresh glow of scientific objectivity and
technological rhetoric. Occasionally this technique was pushed no
farther than the use of a standard cast of determined, lean-jawed
scientists in laboratory smocks, peering into microscopes, holding
test tubes, or waving at the reader a set of dentist's probes. Serving
a similarly decorative purpose were the hair-splitting statistic
(Listerine reduces germs "up to 96.7%"), the smell of the chemis-

12. Mark O'Dea, in *P.I.* (Sept. 17, 1936), p. 44 (italics mine). O'Dea's views,
of which this is representative, assume some importance from the fact that, having
been invited to contribute a weekly column to *P.I.* from Sept. 1936 to Sept. 1937,
he was soon hailed by a large number of readers (writing to the journal) as the
most sensible, intelligent, and capable commentator on advertising to have appeared in a long time; reprints of his articles were in demand.

13. *A.S.* (Dec. 1941), p. 108.

try table (Listerine toothpaste is "charged with Luster-Foam detergent $C_{14}H_{27}O_5SNa$ . . ."; Old Golds, tested in an "Oxygen Bomb Calorimeter," produced "less B.T.U.'s"), and a host of other devices to flag the reader's attention and establish simultaneously an impression of deliberate, prosaic veracity.[14] More significant in appearing to narrow the gap between plausibility and accuracy was the practice of offering the general reader a needlessly technical, though correct, description of a complex product which few were likely to purchase until they had satisfied themselves that they had scrutinized it with sober reason and informed judgment. (Victor radios possess a "super-efficient Super-Heterodyne circuit," a "continuous band-pass variable tone control," "impregnated condensers," a "pentode tube with push-pull amplification.") [15]

Advertising of this sort became celebrated within the industry and soon took on the proportions of a fad; those who favored it tended to see in it both a concession and a foil to the consumer movement. The rationality in "reason-why" copy was, of course, no greater than the rationality in any other type of copy; it was merely made to seem so. Few were as frank in describing this technique as was a *Printers' Ink* staff writer in 1925, but the attitude which underlay his defense was even then unremarkable and would soon become commonplace. Advertisements which employed the technical and difficult language of engineering and science, he declared, were suitable even for the uneducated readers who would not understand them, for they compelled attention, left an impression of efficiency and competence, and flattered readers by pretending to assume that readers were intelligent and discriminating.[16] Yet the uses of "reason-why" copy were limited. Advertising men had long believed that to gain for a product the consumer's intellectual acceptance was a more difficult and less rewarding task than to gain his emotional ac-

14. On the subject of the B.T.U. claim for Old Golds see *P.I.* (July 28, 1932), p. 10, which exposes it as pseudoscience.
15. *P.I.* (Sept. 1, 1932), p. 17.
16. *P.I.* (June 11, 1925), p. 41. See also *P.I.* (Mar. 24, 1927), p. 127; (Jan. 15, 1931), p. 3; (Feb. 12, 1931), p. 17; (Feb. 26, 1931), p. 25; (Mar. 19, 1931), p. 3; (July 9, 1931), p. 12; (Aug. 20, 1931), p. 3; (Nov. 24, 1932), p. 68; (Apr. 27, 1933), p. 32.

ceptance, and psychologists, it has been shown, could offer advertisers the satisfaction of feeling that this belief was a valid one.

The forces which contributed to the decline of "reason-why" copy can clearly be seen in the advertising for the automobile industry toward the end of the 1930's. During the Depression the intangible, emotional appeals of the previous decade had given way to an equally irrational enthusiasm for the prosy recital of facts. Advertisements for Plymouth cars, and to a lesser extent for Fords, Packards, and Buicks, attempted to engulf the reader in a massive profusion of technical jargon, statistics, and diagrams to describe transmission, engine, chassis, wheelbase, and horsepower. Those who had developed this technique were soon classified as belonging to the "nuts and bolts" school of appeal; the technique derived its popularity from the fact that, in pretending to reveal more than it actually did, it was deliberately aimed at those lower-class readers whose literary tastes had been fashioned by tabloid newspapers, who were coming to dominate the market for low priced cars, who preferred to exercise great care in buying, and who were presumed to be easily impressed with "factual" information. Formal and detailed investigation of the motives which impelled consumers to prefer one make of car to another, however, eventually convinced the leading proponents of the "nuts and bolts" school that a more intangible and emotional appeal would prove more successful. Modification of the "nuts and bolts" approach was made still more likely by an extensive federal investigation of the automobile industry, in the course of which the FTC had ruled against a number of pseudoscientific claims of the "nuts and bolts" sort which, being specific and tangible, were often open to objective verification.[17] By 1940 the leading automobile companies had replaced reason-why copy with cautious and cloudly generalities which consciously exploited humor, entertainment, romance, "pride of ownership," the fun and prestige of driving, and the smartness of new models. (Beneath a photograph of a young couple gazing at a gleaming Ply-

17. A.S. (Apr. 1940), p. 22; (May 1940), p. 64. As a result of its labor troubles in 1937, the automobile industry was also in that year more than ordinarily sensitive to the impact of its advertising.

mouth was the explanation: "We stood there all excited . . .") [18]
Advertising of this sort was hardly likely to arouse the attention
of a federal investigator or the probing criticism of a Consumers'
Union report. Consumers, as one advertising man shrewdly observed, could easily "debunk" a health claim for a chocolate cake
mix, but a glowing four-color reproduction of such a cake was
practically invulnerable to assault.[19]

In support of the conviction that the intellectually reasonable
form of appeal could become more of a liability than an asset
were to be found some well-articulated assumptions about the
average consumer. Derived in part from the supposed findings
of "intelligence" tests and the statements of psychologists in the
years following the first World War, they soon gained great vogue
in the advertising industry, where such views were likely to flourish even without the apparent support of science. Because two
thirds of the American people possess no more than the intelligence of a seventh grade child, reported a Columbia University
psychologist to a gathering of advertising men in 1920, advertisements ought to be kept simple, primitive, and emotional.[20]
Within a few years this conception had become almost a cliché
among advertising experts. The average consumer—echoed William L. Day, an executive of the J. Walter Thompson agency—is
a "fourteen-year-old human animal" who displayed in his daily
actions "inexplicable whims," a "careless, uncomprehending men-
tality," and "crude and often false standards of measurement." [21]
Such an animal was consequently to be influenced only "through
his senses and appetites"; he was no "earth-bound angel to be
reached through his feeble intellect." [22] "The mass mind," declared another speaker by way of reassuring a convention of advertisers in 1925, is "thoroughly incapable of nice distinctions
in anything approaching a technical problem, and always acting

18. A.S. (July 1940), p. 54; (Apr. 1940), p. 22; (May, 1940), p. 64.
19. P.I. (Aug. 2, 1940), p. 13.
20. A. I. Gates, reported in A.S. (June 19, 1920), p. 3.
21. P.I. (Apr. 21, 1932), p. 71. William L. Day was primarily responsible for
the advertising of Fleischmann's Yeast and Pond's Creams.
22. Day, in an address at the annual convention of the AAAA in 1936: A.S.
(May 7, 1936), p. 33.

upon impressions and impulse rather than upon facts and logic." [23]
Self-evident "truths" of this type held important implications for
the operations of the advertising man as well as for the theories
he espoused. Because the public did not care to know about
"every nut and bolt in a car engine," but preferred to be "sold"
on "intangibles," the copy writer did not need to know all about
the car engine either. It followed, in fact, that the copy writer
could know so much that he might become, like an intelligent
man in a scholastic debate, debilitatingly convinced of the soundness of his opponent's arguments. "The more you know," warned
one seasoned commentator, "the more you know you don't
know. *And a copy writer's job is to create* confidence in a product. . . ." [24] Finally, it was often asserted that the small group
of intelligent people who insisted on buying according to reason
and information should in no sense be confused with the "public,"
who bought only by whim and on emotional impulse, who wanted
in their advertising not facts but "entertainment," a magic world
of dreams, an escape: copy writers should therefore forget about
being informative and try instead to be entertaining. [25]

If one assumed that most consumers were incapable of making
rational decisions and that readers did not need to believe advertisements in order to be influenced by them, it was not hard,
in fact, to think that advertisements ought to be constructed according to principles of entertainment and fiction. It was in all
probability more accurate and certainly more reassuring to attribute an apparent public indifference toward advertising appeals not so much to consumer disbelief or to ethical revulsion
as to sheer boredom. The jaded appetites of a generation of
tabloid readers, movie goers, and radio listeners, it was suggested,
could scarcely be aroused by anything less than the sort of nourishment which had become the stock offering of the mass media;
by 1930 nothing about copy writing was more widely recognized
than that advertisements had to compete with their own media

23. *P.I.* (June 18, 1925), p. 117.
24. *P.I.* (Jan. 10, 1935), p. 33 (italics mine).
25. For example, Gilbert Hodges, of the executive board of the New York *Sun*,
to a convention of the American Home Economics Association: *P.I.* (July 5,
1934), p. 60.

for the reader's attention. Advertising men had already begun to urge each other to develop hard-hitting appeals of unfailing human interest and to utilize humor, stories, bizarre puzzles, recipes, celebrities, and even straight news to attract the reader's eye, hold his curiosity, and lead him to look for similarly rewarding diversions in subsequent advertisements for the same product.[26] Successful examples of commercial entertainment were already numerous: advertisements for Old Gold cigarettes featured the work of Claire Briggs, a celebrated cartoonist; Eveready batteries were depicted in a series of purportedly "real-life" stories, grim and startling in circumstance, as having enabled those who depended on the batteries to escape imminent danger; and the Swift Packing Company presented timely features of journalistic interest, such as the return of Commander McMillan from the Arctic. Within another decade the pace had increased. Advertisements for Hudson cars were featuring tales of "how I escaped alive," the Coffee Association and American Airlines attempted to fix their "sales points" in readers' minds by presenting them in the form of true-false quizzes, and Spud cigarettes (as did countless other products) exploited a powerful and carefully cultivated public interest in stage and screen "stars" by offering the face of Bert Lahr in a pantomine sequence that testified eloquently to the pleasure he derived from smoking. In such manner it was thought that a reader, having been induced to read advertisements for their own sake, could not help being affected by exposure to the commercial message which surrounded or was woven implicitly into the entertainment which had initially attracted his interest.

Among the important national advertisers in the 1930's no one exploited this theory of commercial entertainment more consistently or conspicuously than the Reynolds Tobacco Company in advertisements for Camel cigarettes. Its initial foray into commercial entertainment was a series of advertisements which dis-

26. *P.I.* (Apr. 6, 1922), p. 94; (Apr. 13, 1922), p. 18; (Aug. 21, 1924), p. 79; (Oct. 30, 1924), p. 87. In a number of articles, it was urged that newspaper reporters and feature editors would make admirable copy writers.

Similar evidence for the 1930's may be found in *P.I.* (May 14, 1936), p. 76; (Dec. 9, 1937), p. 89; (July 28, 1939), p. 13.

played the performances and tricks of professional magicians. Explanations of well-known tricks easily caught and sustained the reader's attention; only at the bottom of the page did there appear a reference to Camels, usually with the message that there were no tricks or sleight-of-hand deceptions in claims for Camel cigarettes. The Reynolds Company followed this series with a second which continued five years and featured a tireless number of authentic sportsmen and athletes, each of whom performed for the reader in a strip of four-color panels underscored with captions, and each of whom concluded by recommending Camels as a way to "get a lift," renew one's vitality, and steady one's nerves. Bush pilots flew the mails through lightning-stabbed sky ("it takes healthier nerves to fly the mail"); champion ski-jumpers and speed skaters broke records against tough odds, but were able to face the reader in the final panel and testify that a Camel "seemed" to restore their energy; helmeted auto racers, high diving stunt artists, deep-sea fishermen, big-game hunters, circus performers, polo players and screen stars alike skirted danger or courted death from unexpected mishaps before coming to rest, Camel in hand.

The steady, unvarying formula of Reynolds advertisements provided millions of newspaper and magazine readers with a number of important ingredients for accepted journalistic entertainment: the actions of athletic celebrities, the sporting thrill, the simple sequence of a "comic strip" (dilemma, disaster, escape), the opportunity to experience vicariously the deliberate risk of danger for its own sake or for the sake of the "game," and a commercial message hidden enough to avoid intruding on the entertainment until the very end, but then direct enough to be clear to the dullest-witted reader. Even clearer to advertising men was an upward trend in the sales of Camel cigarettes from 1933 to 1939. During the previous five years Camel sales had run second to Lucky Strikes; in that period Lucky Strike advertising had featured testimonials, dramatic incidents vigorously illustrated by prominent artists, and other varieties of entertainment, while Camels had been advertised with conservative caution and with no memorable claims. Beginning in 1933, however, with Camel's magic tricks, the advertising techniques for the two cigarettes were reversed, and Camels thereupon forged ahead of Lucky Strikes and stayed ahead until the war. Surveys also reported that of all cigarette advertising, that for Camels drew the highest and most consistent readership.[27] Nor did advertisers overlook the fact that Camel advertising depended on the testimonial without essentially seeming to; it was more difficult, after experiencing entertainment, to nourish serious doubts of the authenticity of these testimonials, than it had been, for example, upon reading of Lady Grace Drummond Hay and the Graf Zeppelin.[28]

The use of entertainment was often expected to fulfill a wider function. Advertisers occasionally found it necessary, before they could hope to convey a sales message, to disarm the reader of particular suspicions and prejudices concerning the product or even the company. If the reader could be made to smile or laugh, or if he could be induced to read copy which entertained him and thus to avoid the controversial issues which might have given rise to his suspicions, he was considered a more likely target for successful persuasion. In its broadest sense this use of entertainment could be considered public relations advertising; it was presumably hoped, for example, that the warm glow of appreciation which readers experienced when reading of the adventures of "Elsie the Cow" would spill over to include the Borden Milk Company for whom Elsie worked.

Few readers were likely to bring any deep-seated suspicions to their perusal of advertisements for milk; but it was otherwise with liquor. No industry found itself in the 1930's with as delicate a "problem" of public relations as did the liquor industry, and no industry was more careful to evolve a deliberate code of advertising appeals based on entertaining and disarming euphemism and on an almost complete absence of direct claims. Not only did the liquor industry openly announce a self-imposed body of copy rules, such as, for example, those which prohibited the appearance of women and children in liquor advertisements and discouraged direct references to the pleasurable effects of drinking; it generally, though grudgingly, obeyed these rules as em-

27. A.S. (Dec. 1938), p. 36.
28. See above, p. 62.

bodied in the decisions of a special federal regulatory body. The potency of liquor now hid behind such verbal ambiguities as "smooth," "velvety," "mellow," "rich," "light," "full-bodied," while the pictorial content of its advertising was apt to consist of almost anything except matters relating to the product or its use. Scenes of American history (Cumberland Gap, Mount Vernon), regional iconography (horses, sleigh, snow, an old Vermonter, a Blue-Grass racing stable), and stereotypes of social classes (men gathered in the Hunt Club, the Country Club, the Trophy Room) alternated with artistically impressive four-color photographs of horses, dogs, roses, gold tea services, crystal glassware, or panoramas of sport and adventure in far-off places (a Swiss chalet where competent-looking skiers relaxed with glasses of Canadian Club). Even where illustrations were used to convey a message unacceptable when expressed in words, they were made as disarmingly pleasant and inoffensive as possible (beer was often pictured as an "appetizing" and thirst-quenching food suitable for picnics, parties, and home entertainment, and as a drink for active sportsmen in a wholesome outdoor life). In a few instances the central problem of liquor was offset in the advertisement by self-conscious, deprecatory slogans of public service ("Have a head for quality, not from quantity." "Don't run away with it and it won't run away with you." "We who make whiskey say drinking and driving do not mix.") By 1937 the three biggest liquor firms (Seagram's, Schenley's, and National) had arrived among the eleven biggest national advertisers, but none of these firms, nor the industry as a whole, could forget how short a time they had been allowed to advertise or how powerful remained the opposition to their product. In offering entertainment and technically innocuous appeals, the liquor industry hoped to pacify its opponents, or at least distract their attention, while winning for its wares the customers who could be expected to respond not only to the entertainment but to the messages hidden within it.[29]

29. References to liquor advertising were derived from a survey of such advertisements found in twenty issues of *Time Magazine*, 1934 and 1937, and ten issues of the New Haven (Conn.) *Register*, 1937 and 1938. See also *P.I.* (Sept. 20,

One of the most spectacular and disarming techniques of entertainment which advertisers adopted from the mass media was the general form of "continuity" strip, whether the images were cartoons, comics, photographs, sketches, or some other visual device. The sudden popularity of the "continuity" sequence in the early 1930's was due partly to a study of newspaper reading habits which George Gallup conducted in 1931. Gallup had concluded from his study that 70 per cent of the adults who read a Sunday paper read the comic strips, whereas no more than 25 per cent read the second most popular feature of any paper. His survey further revealed that the proportion of comic strip readers was highest among children (99 per cent) and among low income families, both regarded increasingly as important consumer groups.[30] Shortly thereafter the General Foods Corporation, at the instigation of Hawley Turner, executive editor of Hearst's *Comic Weekly,* gambled on the use of a comic sequence advertisement for Grape-Nuts, a product that had not been selling well. Grape-Nuts was saved, the commercial use of strips seemed vindicated, and in six years the annual expenditures by national advertisers on continuity strip advertising jumped from under $1,000 to

---

1940), p. 61. The liquor industry voluntarily policed its own advertising through its principal trade association, the Distilled Spirits Institute (DSI). In 1937 the DSI was headed by W. F. Morgan (former Treasurer of the Democratic National Committee and a nephew of J. P. Morgan), for which he was paid $50,000 a year and requested to enforce discipline by every means at his command. Morgan's task was apparently a hard one, for there had been many "recalcitrant" members of the industry: *P.I.* (Mar. 25, 1937), p. 6. But he had the support of the Federal Alcohol Control Administration, an official body that promulgated and enforced legal regulations for liquor advertising, and the National Conference of State Liquor Administrators, whose power within many states was forceful and direct. The minimum federal regulations provided that every advertisement had to include the manufacturer's name and address and the type of whiskey, and was prohibited from making disparaging remarks about other liquors or any claims of therapeutic benefit. Reprinted in *P.I.* (Jan. 24, 1935), p. 20. In practice the Federal Administrator was even stricter: no whiskey could be claimed as "wholesome" or "soothing," or as improving appetite or reducing hangover. *P.I.* (Mar. 25, 1937), p. 6. The DSI attempted to add further "taboos": no copy could be directed at women or children or feature them in it; no bars or saloons, or excessively convivial drinking scenes; no reference of any kind to the pleasures of being drunk or to sexual or religious matters. Ibid.

30. *P.I.* (Apr. 28, 1932), p. 3.

$16,500,000.[31] Advertising men confidently attributed its success to an insatiable public appetite for entertainment and foresaw no end to its popularity.[32]

For those who felt that advertising had remained too rational and was insufficiently geared to fundamental human drives the comic strip seemed well suited for garbing sales messages in simple and direct emotions. The formula seldom varied: women lose their lovers or waste away over washboards, men fail to win prestige, boys and girls become troubled and insecure; enter the product; love is restored, washing becomes easy, men find popularity, boys and girls are made happy. That such a formula seldom varied proved no disadvantage, for readers of comic strips were generally found to have derived much of their satisfaction and pleasure from being able to anticipate what was coming. Comic strips, furthermore, stressed themes elemental enough to bear endless repetition (love, fear, hate, aggression, insecurity) and employed the techniques characteristic of the bedtime story, whose plot is peopled with personalities which are for the most part either black or white and devoid of any complicated pattern of thought that might invite only perplexity and puzzlement. Finally, and of particular significance, advertisers regarded continuity strips as an effective and inoffensive way to present appeals which had been thought otherwise too blatant and too crude for public tolerance. Comics, stated one advertising agent, "help to make testimonials more convincing. . . . Usually the testimonial statement is made by one character to another character in the strip—and the reader 'overhears' what is being said. It needs a lot of sales resistance to overcome the insidious effect of testimonial, word-of-mouth, and disinterested third-person-selling all rolled into one." [33] Cartoon advertising, affirmed an editorial in *Advertising and Selling*, "has the undoubted advantage that its tongue-in-cheek claims can sidestep taboos against factual misstatements imposed by the F.T.C." [34] In short, continuity strips

31. *A.S.* (Apr. 1938), p. 21.
32. *P.I.* (Apr. 28, 1932), p. 3.
33. Ibid.
34. *A.S.* (Dec. 1941), p. 14. See also *P.I.* (Dec. 19, 1935), p. 37, and a special report, "Funny Paper Advts. [*sic*]," *Fortune Magazine* (Apr. 1933), p. 98.

recommended themselves to the industry as a means for rendering exaggeration more palatable, for stating claims and presenting ideas that would seem otherwise less credible, and for enabling the advertiser to put such claims and ideas within the grasp of a large semiliterate public that had previously been less accessible to them. "As citizens," remarked one agent in 1932, "we may despair that [comic strips] should be so popular, but as advertising men we must note objectively the fact that comic strips and continuities provide an extraordinarily potent means of attracting reader attention." [35]

With increasing sophistication advertising men exploited devices of entertainment. Borrowing techniques from tabloid journalism, from "slick" fiction, and even from motion pictures, they gradually learned not only to arrest the attention but to provoke a response closely related to the product. The camouflage which entertainment placed on sales messages, of course, varied in effectiveness, and it became clear that the more directly and integrally the particular entertainment was related to the product or the message about it the more effectively it would aid in selling the product or in conveying the message. Thus a "real-life" story concerning a husband and wife saved from imminent (and plausible) peril by the dependability of their Eveready flashlight batteries might be expected to arouse in a reader a more effective response than would, for example, a sequence of cartoon panels which merely demonstrated the trade secrets of professional magicians while attempting to make the reader aware of Camel cigarettes. In the first instance the average reader might respond to the entertainment with a vicarious feeling of insecurity which the product alleviates; the entertainment arouses the reader's imaginative interest and sustains it even through the actual sales message, for the two are so intertwined that the reader's response to the first readily transfers itself to the second. In the case of the magicians and Camel cigarettes, however, the reader's response to the entertainment might be both strong and dependable ("I am consumed with curiosity to know how they appear to saw people in half; besides I like to be 'in the know'—it makes me feel important"), but there is little assurance that this response

35. *P.I.* (Apr. 28, 1932), p. 3.

will induce any change in attitude toward Camels. In fact upon satisfying his curiosity the reader might stop short of the end of the page and thus never see the word "Camel." The advertisement for Eveready batteries would clearly seem more capable of affecting the reader's attitude toward the product than the advertisement for Camels. Better than either would be an advertisement so constructed as to invoke in the reader the very response he would be most likely to make in the physical presence of the product itself, as, for example, a four-color photograph of a raspberry sundae, or a series of photographs which takes the reader through a hot, dry day of work, deposits him in a cool drugstore on his way home, and shows him in the act of placing the first spoonful of the raspberry sundae in his mouth.[36]

With such "mouth-watering" techniques the addition of entertainment was often superfluous, and, to be sure, during the decade of Depression and recovery a greater proportion of magazine advertisements than in the 1920's remained prosaic and uncomplicated; they pictured the product with alluring fidelity but with little or no secondary stimulus of entertainment. The theory of direct stimulus, however, received its most spectacular trial with the sudden and comprehensive exploitation, in the mid-1930's, of sexual and erotic appeals and similarly compelling stimuli. By this I do not mean merely journalistic devices for attracting attention, as, for example, a "cheesecake" photograph placed on the front page of a tabloid in order to sell more copies on the newsstand. Rather, as in the hypothetical case of the raspberry sundae, I mean the ways in which the reader was induced to undergo a vicarious emotional experience which aimed at arousing a desired response in him strong enough to overcome even his considered, rational opposition.[37]

By way of illustration it may be worth while to describe the

36. For an excellent analysis of the theoretical distinction just described see Leonard W. Doob, *Public Opinion and Propaganda* (New York, Henry Holt, 1948), pp. 320–53.

37. To determine roughly what sort of changes, if any, could be detected in advertising appeals in the period of the 1930's, I analyzed, in a fashion similar to the one described above, p. 38, n. 44, seven issues of *Woman's Home Companion*: May 1928, Feb. 1929, Sept. 1929, and Feb., Mar., Sept., Oct. 1939. Totaling the number of "points" (see above, p. 38, n. 44) for the four issues of 1939, and

structure and content of three typical magazine advertisements of the late 1930's. One is an advertisement for Cashmere Bouquet soap. A handsome male is photographed caressing with his lips the ear of a glamorous woman. Her eyes are half-closed as she smiles with pleasurable anticipation. The copy reads in part as follows:

> Success in love turns on such unexpected things! Just when you feel victory is yours, your luck deserts you—something happens to transform your confidence into confusion. Nine times out of ten you blame the you that is deep in you. Your whole personality goes vacant and hopeless.
>
> But, such disillusionments should only be temporary. Too bad, most women take them deeply to heart, when the trouble can be so easily avoided. . . .
>
> Yes, go by the "smell test" when you buy soap to overcome body odor. . . . Instinctively, you will prefer the costly perfume of Cashmere Bouquet. . . . It's a fragrance men love! A fragrance with a peculiar affinity for the senses of men.
>
> Massage each tiny ripple of your body daily with this delicate, penetrating lather! Glory in the departure of un-

---

setting this value at 100, I classified the advertisements into the following themes and calculated the "percentage" which each represented of the total for each year:

Theme, by Content and Technique	1939	1929
a. Simple reproduction of product—little or no secondary association or appeals	39	32
b. Appeals of romance, emotional satisfaction, desire to be secure, popular, attractive, sexually competent	28	15
c. Comfort, leisure, prestige, highly valued middle-class stereotypes, family and home life, conspicuous consumption	15	23
d. Institutional, general public relations, appeals of protection and security	9	7
e. Product as a conspicuous aid to health, otherwise in danger	3	13
f. Others	6	10
	100	100

The type of advertising to emerge most spectacularly in the 1930's was type *a* (above), even though type *a* led the total percentages. The proportions thus determined are to some degree peculiar to a woman's magazine. The *Saturday Evening Post*, for example, included in 1939 a higher proportion of types, *a, c,* and *d,* but the change from 1929 to 1939 in any category for the *Post* was roughly comparable to that found in the *Woman's Home Companion*.

welcome body odor! Thrill as your senses are kissed by Cashmere Bouquet's exquisite perfume . . [its] gentle, caressing
lather. . . . Be radiant, and confident to face the world.[38]

A second example is an advertisement for Palmolive soap. It
features a photograph of a statuesque nude standing in semidark-
ness, outlined with heavy shadows and a discreet pattern of light.
Underneath is a caption: "All alone, and the night was made for
love!" A smaller picture is placed elsewhere on the page: in it a
man and woman (fully clothed) are embracing. The text explains
that the woman switched to Palmolive soap.[39]

Third is an advertisement for Pond's Creams. It is divided into
two sections; each consists of a series of photographs with captions designed to resemble the pictorial features of *Life* magazine.
The first series comprises an interview with an unmarried working girl. She is presented as a real person and is testifying that she
uses Pond's Creams. Revealed as a bookkeeper who lives in a single apartment in Washington, D.C., she is shown to be attractive
and about twenty years of age. The advertisement pictures her on
a leisurely Sunday with a "date." They hire a canoe for an after-
noon in the park; in the evening before parting they kiss good-
night on her doorstep. The second series of photographs presents
an interview with Mrs. A. J. Drexel, III, of Philadelphia. She is
pictured as belonging to a "young married set." She appears attractive, well-dressed, and sophisticated in manner. She is shown
yachting, entertaining guests at a party, and dressed in costume
at a masquerade ball. She also testifies to her use of Pond's
Creams. The two series of photographs are so juxtaposed as to induce the reader to compare both women throughout.[40]

These advertisements, each in a slightly different way, were
designed to combine high attention value with direct evocation of
a response favorable to the reception of the product. The first
advertisement provided a stimulus which closely reproduced
romantic scenes in contemporary films. The second advertisement
relied on a fairly dependable (and, by 1936, a widely used) stimu-

38. Released for fall, 1939.
39. Released for fall, 1936.
40. Released for fall, 1939.

lus for attracting attention in newspapers and magazines: a nude.[41] The third provided an entertaining and journalistic story of "human interest" in the form of candid camera sequences of a sort which a number of "pictorial" magazines were beginning to find popular and profitable. In the third advertisement, it might be observed, the text was in part superfluous: a person with no ability to read could still have "understood" most of the advertisement for Pond's. All three advertisements attempted to offer the reader (presumably a woman) a vicarious experience of a desire, in the first two instances sexual, in the last a more generalized desire for security, prestige, and companionship with sexual connotations. The vicarious experience in each case served a number of possible functions. It helped to convey, in one instance, the impression that a cake of soap could be used as an aphrodisiac (a claim that, had it been stated in so many words, would probably have inspired disbelief among readers and almost certain retribution from the FTC); presumably by reading the ambiguous message for Cashmere Bouquet soap the reader would undergo an experience approximating that claimed to result from using the soap, an experience of a sort which would make her less likely to subject the initial claim to rational scrutiny. The Palmolive advertisement was calculated to render a more simple message: if you are now deprived of sexual fulfillment you need only use Palmolive to win the man who will enable you to experience it. The appeal depended on making the reader feel simultaneously both deprivation and desire. The dual testimonial for Pond's Creams suggested implicitly that the young, simple bookkeeper could not ask for anything better, even if she were young Mrs. Drexel, than the opportunity to use Pond's. If she continued to use Pond's, it was fairly clear, she might find in life all that Mrs. Drexel had found, particularly if she attracted the right man. The explicit comparison of her life with the leisure life of high prestige and security made the ordinary reader's identification with Mrs. Drexel easier and more plausible. Each of the advertisements surrounded its product with its emotional stimuli skillfully arranged to reduce the probability of rational response.

41. For an analytical comment on this "fad" in national advertising see A.S. (Dec. 3, 1936), p. 31; (Mar. 25, 1937), p. 29.

Each stressed a theme common to most advertising in a modern consumer's society, that it was possible to achieve desirable personal and social relations simply by consuming the right material goods. Above all, each of them rested on the theory that the consumer could be led to desire those goods by being induced to participate vicariously in powerful sense experiences which the advertisement could offer him and which would lead him almost irresistibly to accept the evaluation which the advertiser himself put on his own wares.

By the middle of the 1930's national advertising had become a formidable process of social communication. Nourished in part on psychology, it communicated not merely sales messages for products but graphic instructions and carefully-wrought suggestions for social behavior. And hand-in-hand with national advertising went the media which published it. These two powerful systems of communication were seldom rivals, and seldom did they offer readers a choice of proposals or attitudes. But the presence of overt conspiracy, or a combination in restraint of thought, was unlikely and unnecessary. Both systems were prisoners of the fundamental requirement that they attract and hold a large number of readers. Each partially reflected the harmony of interest which bound together commercial publishers and businessmen in a modern capitalistic society. And more often than not, each was subject to the same self-imposed criteria of mass persuasion: verbal arguments, for example, were best made short and simple, stripped of complexities and qualifications; appeals were best rendered in stereotyped images and unequivocal symbols, preferably based on fundamental emotional drives; and ideas were to be presented, wherever possible, in the dress of personalities or through the framework of a conflict between good and evil. For several generations criteria of this sort had been standard in popular journalism, and in countless ways the modern advertising industry was a child of the modern press.

Inevitably, then, and often unwittingly, the editorial features of the mass media reinforced the system of communication embodied in advertisements. Negatively the commercial press avoided publishing views which were likely to arouse the permanent or serious resistance of consumers to the reception of advertising appeals. The press never challenged the fundamental premises of modern advertising. Its journalistic and its fictional accounts of the industry often poked fun at it, but in such a manner as to leave its social and economic role enhanced or to cast a glow of sophistication and prestige over its legendary personnel. (Few business enterprises, in fact, have ever appeared in fiction so glamorized as the national advertising agency.) The presence of fiction itself, moreover, was regarded as an asset to the advertisements which appeared in adjacent columns. A constant reader of fiction, reflected one agency executive in 1936, was a "conditioned prospect" for advertising, because he was likely to crave imaginary situations of romance with which he could readily identify himself; such readers, he suggested, found it less difficult "to imagine throwing out the old ice box and installing a Frigidaire." [42] A more subtle but no less significant aid to the consumer advertisement was the prevailing formula of success around which fictional stories and serials were commonly built. As Leonard Doob has expressed it:

> . . . The happy-ending, the boy-meets-and-marries-girl, the poor-lad-becomes-rich, the louse-gets-it-in-the-neck, or many of the other themes which saturate most magazine fiction serve to reinforce the reader's drive to patronize the advertiser of consumer goods so that he too can find his salvation. . . . The way of life in our society fostered by the glib formulas for [periodical] stories and articles . . . is an almost exact reproduction of those conditions which must exist if most advertisers are to continue to produce and distribute their products or services.[43]

Even in the nonfictional features of the commercial press the consumer could find no crevice in the monolithic structure of advice which came at him from every page, urging him simply to acquiesce, to accept, and to consume. Purporting to offer the consumer a defense against his own ignorance, *Good Housekeeping*, for example, conducted for its readers a monthly column of

42. Mark O'Dea, *P.I.*, May 28, 1936. See n. 12, above.
43. Doob, *Public Opinion and Propaganda*, p. 454.

"advice" about products tested in its "Institute" for consumers. Rarely detailed or specific, this column seldom criticized a product, nor were individual products ever singled out for comment by name. The column merely reinforced the heavy burden of advertising which swamped over half the total space of every issue: anything advertised is good; consume it if you possibly can; if you cannot, try to expand your desires and your standard of living; buy an electric mixer, get a new iron, eat oranges and lemons, eat more meat, wear more clothes; above all, rely on our Institute for worth-while advice; the consumer has a right to know the facts, and the press has an obligation to provide them.[44] Other media for national advertisements were generally less self-conscious about their services to the consumer and seldom operated such elaborate paraphernalia with which to persuade him of their good intentions; but none of them differed significantly in their willingness to offer solid support to the advertising industry in its efforts to gain the consent and patronage of the reading public. By 1940 the editorial, the feature, and the advertising pages in some national printed media had become so like-minded that it was frequently hard to tell one from another, and in almost no media was the general social impact of national advertisements ever confronted with effective challenge or dissent. The press served to create an atmosphere of acceptance for its advertisements; in such an atmosphere, the probing curiosity of a rational mind, the tendency for consumers to ask questions, were made to seem marks of eccentricity, even ill-will. Advertisers and the press alike strove to lull critical faculties to a point where simple assertions could be accepted for argument, demonstration, or logic.

Thus by 1940 the national advertising industry had consolidated its position. For twenty years it had been developing a theory whereby, in lieu of submitting to the rational demands of consumers, it should instead attempt to control their nonrational behavior. As advertising men gained in an understanding of their markets and the behavior of their readers, their advertisements in practice became more subtle and less easy to resist. The con-

44. Based on an examination of *Good Housekeeping*, issues of July 1937–June 1938, Sept. 1941–Jan. 1942.

sumer movement and the Wheeler-Lea Act encouraged them to make their appeals still more plausible, to avoid overt offenses against accepted taste, and to adhere to a minimum canon of technical honesty; and without impairing the power of their advertisements, copy writers had managed to reduce greatly the likelihood of formal complaint. Practicing psychologists urged them, even at the risk of occasional misrepresentation, to associate with their products qualities which their research had told them consumers urgently desired. By the use of pseudoscience it was possible for some advertisers to obscure from the consumer precisely the sort of information which they were pretending to offer him. Others, by providing popular entertainment and the means for experiencing vicariously the rewards which were attributed to the product, attempted to sway consumers by appealing to basic emotional and physical drives in an effort to circumvent the rational perceptions which might have led to doubt or hesitation. One might justifiably conclude that the consumer, as a consequence, was less and less likely to be able successfully to exercise rational discrimination toward statements and insinuations couched in such disarming guise. Nor did he have at his elbow, to warn him of the tricks played on him, the staffs of psychologists that were making themselves available to agency executives, rendering their tricks more foolproof and providing them with a welcome set of rationalizations concerning the nature of consumers ("fourteen-year-olds"), and the tactics of mass persuasion ("the public wants entertainment"; "avoid their minds"; "not truth but credibility"). Measured against the weapons of the national advertising industry, it would seem that on the eve of the second World War the consumer's defenses were weakening.

It was by no means certain, of course, that consumers had been left in as dire a position as many of them feared. By 1940, inexorable though the trend may have been toward nonrational advertisements, there is little doubt that the appeals on which the bulk of American advertising depended were still more rational than nonrational: if the old order was dying, it was by no means dead. Critics of advertising tended to confuse the problem of rationality in buying with the less frightening problem of rationality in advertisements. Appeals which depended on what appeared to be a nonrational response were often, in fact, no more than eloquent literary or pictorial devices which were intended to enhance the persuasiveness of the advertisement but which did not necessarily encourage irrationality in consumption. (A photograph of a field of snow under a crisp winter sky can serve to attract attention to an air conditioner which might then be advertised with a rational presentation of facts.) Consumer critics who failed to make such a distinction might easily have been led to unwarranted despair lest they ever gain support in the advertising industry for rational consumption when that industry was so quick to defend its "right" to create nonrational appeals. Nor was it precisely clear how one ought to view the willing conversion of a few professional psychologists into advertising men. The achievements of psychological research promised to make the work of the agency executive easier and brought his goals more readily within reach; they may even have suggested to him additional goals that heretofore had been thought unattainable. Yet the existence of new techniques by themselves were not originally responsible for suggesting that the primary goal of modern advertising ought to be to turn a reader into a spontaneous, unreflecting consumer.

The consumer movement was directed, to be sure, not against consumption as such but against the way that advertisers, seeking mass markets among mass readers, tended deliberately to persuade consumers through nonrational stimuli that their products were better than they actually were. National advertising, however, was directed heavily toward the promotion of brand-name identification among masses of consumers, and it was brand-name buying which at least in theory threatened to deprive this criticism of its sting. Brand advertising supposedly forced the manufacturer to maintain consistency of quality and thereby enabled the consumer to depend on the name of the brand and not on his own processes of reason or on factual statements about the product in its advertising: the branded product had in effect been rationalized for him, and, therefore, provided he bought well-known brands, the modern consumer could consequently afford the luxury of nonrational advertising. Thus, as the producer himself became more responsible, the responsibility demanded of his advertisements became more irrelevant.

However hopeful such possibilities might seem, nevertheless, the primary function of the American advertising industry—to stimulate consumption—tended to produce effects which were unforeseeable and for which no one could in practice be held responsible. Relentlessly and unwaveringly it tended to foster a universal faith in the efficacy and growth of consumption and in the particular economic institutions on which that growth seemed to depend. The social implications of this faith have sometimes been as far-reaching as they have been uncontrollable. Should the federal government ever wish to reduce the national propensity to consume for the purpose of controlling inflation, for example, its weapons are likely to be confined to the manipulation of credit, and the application of this single brake would have to overcome the continued full throttle of advertising and marketing. Although in theory it might be possible to discourage advertising by a reversal of current tax policies, in practice such a course, striking first at the publishing industry and the mass media, would appear to the ordinary politician as an almost certain form of suicide. The financial relationship of advertising to media, it might be said with relief, has made the mass media peculiarly independent of direct political control and perhaps even of indirect manipulation. At the same time, it has placed advertising politically in an almost invulnerable position.

These attributes of the advertising industry have developed almost incidentally to its principal purpose. Individual advertisers have scarcely been able to foresee or to anticipate the cumulative effects of what they do, and it would be difficult if not irrelevant to ascribe to them special motives or deliberate intentions for the ultimate social impact of advertising. In less than two generations the effects of this structure of power have been momentous, but by 1940 the responsibility for its operations had already become so permanently entangled within the larger structure of society as to remain almost hidden from sight and impervious to definition.

8

Conclusion

I HAVE ATTEMPTED in this study to suggest the extent to which concepts of public responsibility existed in the national advertising industry as a part of its basic intellectual assumptions during the critical period of its recent growth and the relation which these concepts and assumptions bore to advertising behavior.

National advertising in the period 1920–40 became a continuous, powerful technique for mass persuasion, employed to inculcate specific goals and values. It grew in response to the needs of an industrial society which had achieved efficient methods of mass production and distribution but which had not yet developed standards of consumption sufficiently lavish to maintain that production. Not only did it seek to stimulate a lagging market; it attempted to create a revolution in social attitudes toward consumption—to teach the public what to consume and how to consume. From its beginning, national adver-

tising was used as a manufacturer's weapon for gaining control
of his market. It also proved to be a convenient device for the
financial stabilization of the press; in fact the men who first encouraged the manufacturer to use national advertising to gain
control of his market were generally agents representing the
interests of the press. National advertising developed its techniques of persuasion in conjunction with modern commercial
journalism and developed them most fully for products whose
values could not readily be measured by rational judgment. The
marketing of such products, as a consequence, tended to remain
in the control of their manufacturers rather than their distributors,
and tended to exploit the high degree of consumer ignorance
about such products. National advertising, furthermore, was produced by an increasingly powerful and unified body of men who
seldom failed to encourage new uses for advertising, to sell it,
advertise it, and defend it against all forms of competition. This
body of men depicted their trade as one that served producers in
a society of consumers, that lessened public reluctance to consume,
and that helped to reduce public skepticism of business enterprise.

These men were generally agreed that if advertising were to
prove effective in controlling consumer behavior, it required the
constant cultivation of favorable public relations. They had reason
to hold this view. In the period from 1920 to 1940, a number of
determined consumer organizations and a small but articulate
group of critics confronted the national advertising industry with
a serious challenge to its power. This challenge was embodied in
a persistent public questioning of the validity and social benefit
of advertising and in a partially successful effort to assure the
technical truthfulness of advertising by federal regulation. To
most of the industry this challenge seemed to threaten their very
security. Critics were demanding that consumers be presented
with advertising from which they could derive useful information
and rational judgments; failing that, critics were proposing to
counteract national advertising with propaganda and information
designed to reduce its control over the market. The threat of
regulation seemed to promise a curtailment of advertising volume, conceivably with catastrophic effects on the commercial

press, with a restriction on the marketing procedures of many products, and with a resulting loss of profits to the advertising industry.

Those who offered this challenge spoke in the rhetoric of social reformers. They comprised, it is true, a diverse group (retailers, medical scientists, governmental agencies, intellectual critics, organizations of consumers), and many of them were by no means challenging either the basic message (greater consumption) or the prevailing structure of values within most advertisements. Preponderantly they were bothered by the misrepresentation and the waste in the production of advertisements and in the operations of the market which advertising so strongly affected. But challenge even on these counts distinctly signified a determination to increase consumer skepticism and distrust of advertisements.

Faced with this challenge the advertising industry defended its behavior by making articulate its own views of its social responsibility.

Advertising men contended principally that their responsible behavior was assured by an effective structure of control within the industry. They pointed to such devices as local and state regulations, the *P.I.* Statute, the Better Business Bureaus, the association of national advertisers, their agents, and the press. They publicized codes of behavior and resolutions which condemned practices that were plainly irresponsible and damaging to the public. They reminded the public that advertising had "improved" steadily through the years, that improvement was often slow, and that no one was perfect. They took pains to distinguish between the discontent with advertising which a few radical consumer spokesmen manifested and the passive acceptance of advertisements with which most ordinary readers responded. They rejected any suggestion that their responsibility extended beyond the rendering of ethical service to those who sponsored the advertisements or beyond the securing of the effectiveness and public repute of advertising as a whole; responsibility to the public was automatically assured by responsibility to the "profession" of advertising. And, not least, they took refuge in the explanation that the self-regulating mechanism of a competitive market assured the public that it would get only the sort of advertisements it wanted: an unethical or irresponsible advertiser would lose out to his honest competitor; no advertising man could remain in business unless his wares pleased the public. The industry, consequently, possessed within itself the mechanism which guaranteed the public good.

The structure of internal control cited in such fashion, however, operated with effectiveness to curb only behavior found objectionable by those within the industry, and even in this relatively narrow sphere of action the forces for internal control were generally of small effect. Comments which disparaged competitors comprised most of the practices to come under internal discipline. But disparaging copy was not the principal concern of the forces outside the industry which were demanding a larger degree of public responsibility from it. Indignant over the widespread existence of technically truthful insinuations of untruth, the devices of the "borderline" and similar evasions of candor, they were principally concerned that consumers be permitted to exercise rational judgment on the basis of information supplied them in advertisements.

Advertising men did not consider it their responsibility to heed a public demand of this sort. Faced with the hostility of reformers, they displayed in their turn the outlook of missionaries preaching the equally reformist doctrine of uninhibited consumption to a society steeped in the outmoded assumptions of scarcity. For every phase of their trade they constructed a rationale with which to counter the arguments of their critics and to discredit their motives. The consumer movement was plainly handicapped by the fact that it had never secured a broad public support, and it was to some extent exploited by men who were more concerned with creating public distrust of capitalism than with gaining advantages for the consumer. More important, however, was the fact that while the consumer movement was forced to attack advertising on the issue of its literal truthfulness, the advertising industry itself recognized that the question of literal truth or falsity was largely irrelevant, since the appeal of the advertisement lay not in the factual assertions of its contents but in the associations which it set up in the mind of the reader. This psychological factor to a great extent shifted the battle to a field where the critics were then deprived of all reasonable social weapons with which to oppose advertising, more specifically, a field where the barrier between literal truth and literal falsity was obscured and where, in consequence, it lost much of its effectiveness.

Thus the industry was left almost wholly free to decide for itself how it would use its influence, and its practices offered only partial and infrequent concessions to consumer demand. A few of them were wrung from the industry by law, but they represented tactical changes of form more often than basic alterations of principle. If there were to be any fundamental changes in the public policies of advertising men or in the principles or practices of their trade, these changes would occur, apparently, only because advances in the techniques of persuasion and in the body of advertising skills rendered older practices outmoded. The improved techniques available to the advertiser might, indeed, render unnecessary any fundamental changes in policy; it was hoped that advertising could be made skillful enough to win not only the public's patronage for the advertised product but also the public's enthusiasm (or at least its tolerance) for the institution of advertising itself. But though such a process would reduce the threat of censure, and would relieve the advertising industry of the problems caused by a steady fire of adverse criticism, it was scarcely adequate to resolve any of the social problems which had inspired this criticism in the first place.

The practices of advertising men merely confirmed the suspicion that there existed in the industry no operating concept which would encourage the public to exercise free or rational judgments as consumers. The future was scarcely more hopeful. With the coming of the second World War some of the forces actively in opposition to the structure of national advertising diminished: under the heat of prosperity the consumer movement withered and did not again recover its earlier vigor or its former capacity for effective challenge; advertising men themselves continued to operate as before, now clothed with the impeccable prestige of being asked to help forge public unanimity for survival in time of war; and even less than in an earlier day did they feel any obligation to encourage intellectual dissent from their apparatus of mass persuasion. Indeed, with improved techniques of advertising, they continued their efforts to render such dissent useless. In the next decade would come television and such a proficient expansion of psychological research into the motives and behavior of consumers as to render the findings of the prewar era almost elementary in contrast.

The experience and growth of that era had placed advertising in a formidable position in American society. Combined with the commercial press no other institution could rival its services, and no other industry had packaged the techniques of mass persuasion so efficiently or had offered them on such reasonable terms. Nor had any industry in modern times attempted more effectively to manipulate the process of consumption in an economy which had constantly to increase its consumption or crash. Indeed it might further be argued that no institution had done more to circumvent the process and operation of rational thought in a free society. Surely, none of the triumphs of capitalism in the 1920's and 1930's was more extensive or significant than the triumphs of American advertising. How the consumer was to fare at its hands would seem to depend less on the consumer than on forces within the industry itself. So pervasive and skillful had advertising become by the 1940's that it seemed doubtful whether it could ever be forced to develop a concept of public responsibility more rigorous than the modest one which had characterized its earlier growth.

Bibliographical Essay

IN EXPLORING the subject of this book I found one general source uniquely relevant and available: the collective record of the significant attitudes and views which advertising men expressed about advertising, its behavior and its social role. The record included, on the one hand, published statements, articles, speeches, and memoirs, as well as formal resolutions, codes, pronouncements of policy, and official or quasi-official records both individual and institutional; and, on the other hand, occasional private interviews and published business records.

Innumerable writings of advertising men, as well as the official record of their views—a surprisingly voluminous source—are to be found in the trade journals of the advertising and publishing industries. Oldest and most important among the journals is *Printers' Ink,* a weekly magazine begun in 1888. It provides a continuous survey of those events and developments in national and retail advertising of sufficient general importance to hold the interest of readers in every phase of the industry. Between 1920 and 1940 its staff consisted of five or six editors and about as many permanent "correspondents" and reporters. Most issues of the journal characteristically presented the following fare: a half dozen feature articles, written as often by advertisers or agents as by the journal's staff, which described examples of successful advertising and occasionally the theories behind them, posed problems of technique and management, and offered thinly disguised publicity for various companies and their views on advertising; three or four articles and a host of "notices," which reported news of individuals, firms, media, important business events, consumer criticism, and federal and state legislation; an editorial page, which was generally devoted to ethical questions arising from the relations of the advertising industry to its society; and, rounding out most issues, columns of advice on how to write copy, sell products, and plan campaigns.

Almost as valuable as a source for the record of the industry between 1920 and 1940 was *Advertising and Selling*, published monthly from 1894 to 1918, weekly to 1923, byweekly to 1938, and monthly from 1938 (re-named *Advertising Agency* in 1948). It compensated for a smaller staff and narrower coverage of the industry by providing frequently a more sophisticated assessment of the business of advertising, and its editorial attitude tended to be less self-conscious and didactic.

Corroborative and supplementary data on specific events in the history of the advertising industry can be found in a number of other trade journals. *Tide*, published monthly from 1927 to 1936 and semimonthly after 1936, was begun as an enterprise of *Time,* Inc., but was published independently after 1930. It did not attempt at first to cover the entire industry but concentrated on reporting particular developments of unusual interest as they arose. Regarding ethical matters, its early issues affected a relatively neutral and deprecatory attitude. *Advertising Age*, a weekly begun in 1930 and published in Chicago, offered an eclectic weekly survey of the industry, frequently with an emphasis on the Middle West. *Printers' Ink Monthly*, published by Printers' Ink Publishing Co. from 1919 to 1940 as an independent magazine, supplemented *Printers' Ink* with general articles and art work in a larger format. *Associated Advertising,* published monthly by the AACW, 1910–26, served largely as a personality and publicity organ for the leading association in the so-called Truth-in-Advertising movement, and its usefulness was correspondingly restricted. *Editor and Publisher,* published weekly since 1901, has remained the leading journal for the newspaper industry in America, and was found to be a supplementary source of immense value.

These trade journals of advertising have proved exceptionally useful because of the attitudes of advertising men expressed in them as well as the record of campaigns, legislation, and other matters important to the industry. In varying degrees the journals served in the 1920's and 1930's as semiprivate forums in which advertising men exchanged views. Fundamentally, though often inconspicuously, the journals reflected the prevailing views of their readers (who were for the most part advertising men), and almost any aspect of the advertising industry which its members were willing to discuss among themselves—except private agency affairs and competitive business plans—was apt to be aired in these organs, often with a considerable degree of candor. And even where candor was absent, attitudes were frequently obvious. At times, indeed, contributors attempted to outdo one another in affirming their common faith, a faith which the journals were always willing to make articulate.

To provide an essential perspective on material found in trade journals I turned in part to three particular sources of striking general value: personal interviews, periodical journals, and an outstanding scholarly study. George F. Thomson, René Clarke, Warren Rebell, and Roger Brown of the Calkins and Holden advertising firm provided me opportunities to interview them and examine material concerning a number of matters pertinent to the advertising industry in the period between the wars; these materials corroborated in important ways my findings in the published literature of advertising. For further information on some of the well-publicized developments in American advertising and its relations to the public, I made extensive use of the New York *Times* (from 1918), *Business Week* (from 1937), *Fortune* (from 1930), *Time* (from 1926), the *Nation* (from 1916), and the *New Republic* (from 1923) all of which, among periodicals of general circulation in the United States, I found uniquely valuable. The *Harvard Business Review* (from 1922) and the *Journal of Marketing* (from 1936) provided occasional articles and interpretive data.

Of still greater usefulness for the present study as a whole was Ralph M. Hower's thorough and competent monograph, *The History of an Advertising Agency: N. W. Ayer and Son at Work, 1869–1949*, Cambridge, Mass., 1949. His investigation of one of the largest, oldest, and most conservative national agencies was based on a careful perusal of the unpublished records of that firm. Undertaken as a project in entrepreneurial history, it may be said, nevertheless, to offer an insight into the entire field of advertising. To produce results more widely relevant and significantly more detailed would call for a formidable cooperative investigation.

Important bibliographical aids and reference works are available to simplify the task of threading a path through the published data. Foremost for scholars in the field of propaganda and communications are the two works by Harold D. Lasswell, Ralph D. Casey, and Bruce L. Smith: *Propaganda and Promotional Activities*, Minneapolis, 1935, and *Propaganda, Communication, and Public Opinion*, Princeton, 1946. The first provides a briefly annotated list of 4,000 books, articles, and previous bibliographies, in all languages, on all aspects of propaganda through 1943. It classifies its entries under each of several headings, which include particular techniques, promoting groups, and channels of propaganda. The second is an excellent and thoroughly annotated bibliography of 3,000 titles published between 1934 and 1946, and combines with it four essays of varying value on the media of communication, the measurement of the content and effectiveness of communication, and the agents of communication. The bibliography is arranged in substantially the same way as in the earlier book but with greater refinement. The field of advertising is covered adequately under several appropriate headings.

The *Journalism Quarterly* (published since 1924) provides in each issue a comprehensive bibliography of periodical and newspaper articles on advertising. I found this an indispensable guide to published sources. More selective is the United States Library of Congress, Division of Bibliography, *Selected List of Recent References on Advertising* (mimeographed, May 1940), which lists over 400 items, including periodical articles published since 1931. I also found useful the compilation by the United States Department of Commerce, *Market Research Sources*, Washington, D.C., revised, 1940.

Comprehensive statistical information and other information of a quantitative nature on American advertising may readily be found in the *Printers' Ink Guide to Marketing*, published as an annual supplement to *Printers' Ink*. I had occasion as well to resort to the *Standard Advertising Register and Agency List*, published three times each year, and to *National Advertising Records*, published monthly. The first provides lists of all national advertisers and all "recognized" advertising agencies, including personnel and clients; the second records the size and cost of space used by national advertisers and for individual products each month in each of 150 magazines. Information on which to make meaningful international comparisons among advertising enterprises is extremely meager, but reliable data on advertising in Great Britain is available in N. Kaldor and R. Silverman, *A Statistical Analysis of Advertising Expenditure and of the Revenue of the Press*, Cambridge, England, 1948. Comparative studies of foreign advertising with American advertising are badly needed.

My sources for the national advertisements discussed or analyzed in this study consisted for the most part of the files for the period between 1910 and 1942 of the *Saturday Evening Post, Good Housekeeping, Ladies' Home Journal, Woman's Home Companion, Collier's Weekly, Life* (from 1936), *Time* (from 1923), the New York *Times,* and the New Haven (Conn.) *Register.*

Origins and Growth of American Advertising

Anyone wishing today to write a comprehensive history of the origins and growth of American advertising would have to build it in part on the mass of unpublished records and correspondence of the major firms, trade associations, and key individuals within the field. This material is largely unmapped, though there exist a few aerial surveys—made from varying heights, as it were, and consequently of varying reliability and usefulness.

The two most illuminating studies of advertising which have yet appeared are by Ralph Hower and Neil H. Borden, both of the Harvard Graduate School of Business Administration. Hower's I have just described, and Borden's is discussed briefly in Chapter 6, above. Titled *The Economic Effects of Advertising*, it is based on the careful research of a team of economists concerned with the economic background of advertising and with both its theoretical and empirical role in the capitalistic market structure of the United States since the midnineteenth century. Special sections explore the relations of advertising to costs, prices, quality, and range of consumer products, and to national income. Chapters on the attitudes of consumers toward the ethics of advertising set forth the findings of two elaborate polls and have been justly described as an outstanding contribution to the study of the social relations of advertising in the United States.

Historians of advertising must stand indebted to at least three superior studies of the development of the printed media in America: Frank Luther Mott, *A History of American Magazines*, Cambridge, Mass., 1938, to which was added in 1957 a fourth volume, the whole comprising in 2500 pages a massive compendium of information about magazines, including their relationship to advertising, from 1741 to 1905; *American Journalism*, New York, 1941, by the same author, necessarily probes less deeply into 250 years of newspaper publication; Alfred McClung Lee, *The Daily Newspaper in America*, New York, 1938, a perceptive and even caustic study of the institutional structure of American newspapers, which I found particularly valuable in tracing the growth of journalism as a major business enterprise. Of special value to this study was Edward Jackson Baur's unpublished doctoral dissertation, "Voluntary Control in the Advertising Industry," University of Chicago, 1942. Baur has sought to explore the structure of trade organizations and the rationale for "collective action" in the highly competitive business of advertising from the 1880's to 1925.

In 1929 there appeared a lavishly illustrated *History and Development of Advertising* (New York) by Frank Presbrey. Conveying almost an air of piety, it still possesses the character of a monument, appropriate to the year in which it appeared, and could be described as a sort of unofficial "court history" of advertising for advertising men by one of their own number. Presbrey has compiled a unique summary of advertising activity from antiquity to the date of writing, with an emphasis on American advertising since 1860. It is more useful than it appears. Its principal value lies in the multitude of facsimiles and photographs, together with comments, to demonstrate the changing styles and substance of advertisements. The author keeps his own obvious enthusiasm for the traditions and accomplishments of his craft on a reasonably tight leash until the last chapters, where, in discussing advertising in the 1920's, there appears an unambiguous strain of the rhapsodic which scholars might find disconcerting were it not so instructive.

For information about the early years of advertising, I found four other works to be of some use: Sidney A. Sherman, "Advertising in the United States," *Publications of the American Statistical Association*, 7 (1900), 119–206; George B. Hotchkiss, *Milestones of Marketing*, New York, 1938, a short survey of the growth of marketing institutions; Frank A. Burt, *American Advertising Agencies*, New York, 1940, a brief review of their origins, growth, and functions; and *Printers' Ink: Fifty Years, 1888–1938*, New York, 1938, an unexpectedly sophisticated narrative summary of the principal features in the growth of advertising as condensed from the pages of that trade journal.

In varying degrees the personal reminiscences and memoirs of a few advertising men offered insight into the attitudes and goals of early advertising. Despite the fact that the historian is likely to discover in these memoirs less than meets the eye, he will find at least three of uncommon interest: George P. Rowell, *Forty Years an Advertising Agent, 1865–1905*, New York, 1906; Joseph H. Appel, *Growing Up with Advertising*, New York, 1940; and the partial transcript of a taped interview with Albert Lasker conducted by Allan Nevins and Dean Albertson, published in *American Heritage*, 6 (Dec. 1954), 74 ff., from which it becomes plain that even in his last years the man most responsible for the advertising of the American Tobacco Company had lost none of his capacity for the hyperbolic overstatement. The memoirs of Claude C. Hopkins, who gave the world the phrase "shot from guns" as a tribute to the qualities of a breakfast food, are entitled

My Life in Advertising (New York, 1927) and are frustratingly brief. George Creel was not properly an advertising man, but his testimony of *How We Advertised America* (New York, 1920) contains his assessment of the role advertising men played in the Great Crusade. Earnest Elmo Calkins, *"And Hearing Not—": Annals of an Adman* (New York, 1946), however delightful a reminiscence in other ways, is disappointingly unspecific about the agency matters on which he was most able to write with authority; while Gerard Lambert, *All Out of Step* (New York, 1956) devotes approximately thirty antiseptic pages to a discussion of his justly memorable career as the promoter of a "cure" for "halitosis," surely one of the most significant and triumphant examples of the powers of advertising in modern society. Concerning Lambert's failure to tell more about his career in advertising, John Kenneth Galbraith has aptly observed that it was as though Lord Nelson had survived Trafalgar but confined his memoirs to his gardening and his recollections of Lady Hamilton.

One can gain a precise sense of the evolving image which advertising men have held of their business by an examination of the leading textbooks and surveys of advertising published in the past fifty years. For this purpose I selected from a ponderous quantity of works seven of the more important ones, appropriately spaced in years: Earnest Elmo Calkins and Ralph Holden, *Modern Advertising*, New York, 1905; Calkins, *The Business of Advertising*, New York, 1915; Daniel Starch, *Principles of Advertising*, New York, 1923; George French, *Twentieth Century Advertising*, New York, 1926; George B. Hotchkiss, *An Outline of Advertising*, New York, 1933; Harry Hepner, *Effective Advertising*, New York, 1941; and Albert W. Frey, *Advertising*, New York, 1947. Each exposes to view a comprehensive cross section of the industry, its operations, ideals, and assumptions concerning the actual role and responsibilities of advertising.

Self-Regulation and Public Regulation

The most useful single source of information concerning the issues of internal control and external regulations consists of the four leading trade journals, previously described, whose interest in the problem was intense and whose coverage (for the benefit of the advertising men who read them) was apt to be scrupulous. I also consulted the New York *Times* wherever pertinent, together with the aforementioned accounts by Borden, Hower, Lee, and Baur. The records of Congressional hearings proved an essential source of data on the controversy over federal regulation of advertising which erupted in the mid-1930's. To the hearings there came witnesses to testify for and against a large number of differing legislative proposals, and there they revealed in consequence important attitudes on the subject of advertising which had nowhere else been made so plain. The pertinent documents are as follows: United States Congress, Senate Committee on Commerce, 73d Cong. 2d Sess., *Hearings . . . on S-1944*, Dec. 7–8, 1933; *Hearings . . . on S-2800*, Feb. 27–Mar. 3, 1934; 74th Cong., 1st Sess., *Hearings . . . on S-5*, Mar. 2–9, 1935. I also made use of the United States Federal Trade Commission, *Decisions, 29*, 1446 ff., in connection with the Lambert Pharmacal Co. Concerning the problem of overtly false advertising, I found two other sources of interest: Milton Handler, "False and Misleading Advertising," *Yale Law Journal, 39* (1929), 22, a general essay; and John R. Doubman, *An Analysis of Display Advertising in Philadelphia Newspapers*, Philadelphia, 1926, which concluded upon careful investigation that among consumers, merchants, and officials of the Better Business Bureau, consumers were the most "docile," merchants the least so, over "unfair" practices.

On the subject of internal control a small but suggestive body of literature exists. Three studies, by nature of their purposes and authorship, possess value as sources. Lawrence Valenstein and E. B. Weiss wrote *Business under the Recovery Act* (New York, 1933) to urge the advertising industry to welcome rather than fear the NIRA. In the same year James W. Young, a leading figure in the field of advertising, wrote an influential report upholding the existing financial relationships among agencies, advertisers, and publishers; called *Advertising Agency Compensation* (Chicago, 1933), it found favor among agency executives and publishers. The ANA disagreed with its conclusions and subsidized a divergent study by Albert E. Haase, whose findings, embodied in *Advertising Agency Compensation: Theory, Law, and Practice* (New York, 1934), differed radically from Young's. Neither book was disinterested, but both sought capably to present an important issue concerning the growing problem of self-regulation. Secondary studies which touch on the problem include Carl F. Taeusch, *Policy and Ethics in Business,* New York, 1931, and James W. Prothro, *The Dollar Decade,* Baton Rouge, 1954. Edwin Emery, *History of the American Newspaper Publishers Association* (Minneapolis, 1950) presents well-researched facts about a leading trade organization important to the advertising industry; his account, however, is virtually bare of interpretation.

Phases of the external regulation of advertising have been explored in the following works: Bert W. Roper, *State Advertising Legislation,* New York, 1945, which offers a digest of 2,000 state state statutes; Max A. Geller, "The Federal Regulation of Advertising," unpublished dissertation, New York University, 1951, a study of the recent role of administrative agencies in enforcing legislation; and C. C. Regier, *The Era of the Muckrakers,* Chapel Hill, 1932, a useful study of the reform pressures on business from journalists and the public during the Progressive era. Important writings on the federal laws passed in the 1930's to regulate advertising include articles by D. F. Cavers and others in *Law and Contemporary Problems* (Durham), *1* (Dec. 1933) and *6* (Jan. 1939). Thomas B. Clarke, *The Advertising Smokescreen,* New York, 1944, is a popular account of the adverse findings of the FTC with respect to tobacco, cosmetics, and drug advertising. Of great importance is Llewellyn White, *The American Radio,* Chicago, 1947, an extremely competent report on the growth and regulation of broadcasting from 1920 through 1946. It was undertaken as part of the general study of mass communications by the Commission on Freedom of the Press.

The Critical Attack on Advertising

The so-called "consumer's movement" of the 1920's and 1930's, and its continuing influence, richly deserves a competent general history. He who writes it ideally should possess in judicious combination the qualifications of an economist, an intellectual historian, and a political scientist. His sources would derive in large part from interviews with the principal actors in the movement (most of whom are at present living), their private papers and correspondence, the records and files of the testing agencies, the published writings of these unusually articulate men and women, the records of some of the New Deal agencies and bureaus, and the proceedings of Congressional investigations into the relations of the consumer movement to left-wing political programs. Such a full history has yet to be written.

My interest in the consumer movement for the purposes of this study was much more modest, being confined to its existence as an important source of hostility to advertising and to its public literature of attack. Some of this literature appeared in the *Nation* and the *New Republic*. Two leading independent testing organizations, which represented the practical heart of the movement, published periodicals of widespread importance to the self-conscious consumer. *Consumers' Research Bulletin* has been issued monthly since 1931 by Consumers' Research. *Consumers Union Reports* has been issued monthly since 1936. Both are major sources for the growth and preoccupation of the consumer movement. The movement also fed in part on books which strongly criticized the manufacturing and selling practices of a number of American businesses. Leading off were Stuart Chase and Frederick J. Schlink, *Your Money's Worth*, New York, 1927. They were followed by Arthur Kallet and Frederick J. Schlink, *100,000,000 Guinea Pigs*, New York, 1933; T. Swann Harding, *The Joy of Ignorance*, New York, 1932; *The Popular Practice of Fraud*, New York, 1935; and two articles by Harding in *Commonweal*: "The Truth Is Not Enough," *19* (1934), 491, and "The Consumer Demurs," *22* (1935), 419. Probing attacks continued with the publication of *The Ultimate Consumer: a Study in Economic Illiteracy* as one of the *Annals of the American Academy of Political and Social Science, 173* (1934); and a celebrated study by Rachel L. Palmer and Isadore M. Alpher, *40,000,000 Guinea Pig Children*, New York, 1937, which, when added to the earlier study with roughly similar title, presumably left little of the national population unexamined and unwarned.

A larger number of other books were more specifically critical of the advertising industry and the broader ethics of business itself. Ralph Borsodi, *The Distribution Age*, New York, 1927, offered a constructive proposal for the enlargement of the retailer's power to offset the influence of national advertising in the market process. Max Radin, *The Lawful Pursuit of Gain*, Boston, 1931, is a short and persuasive essay on the moral contradictions involved in the business creed of *caveat emptor*, contradictions which are compounded by what he views as the inherently deceitful nature of all advertising. Upton Sinclair, *The Brass Check: a Study of American Journalism*, rev. ed. Pasadena, 1931, makes the classically oversimplified contention that the advertisers who support the mass media call their tunes. James Rorty, *Our Master's Voice, Advertising*, New York, 1934, writing as a "disillusioned" advertising man, offers a far abler and more sophisticated argument to the same effect, and his Veblenesque dissection of the advertising world is conveyed in a tone more of pity than anger. A. S. J. Baster, *Advertising Reconsidered*, London, 1935, represents a similar strain of polemic to be found among British critics of a national industry almost as fully developed as our own. Tiresome as a tirade against the excesses of hucksterism and written with pseudo-Marxist overtones is J. B. Matthews and R. E. Shallcross, *Partners in Plunder*, New York, 1935, published while Matthews was working for the far left. Far calmer and more judicious are the frequently entertaining revelations by Helen Woodward, *It's an Art!* New York, 1938, in which she discusses her former occupation of advertising in disjointed fashion but with few traces of bitterness. William Allen White, "The Ethics of Advertising," *Atlantic Monthly, 164* (Nov. 1939), 665, carries weight because of the career and reputation of its author. He purports to have found many desirable changes but little total improvement in fifty years of advertising.

In 1938 and 1939 the House (Dies) Committee on Un-American Activities heard a number of special witnesses—the most important of whom was J. B. Matthews—testify concerning an alleged affiliation between the Communist party and the consumer movement. As a consequence the records of the Dies Committee hearings contain assertions, yet to be evaluated, concerning the consumer movement. The testimony of Matthews and others are scattered through the following records of the House Special Committee on Un-American Activities: *Hearings, 1, 3,* and *4,* and supplement to *4* (75th Cong., 1938–1939); *Executive Hearings,*

4 and 7 (76th and 77th Cong., 1940–42); *Appendix to Hearings,*
Pt. 9 (78th Cong., 1944); 76th Cong., House Report 1476 (1940);
78th Cong., House Report 1311 (1944). Concerning the controversial "Matthews Report" bearing the Committee's imprint,
dated Dec. 10, 1939, but missing from the official records of the
Committee, I have relied in large part on information derived
from the New York *Times* and from Jerry Voorhis, *Confessions of
a Congressman,* New York, 1948. Matthews' autobiography,
Odyssey of a Fellow Traveler, Mt. Vernon, 1938, asserts that the
turning point in his career was the occasion of the famous strike
at Consumers' Research, from which was formed Consumers'
Union, an event on which Matthews dwells at length.

Secondary studies of the consumer movement are meager and of
varying competence. Perhaps the most discerning and comprehensive survey has been Margaret G. Reid's, *Consumers and the
Market,* rev. ed. New York, 1942. Helen Sorenson, *The Consumer
Movement,* New York, 1941, sponsored by the Stephens College
(Missouri) Institute for Consumer Education, is useful, though
perfunctory as history and ardently sympathetic. Persia Campbell,
Consumer Representation in the New Deal, New York, 1940,
partly because of the author's obvious sympathies, presents what
becomes a sort of case study in political frustration. S. P. Kaidanovsky and Alice L. Edwards, *Consumer Standards,* Washington,
1941, is a short, technical monograph, and Vol. 209 of the *Annals
of the American Academy of Political and Social Science,* entitled
Marketing in Our American Economy (1940), brings together a
number of essays, both friendly and critical, on the problems
which a modern economy poses alike for the seller and consumer.

The Developing Rationale of Advertising

The advertising industry has produced a vast literature of defense and self-justification. Much of this literature is to be found in
the trade journals, particularly in *Printers' Ink, Tide,* and *Advertising and Selling.* Week after week on editorial pages, in signed
articles, and in reports of convention proceedings, the journals
sought to hammer out a position on the validity and role of advertising. Another major source consists of textbooks, memoirs,
and "histories," which have attempted to offer a favorable image

of advertising as a social and historical institution. Testimony at Congressional hearings constitute a still further source.

These sources have already been described and their nature discussed. There remain for consideration a number of others.

Of special importance for the development of a conscious policy of public relations by a major advertising association are the files of the Committee for Consumer Relations in Advertising, an organization which operated from 1939 to 1950 under the sponsorship of the AAAA. The principal item of value in the files is an unpublished "Report on the CCRA, Inc.," dated Feb. 1, 1950. Of related interest is a folder of materials which bear on the influence which publications of the CCRA were said to have had among educational institutions.

Published articles and the published proceedings of conventions have been standard vehicles for the dissemination of the views of advertising men concerning their own role and responsibilities. N. T. Praigg and J. C. Oswald, eds., *The Advertising Yearbook*, 5 vols. New York, 1921–25, present comprehensive digests of papers and addresses at five conventions of the AACW. Proceedings of the AAAA annual meetings were generally reported in *Printers' Ink*, but a special report, *Papers of the AAAA*, New York, 1927, was published for the year 1927. A series of public lectures at Northwestern University in 1931, delivered for the most part by advertising men, was published as a book, *The Ethical Problems of Modern Advertising*, New York, 1931. Caustic and hard-boiled in his defense of advertising against doubting Thomases within as well as without the industry is E. T. Gundlach's *Facts and Fetishes in Advertising*, Chicago, 1931. H. J. Kenner, *The Fight for Truth in Advertising*, New York, 1936, sponsored by the AFA for its twenty-fifth anniversary celebration of the Truth-in-Advertising Movement, is a revealing piece of promotional enthusiasm for the efficacy of self-regulation. Far more judicious and balanced in their perception of the ethical dilemmas involved are H. A. Batten, "An Advertising Man Looks at Advertising," *Atlantic Monthly, 150* (July 1932), 53; Melvin Anshen, "The Rediscovery of the Consumer," *Journal of Marketing, 5* (Jan. 1941), 248; and Kenneth Dameron, "Advertising and the Consumer Movement," ibid., *5* (Jan. 1941), 234. Dameron was director of the CCRA, and his views may be said to have represented accurately the position of most of the "moderates" within the industry on the question of making a reasonable response to the consumer movement. (For further references to "internal" views of advertising, see note 26 to Chapter 6, above.)

Advertising Reaches Outward

During the past two decades Americans have exhibited mounting fascination and concern over the activities of their advertising industry. Their attention has been fixed in particular on three segments of the rim which joins advertising to a wider band of publicly influential institutions. At one segment of this rim stands the growing science of psychology; at another, the business of public relations. Elsewhere the rim touches radio, television, and printed media. Across each segment flows a two-way traffic of heavy freight, in a few places so heavy that the rim itself has disappeared to leave an almost unbroken gradation. It is important to observe that the central operations of the advertising industry still stand far removed from the rim; yet one of the primary obligations of anyone undertaking to write a comprehensive history of American advertising will be to conduct a meticulous and far-ranging survey of this rim and of the traffic which crosses it.

In the present study for the most part I have been content to survey the rim through secondary writings, reinforced at a number of points with personal interviews and with some published items which possess the character of sources. In exploring the historical relations between the advertising industry and psychological research, I found that a close scrutiny of the *Journal of Applied Psychology* from its founding in 1917 offered rewarding insights into the nature and growth of psychological research useful to sellers. The Journal also provided information about the Psychological Corporation, a private profit-seeking firm of considerable importance for the development of commercial uses for psychological research. Further information was readily supplied by the staff of the Psychological Corporation. Two conspicuous figures in the boundary zone between advertising and psychology were John B. Watson and Henry C. Link. To the best of my

knowledge not many of Watson's views concerning this relationship have been made available; Link's operational views on the
subject were both articulate and revealing, as in *The New Psychology of Selling and Advertising* (New York, 1932) and in occasional articles in the *Journal of Applied Psychology* and *Printers'
Ink*. Comparison of advertising textbooks over a span of time af-
fords another direct insight into the changing relations of advertising to psychology. In this connection I add to the sequence
of texts previously described four specialized ones: Walter Dill
Scott, *The Theory of Advertising*, Boston, 1903, and *The Psychology of Advertising in Theory and Practice*, Boston, 1921; Harold
E. Burtt, *The Psychology of Advertising*, Boston, 1938; and Melvin
Hattwick, *How To Use Psychology for Better Advertising*, New
York, 1950.

Perusal of the standard scholarly journals of psychology—the
Psychological Review (from 1894), the *Journal of General Psychology* (from 1928), the *Journal of Social Psychology* (from
1930), and the *Journal of Psychology* (from 1935)—yielded little
that related to advertising, a fact which in itself speaks eloquently of the small importance which the commercial enterprise
of persuasion has so far represented for the formal and theoretical
science of human behavior.

For secondary materials I relied on scattered but dependable
discussions of the subject in Hower and Borden. The fact of the
matter is that the relationship between advertising and psychological research did not become particularly complex until
the late 1940's. Concerning the more sensational and widely published developments of the past few years, the reader finds an
ever-thickening body of written comment, for the most part in
periodical articles. Two of the more serious, full-length treatments
deserve to be mentioned: George H. Smith, *Motivation Research
in Advertising and Marketing*, New York, 1954, and, for a considerably less complacent view, Vance Packard, *The Hidden
Persuaders*, New York, 1957. It need scarcely be observed that
the subject of psychological research in advertising since 1945
will require a monumental study to exhaust or even circumscribe
it. The subject and its implications fully deserve such a study.

On the long kinship between advertising and public relations

I relied for the most part on information and comment to be found in Hower, in *Printers' Ink,* and in the following special studies: Eric F. Goldman, *Two Way Street: the Emergence of the Public Relations Counsel,* Boston, 1948, a brief exploratory essay on the career of Edward Bernays and other pioneers; S. H. Walker and Paul Sklar, *Business Finds Its Voice,* New York, 1938, based on interviews with business leaders to determine their use of public relations; William H. Whyte and the editors of *Fortune, Is Anybody Listening?,* New York, 1952; and Stanley Kelley, Jr., *Professional Public Relations and Political Power,* Baltimore, 1956. These works stand almost alone in their field; they offer extremely suggestive insights into an area of national activity so far unexplored by historians or other researchers.

The relationship between the advertising industry and the mass media, and the effects of that relationship, stand more urgently in need of a thorough and objective historical investigation than possibly any other phase of the advertising industry. In this study I have depended on a number of carefully chosen secondary works as the basis for hazarding some tentative generalizations. In addition to the general surveys of newspapers and magazines discussed earlier, I made use of the following: Neil F. Borden, *National Advertising in Newspapers,* Cambridge, Mass., 1946; James P. Wood, *Magazines in the United States,* New York, 1949, a popular interpretation; William E. Hocking, *Freedom of the Press,* Chicago, 1947; Morris Ernst, *The First Freedom,* New York, 1946; Herbert Brucker, *Freedom of Information,* New York, 1949; David D. Denker, "The Newspaper PM, 1937–1942," unpublished doctoral dissertation, Yale University, 1951, important for its informed analysis of an extremely important experiment in ad-less journalism; and three of the *Annals of the American Academy of Political and Social Science: Pressure Groups and Propaganda,* 179 (May 1935), *The Press in the Contemporary Scene,* 219 (Jan. 1942), and *Communication and Social Action,* 250 (March 1947). Of related interest and value are two exceedingly competent and persuasive general studies of motion pictures, radio, and television: Charles A. Siepmann, *Radio, Television, and Society,* New York, 1950, and Gilbert Seldes, *The Great Audience,* New York, 1950.

This essay would not be complete without recording my enthusiasm for the fruitful and indispensable insights into the relations of advertising with society which I found in a small number of thoughtful and original writings. Though only one concerns itself with advertising exclusively, all do so explicitly. Two, Walter Lippmann, *Public Opinion*, New York, 1922, and David Riesman, *The Lonely Crowd*, New Haven, 1950, in their widely divergent ways have become classics in the literature of social analysis. Leonard Doob, *Public Opinion and Propaganda*, New York, 1948, analyzes the American advertising industry to great effect as primarily an institution of propaganda. Frank P. Bishop, *The Ethics of Advertising*, London, 1949, engages in a reasoned and temperate discussion of the problems inherent in the formation of any public policy toward an industry hovering with a distinct ambivalence between the demands of a public and a private ethic. Lastly, John Kenneth Galbraith, *American Capitalism: the Concept of Countervailing Power*, Boston, 1952, and David M. Potter, *People of Plenty: Economic Abundance and American Character*, Chicago, 1953, offer penetrating insights of a high order into the cultural implications of the extraordinary and unique expenditures of wealth for advertising which characterizes the most conspicuously lavish and abundant democracy in history. It is Potter's further contention that the principal object for concern over this institution is not its economic influence but its unintentionally vitiating effect on the enterprise and vitality of the modern mass media.

Index

GETTING AND SPENDING:
The Consumer's Dilemma

An Arno Press Collection

Babson, Roger W[ard]. **The Folly of Instalment Buying.** 1938

Bauer, John. **Effective Regulation of Public Utilities.** 1925

Beckman, Theodore N. and Herman C. Nolen. **The Chain Store Problem.** 1938

Berridge, William A., Emma A. Winslow and Richard A. Flinn. **Purchasing Power of the Consumer.** 1925

Borden, Neil H. **The Economic Effects of Advertising.** 1942

Borsodi, Ralph. **The Distribution Age.** 1927

Brainerd, J. G[rist], editor. **The Ultimate Consumer.** 1934

Carson, Gerald. **Cornflake Crusade.** [1957]

Cassels, John M[acIntyre]. **A Study of Fluid Milk Prices.** 1937

Caveat Emptor. 1976

Cherington, Paul Terry. **Advertising as a Business Force.** 1913

Clark, Evans. **Financing the Consumer.** 1933

Cook, James. **Remedies and Rackets:** The Truth About Patent Medicines Today. [1958]

Cover, John H[igson]. **Neighborhood Distribution and Consumption of Meat in Pittsburgh.** [1932]

Federal Trade Commission. **Chain Stores.** 1933

Ferber, Robert and Hugh G. Wales, editors. **Motivation and Market Behavior.** 1958

For Richer or Poorer. 1976

Grether, Ewald T. **Price Control Under Fair Trade Legislation.** 1939

Harding, T. Swann. **The Popular Practice of Fraud.** 1935

Haring, Albert. **Retail Price Cutting and Its Control by Manufacturers.** [1935]

Harris, Emerson P[itt]. **Co-operation:** The Hope of the Consumer. 1918

Hoyt, Elizabeth Ellis. **The Consumption of Wealth.** 1928

Kallen, Horace M[eyer]. **The Decline and Rise of the Consumer.** 1936

Kallet, Arthur and F. J. Schlink. **100,000,000 Guinea Pigs:** Dangers in Everyday Foods, Drugs, and Cosmetics. 1933

Kyrk, Hazel. **A Theory of Consumption.** [1923]

Laird, Donald A[nderson]. **What Makes People Buy.** 1935

Lamb, Ruth deForest. **American Chamber of Horrors:** The Truth About Food and Drugs. [1936]

Lambert, I[saac] E. **The Public Accepts:** Stories Behind Famous Trade-Marks, Names, and Slogans. [1941]

Larrabee, Carroll B. **How to Package for Profit.** 1935

Lough, William H. **High-Level Consumption.** 1935

Lyon, Leverett S[amuel]. **Hand-to-Mouth Buying.** 1929

Means, Gardiner C. **Pricing Power and the Public Interest.** [1962]

Norris, Ruby Turner. **The Theory of Consumer's Demand.** 1952

Nourse, Edwin G. **Price Making in a Democracy.** 1944

Nystrom, Paul H[enry]. **Economic Principles of Consumption.** [1929]

Pancoast, Chalmers Lowell. **Trail Blazers of Advertising.** 1926

Pasdermadjian, H[rant]. **The Department Store.** 1954

Pease, Otis. **The Responsibilities of American Advertising.** 1958

Peixotto, Jessica B[lanche]. **Getting and Spending at the Professional Standard of Living.** 1927

Radin, Max. **The Lawful Pursuit of Gain.** 1931

Reid, Margaret G. **Consumers and the Market.** 1947

Rheinstrom, Carroll. **Psyching the Ads.** [1929]

Rorty, James. **Our Master's Voice:** Advertising. [1934]

Schlink, F. J. **Eat, Drink and Be Wary.** [1935]

Seldin, Joseph J. **The Golden Fleece:** Selling the Good Life to Americans. [1963]

Sheldon, Roy and Egmont Arens. **Consumer Engineering.** 1932

Stewart, Paul W. and J. Frederic Dewhurst. **Does Distribution Cost Too Much?** 1939

Thompson, Carl D. **Confessions of the Power Trust.** 1932

U. S. National Commission on Food Marketing. **Food From Farmer to Consumer.** 1966

U. S. Senate Subcommittee on Anti-Trust and Monopoly of the Committee on the Judiciary. **Administered Prices.** 1963

Waite, Warren C[leland] and Ralph Cassady, Jr. **The Consumer and the Economic Order.** 1939

Washburn, Robert Collyer. **The Life and Times of Lydia E. Pinkham.** 1931

Wiley, Harvey W[ashington]. **The History of a Crime Against the Food Law.** [1929]

Wright, Richardson [Little]. **Hawkers and Walkers in Early America.** 1927

Zimmerman, Carle C[lark]. **Consumption and Standards of Living.** 1936